Warning Signs of Genocide

Warning Signs of Genocide

An Anthropological Perspective

E. N. Anderson and Barbara A. Anderson

LEXINGTON BOOKS
Lanham • Boulder • New York • Toronto • Plymouth, UK

Published by Lexington Books
A wholly owned subsidiary of The Rowman & Littlefield Publishing Group, Inc.
4501 Forbes Boulevard, Suite 200, Lanham, Maryland 20706
www.rowman.com

10 Thornbury Road, Plymouth PL6 7PP, United Kingdom

Copyright © 2013 by Lexington Books

All rights reserved. No part of this book may be reproduced in any form or by any electronic or mechanical means, including information storage and retrieval systems, without written permission from the publisher, except by a reviewer who may quote passages in a review.

British Library Cataloguing in Publication Information Available

Library of Congress Cataloging-in-Publication Data

Anderson, Eugene N. (Eugene Newton), 1941–
Warning signs of genocide : an anthropological perspective / E. N. Anderson and Barbara A. Anderson.
p. cm.
Includes bibliographical references and index.
ISBN 978-0-7391-7514-9 (cloth : alk. paper)—ISBN 978-0-7391-7515-6 (electronic)
1. Genocide. I. Anderson, Barbara A., 1944– II. Title.
HV6322.7.A625 2013
364.15'1—dc23
2012034107

The paper used in this publication meets the minimum requirements of American National Standard for Information Sciences Permanence of Paper for Printed Library Materials, ANSI/NISO Z39.48-1992.

Printed in the United States of America

*To all who believe that hope is audacious
and to those who have lived this hope.*

Contents

Acknowledgments		ix
Preface		xi
1	The Deadly Seeds of Genocide	1
2	Paper Tigers: Fear and Hatred	15
3	From Fear to Hatred	35
4	Animating Tigers: Dehumanization, Justified Violence, and Paper Tigers	59
5	The Tiger Stalks: The Steps of Genocide	75
6	Excursions into History	91
7	Causes and Some Predictions	115
8	Sowing Good Seeds: Sustaining the Soil of Community	127
Appendix I: Statistics of Genocide, with Risk Factors		157
Appendix II: Genocide Compared		187
References		191
Index		207
About the Authors		215

Acknowledgments

There are many persons who have contributed to our knowledge and more importantly, to our sensitivity to all forms of oppression, including genocide. In particular, we would like to acknowledge the fishermen of Hong Kong who told the story of how Communist China changed their ancient world; our friends, refugees of Cambodia and Ethiopia, who allowed us the privilege of sharing their pain; and our colleague, filmmaker and playwright Sharon Williams of the Mahogany Project, who reminds us that our American past does not have to be our present.

Preface

Individually and as a couple, we have traveled the world, witnessed and worked in some of the most impoverished areas of the world, and worked directly with persons whose lives have been altered forever by the horrors of genocide. We have vivid memories of our experiences in Tuol Sleng in Cambodia, Dachau, and Auschwitz. We have had close, personal relationships with people from the Ethiopian, Rwandan, and Burundian diasporas; the Goma refugee camp, Site 2, and Khao-i-Dong camps in Thailand; the dislocated Australian aboriginal people; first nation peoples of America; deeply hurt African Americans; the families of the "disappeared" in El Salvador, Guatemala, and Columbia; Vietnamese first and second generation Americans; and Muslim women of Bosnia. This is not an inclusive list of our experiences as an anthropologist and a public health professor and consultant. On several continents, we have listened to and shared stories of genocide. In our own quest in exploring the question "why genocide," and in the spirit of supporting those incredible human beings whose triumph over overwhelming adversity has inspired us, we write this book.

At present, extremist politics based on hate—especially religious hate, but also ethnic, class, and other forms of group hatred—is increasing worldwide. Much of this is a response to the continuing economic troubles following the 2008 meltdown. Continued economic decline has been a very frequent correlate of genocide in the past. We fear that it will be so now. The warning signs are certainly there: extremist hate-based politics in many countries, violent repression in Syria, Sudan, and several other countries, and increasing disillusionment as economic woes fail to disappear. The United States has not escaped this; extremist rhetoric and action, especially religious and ethnic in nature, have made major inroads into politics and have shaped whole state governments. Media speak of political and economic polarization and paralysis. These are clear warning signs of genocide, and a regime elected with substantial backing from these elements could easily declare a state of emergency, suspend the Constitution, and begin slaughter, as has happened in Argentina, Chile, Guatemala, ex-Yugoslavia, and several other reasonably modern and democratic countries within recent memory. The present time is not one for complacency. It is one in which everyone should know the warning signs, and be prepared to combat extreme political hatreds before they get out of hand.

Since we started this book about ten years ago, there has been an explosion of genocide studies. The present book is not intended as a complete review of genocide studies or anything even remotely close. Genocide studies is a huge and specialized field, and we leave definitions, surveys, overall histories, and political analyses to the experts (references will appear below). We have kept references to a minimum, and we here apologize sincerely to the many excellent scholars whose works have not been cited. As it is, we feel we have to repeat too much that is well known to genocide scholars but that is necessary to cite here to make our case for readers not highly literate in that field. We may take this occasion to recognize the many scholars of genocide, and also Transaction Publishers, a small sociology-focused firm with a sterling role in publishing both pioneering and comprehensive works on genocide; almost half the serious books focusing on comparative and sociological studies of genocide are from this single press. We also recognize two books that appeared in the midst of our work—Ben Kiernan's *Blood and Soil* (2007) and Steven Pinker's *The Better Angels of Our Nature* (2011)—as forcing the biggest rewriting projects the two of us have ever had to undertake in our rather long professional lives! We are grateful to both for moving the study of genocide and violence to a new level. (One reader of our manuscript wished for a full review of all genocide studies, but after Kiernan's book such an effort on our part would be gratuitous.)

A short book is worth bringing forth, however, because we have a new explanation and a hopefully predictive model. The difference between this and other works on genocide is that we take a public health approach. We have been interested in what might be called the epidemiology of genocide. Specifically, we tried to find common factors that lead up to genocide—that predict and explain it. Other books have either stuck to consideration of specific cases, or have explained genocide through broad and general factors such as ethnic hatred, desire for land, and presence of undemocratic regimes. If these were really causal, most countries would have had genocides in recent years and all would have in the past. This is not really the case, by our admittedly rather restrictive definition. Other, more specific factors must be invoked to predict the more specific phenomenon we are considering: systematic, bureaucratically organized murder by a government of large groups of its own people.

Chapter 1 defines genocide. Chapter 2 focuses on what we believe genocide is not, examining the paper tigers of fear and individual hatred. It explores the deliberate development of group hatred as a correlate of genocide. Chapter 3 looks at the development of fear into hate. Chapter 4 tracks the process of dehumanizing a hated group and the justified violence that results: deadly seeds that poison the soil. Chapter 5 looks at the steps in the development of genocide. Chapter 6 is an excursion into the historical roots underlying that development. Chapter 7 addresses social institutions that can be manipulated to support a genocidal regime. Finally, chapter 8 reviews the precursors of genocide, suggests a predictive model of genocide, and offers strategies for prevention. Following frequent practice in anthropology, we have dispensed with endnotes, including references in the text and the full data in a series of appendix tables.

We believe that rational humans can create a world that prevents, rapidly identifies, and acts to eliminate the deadly seeds of genocide before the soil is poisoned. In the past one hundred years, humankind has experienced and historically recorded a huge number of genocides. May we learn from these experiences, pass on this knowledge, and be audacious in hope that our children and their children can live together in peace.

E. N. Anderson and Barbara A. Anderson
Riverside, California, 2012

ONE

The Deadly Seeds of Genocide

Genocide and similar official mass-murder campaigns by governments "killed more than 210 million people during the twentieth century alone and since 2000 more than thirty thousand people have been killed by terrorists" (De Dreu et al., 2010: 1408).

The toll in the twentieth century of wars and democides was in the hundreds of millions. Tilly (2003: 55), estimates about one hundred million directly killed in these episodes, and about as many dying from the indirect effects of war. Others imply far higher figures. Frans de Waal has shown that humans have the biological capacity to be moral, sociable, and helpful, but he also notes that in the twentieth century alone, conservative estimates maintain that almost two hundred million people died through war, genocide, and political repression (de Waal, 2005: 5). Adler et al. (2008) maintain that genocide killed more than malaria, which killed between one hundred and two hundred million people in the twentieth century. Much of this depends on definition; Adler et al. and De Dreu et al. (2010) use the term to cover every mass killing of civilians, even in the heat of combat, whereas others reserve the term for systematic, calm, coolly bureaucratic extermination campaigns. Estimating such events is difficult, and many estimates are too low. Among causes of death, human cruelty and hate ranked just behind heart disease and cancer. Mass murder of innocent populations may have surpassed the combined total of deaths from battles, individual murders, and suicide.

There are also huge indirect costs. Economic damage becomes self-feeding, as genocidal countries become poorer, less well led, and thus more unstable. Paul Collier (2007: 32) finds that civil wars reduce economic growth considerably, and cost the countries involved an average of $64 billion. Wars—largely genocidal—in Africa from 1990 to 2006 have cost an estimated $284 billion in direct damage and lost revenues (Bengali, 2007). The indirect costs would, of course, be even higher. The costs to the world of Hitler's and Stalin's massacres can only be imagined; no one has counted them up.

Obviously, genocides have huge costs. Since genocides are often targeted by the more economically and educationally successful minorities (presumably because of majority jealousy at least in part), the costs can be truly appalling. The extreme case was Cambodia under the Khmer Rouge, where every educated person was systematically hunted down. Guatemala in the 1980s also targeted educated people, as well as aid and development workers of all kinds. Several other genocides have targeted educated people preferentially. Thus educated people flee zones of civil war. A result is seen in a BBC (2008) article about flight of doctors: Mozambique has lost 75 percent of its doctors, Angola 70 percent, Ghana 56 percent, Kenya 51 percent, Rwanda 43 percent, and Sudan 13 percent. Comparable figures hold for nurses, engineers, teachers, and other desperately needed personnel. Of these, Mozambique and Angola were caught in civil war for decades, while Rwanda and Sudan owe their problem to genocide and Kenya to local ethnic killing (though also to more ordinary brain drain due to lack of opportunity).

The twentieth century was notable for an extreme contrast between stunning success of public health, medicine and agricultural sciences at finding cures for diseases, famines, and starvation, and total failure of the world political system in stemming the rising tide of mass murder.

Even so, genocide, as the ultimate example of aggression, is an infrequent event, breaking long peaceful periods and ultimately killing fewer people than humanity's endless feuds over rank, status, loot, and position. Moreover, as Steven Pinker has shown at length and with thorough documentation, violence overall has declined in the last few centuries (Pinker, 2011). This book shows that genocide occurs in quite specific situations and under predictable conditions.

In 1996 Gregory Stanton, in a paper for the US State Department, listed the stages on the path to genocide as classification, symbolization, dehumanization, organization, polarization, preparation, extermination, and denial. This was criticized by Dirk Moses for weak prediction (ibid.), and indeed since it does not say when or who is apt to go down this route. The clean predictor is fear on the part of totalitarian leaders. If they are threatened by war or opponents, or simply are themselves paranoid, the route is taken as far as they feel necessary to stamp out the threat—or unless they are stopped by outside pressure.

There is no evidence for an innate genocidal tendency, or a Nietzschean "will to power" in the violent or warlike sense. Even if aggression, in a general, unfocused sense, is natural to humans, this, alone, does not explain genocide. One cannot explain a variable by a constant. What are the situations and conditions that result in genocide and why does this self-defeating social phenomenon occur? What are the predictive variables that point to this terrible outcome?

CORRELATES OF GENOCIDE

Our findings are straightforward. We have done a comparative survey of genocide events in the twentieth and twenty-first centuries. We find that there are four clear correlates, all of which appear to us to be causal conditions. We propose that genocide will not take place unless at least one is present, and is most deadly when all are present. These are (1) when group hate (ethnic, religious, political) has been whipped up by politicians—usually from extremist movements—or economically powerful people for their own reasons. This is particularly deadly when the hate is part of an ideology to which hatred is central and essential, like the Lenin-Stalin brand of Marxism, the Hitlerian form of fascism, and the extreme forms of religion that have recently been called or miscalled "fundamentalist." (2) When a majority group is downwardly mobile in both economics and prestige. (3) During war, especially civil wars and what we call settler wars—conflicts in which an immigrant or invading group takes over land from a usually smaller and weaker local group. This rises to a very strong likelihood if there is a civil war that was explicitly ethnic or religious, or involved ethnicity or religion as major organizing factors. (4) When an insecure but autocratic government feels threatened—especially, but not only, when it has just seized power—and is desperate to consolidate its hold by any means possible. If such a new government came to power by wielding an extreme ethnic, political, or religious ideology, and using it to marshal supporters in a civil war, the chance of genocide rises to almost 100 percent.

The fourth alone is sufficient to produce genocide; a government in such a situation will almost always resort to whipping up hate, and the other risk factors often follow from the resulting situation. Autocratic governments can seize power in three ways: by coup, by conquest (usually in a civil war), and by instituting dictatorship or at least "extraordinary powers" after having been democratically elected (as Hitler did in Germany and Ferdinand Marcos later did in the Philippines). All these situations are bound to produce major opposition, and it is typically dealt with by indiscriminate mass murder of possible foes.

Clearly, the first three conditions are not necessarily directly causative of genocide. They are, however, the specific factors that set the stage for it. What actually causes it is the fourth. An autocratic government in this position will not always commit genocide, but it often will, and the exceptions are cases in which either the government has been notably successful in stopping economic and political problems or in which the international community has intervened. In other words, one may expect genocide or at least mass political murder in such a situation, and may expect it not to happen in other situations, even when hatred and economic or civil problems are severe.

The above findings allow almost 100 percent perfect prediction of genocide. The major problem with predicting is that totalitarian leaders are individuals, and have their own agendas—often highly irrational ones. There are cases in which a dictator has come near genocide and backed away from the brink (though we believe the two factors mentioned in the last paragraph explain all cases we have noted). There are cases in which a reasonably secure-seeming leader sets off a rapidly spiraling increase of gratuitous killing, often for what appear to be increasingly paranoid reasons; a classic case was that of Zhu Yuanzhang, the founder of the Ming Dynasty in China. However, we find such idiosyncratic stories to be rare. The model outlined above is highly predictive.

It will be noted that *all these are essentially about control, usually of weaker groups, and very often by leaders who feel they are in a position of weakness*. The parallels with domestic violence may need some spelling out. Domestic violence is not a crime of hate, distrust, patriarchy, or economics; it is about control (Barbara Anderson, 2005). It involves a spouse or parent who feels challenged, threatened, or scared, by a family member—usually a supposedly "weaker" one—who is believed to be in a position to hurt the perpetrator. Most serious are cases in which the perpetrator's "honor"—his or her social standing—is at risk. The resemblances of all this to genocide, and the differences of both from war, will become obvious as this book progresses. Genocide often bears an uncanny resemblance to domestic violence, and also to schoolyard bullying. It seems to us to resemble these more than it resembles actual war. (Massacres in the heat of war are an intermediate phenomenon. They seem like genocide, and have been so analyzed by many observers, but we differ on this; they really have a quite different epidemiology.) We shall mention some examples at various points. Decline of domestic violence parallels decline of other forms of violence, including genocide (Pinker 2011: 406–47).

All four of the risk conditions came together in Germany during World War II, in Indonesia in 1965–1966, in Guatemala in the 1980s, and in many (if not most) of the other cases we shall consider. In Germany, full-scale genocide began only when the tides of war began to turn against Hitler. Fearing both the loss of the war and the loss of his government's stability and functionality, he resorted to the "final solution." Rwanda is another case. As analyzed in detail by Scott Straus (2006), it fell into genocide when civil war—typically setting Tutsi against Hutu—had long ravaged the country. The plane carrying the president and several other leaders was shot down, leaving a power vacuum into which the hard-liner Hutu leaders stepped. Needing to consolidate their shaky control, they invoked full-scale genocide. Straus concluded, "I find that an intense civil war, state power, and pre-existing ethnic/racial classifications are the three primary factors that drove the Rwandan genocide" (Straus, 2006: 224); the wording is interesting in that we had reached our conclusions, summarized above, before finding Straus's work.

Every other genocide case in the twentieth century involves some mix of the above problems. External wars that turn bad can precipitate genocide (as in Germany, and in Cambodia in the late 1970s) but civil war is particularly deadly. An identifiable group that is outgunned and losing a civil war can routinely expect to be exterminated, especially if the dominant group can successfully accuse it of "starting" the war.

An additional risk factor pointed out by almost all general works (e.g., Hamburg, 2010; Pinker, 2011) is existence of previous genocide, but this seems less well correlated with genocide in recent years (see below).

The greatest problem for genociders is defining the limits of the groups they wish to exterminate. In the real world, no ethnic or religious groups have neat boundaries. Human groups are fuzzy sets. They inevitably include adopted members, in-marrying outsiders, converts, partial members, partial apostates, and so on. All genociders eventually find the solution that was directly and simply stated by Arnold Amaury, during the Cathar crusade, in 1209 AD: "Kill 'em all, let God sort 'em out" (see below).

Hugh Gusterson (2007) has usefully made the point—summing up a range of literature—that "genocides" usually wind up unleashing mass killing that drifts farther and farther from narrowly targeted ethnic groups. In Rwanda the Tutsi and Hutu were sometimes hard to distinguish, and many perpetrators killed as many of their own people as members of the other group; some of this killing was simply local settling of scores, murder for gain, and the like. Similar patterns seem quite general in genocides. Political campaigns are always hard to keep clearly focused, because there is, ultimately, no sure way to tell the targets from the irrelevant. True genocide kills all available suspects, lest one person escape.

GENOCIDE DEFINED

Those who cannot remember the past are condemned to repeat it.
—George Santayana (from *Reason in Common Sense*, p. 284)

The term "genocide" was coined in 1944 by Raphael Lemkin, a Jewish jurist, to describe Hitler's massacre of the Jewish and Roma peoples (as well as several other targeted groups). Lemkin defined genocide to include attempted as well as full-scale extermination. This was to make sure that any action against genocide would avoid what has actually happened: countries refuse to label a massacre as "genocide," and therefore refuse to act, unless all the members of the target group are killed—after which they still refuse to act, because there is nothing left to be done.

In spite of Lemkin's care in this regard, the Serbian government under Slobodan Milosevich, and several other regimes, got away at least temporarily with genocide by insisting it was not total, and was thus merely "ethnic cleansing" (cf. Naimark, 2001).

Rafael Lemkin, and many others, worked to get the United Nations (UN) to define, and ban, genocide. They were successful—on paper. In fact, the United Nations has never had the ability to enforce it. The election of such nations as China and Sudan to the UN Human Rights Commission, over the years, proves that the United Nations also lacks the will. Many of its member nations are ruled by genocidal regimes, or by regimes that do not want to rule out the option. Genocide continues to flourish abundantly today, with little check. North American Treaty Organization (NATO) forces eventually intervened in the Serbian genocide in Bosnia and Hercegovina, but only after thousands died (Hirsch, 2002).The UN forces in Rwanda were ordered to hold action, and, in fact, were ordered not to use the arms they had; they could only stand by while genocide went on unchecked (Straus, 2006).

The word "genocide" has been variously defined. (On the history of the word and of genocide studies, see Totten and Jacobs 2002; there is an enormous literature on the issue, including much debate over the exact definition of the term, but we see no need to go over the ground when Totten and Jacobs, Kiernan, Heidenreich, and others have done it in great detail.) Following Lemkin and others in his tradition, we use the term to mean *systematic, cold-blooded, bureaucratically administered extermination of entire ethnic, religious, or political groups, by their own national governments, in the absence of anything that a rational external observer could consider an adequate reason*. This is what Rudolph Rummel memorably called "murder by government" (Rummel, 1994, 1998). Lemkin included mass murder for reasons of "race," ethnic or national identity, religion (or lack of it), regional identification, or other similar culturally defined categories. (This would presumably include things he did not really specify, but are highly relevant, like occupational group, or, in Hindu societies, caste.) He originally included cultural repression and political extermination campaigns, but these have sometimes remained separate, and are sometimes called *culturocide* and *politicide* respectively. Politicide—the term was popularized by Charles Tilly (2003)—involves systematic extermination of politically defined groups by their own governments, again in the absence of adequate reason. This becomes genocide, by our definition, when the government starts targeting children (as in Argentina in the 1970s), whole families, or whole groups of people suspected of being sympathetic with real or imagined opponents of the leaders (as in the purges under Stalin and Mao Zidong). On the other hand, such ethnically destructive practices as the forced removal of Australian Aboriginal children to raise them in purely Anglo-Australian cultural settings do count (Heidenrich, 2001; Kiernan, 2007: 11); any measures that forcibly remove children from their culture, or prevent a group from having children, are genocidal (Heidenrich, 2001). We shall follow Lemkin.

We shall also employ the term "politicide" when it is convenient to distinguish purely political killing from purely ethnic and religious campaigns. We only occasionally differentiate "genocide" and "politicide"; our findings are that the two are so universally fused in practice and so similar in motive and course that they cannot be analytically separated. From Hitler to the death squads of Rwanda, genociders have eliminated ethnic and political groups together. The major exception is Communist societies, which have generally engaged in very large-scale politicide but have not always linked it with culturocide. Even they, however, have usually turned to ethnic extermination when they had the chance, notably under Stalin and Mao.

To qualify as genocide, a campaign must involve a systematic attempt to eliminate whole groups, including harmless "critics," innocent families and children, and suspect bystanders. Merely eliminating actual political rivals is not genocide. It is unpleasant, but it is politics-as-usual, carried out everywhere.

A synonym that we will use on occasion is *democide*, a term coined by Rudolph Rummel (1994, 1998). Democide involves the massacre of a large population defined by class, political allegiance, or supposed political sympathies, with the goal of exterminating not only the political dissidents but also their families, sympathizers, and often entire communities. "Democide" is wider than genocide; it includes any large-scale, systematic murder by government of its own people, for whatever reason. It is thus a general term for both politicide and genocide—the latter in the narrow sense of killing groups defined by ethnicity and religion. It is a slightly more general term than genocide, since it does not necessarily imply a desire (or apparent desire) for total extermination.

Genocide, or democide, produces both the most "modern" of mass-murder types and in some ways the most horrific. However, it is not really new. Mass murder of one's own people, for the sole purpose of establishing a reign of terror, has been done before. History records it from ancient Mesopotamia onward. Several Roman emperors, as well as Tamerlane, Qin Shi Huang Di (China's first emperor), Zhu Yuanzhang (the founder of the Ming Dynasty), and many others practiced it.

More important, common, and deadly was use of it to exterminate religious dissenters (Pinker, 2011). The extermination of the Cathars in the Albigensian Crusade in France in the thirteenth century led to the even worse excesses of the Catholic Inquisition. Then came the Religious Wars of the sixteenth and seventeenth centuries, which depopulated whole regions of Europe. Similar persecutions range from mutual massacres of Muslims by Hindus and vice versa in medieval and modern India to the suppression of Buddhists, Daoists, and sectarians in medieval China and of Muslims in nineteenth-century China. (We will discuss and document these cases below.) All these qualify as genocide, or at least democide, to the extent that the government systematically exterminated peaceful and innocent people as a matter of routine policy—as opposed to random violence by disorganized sectaries or troops.

However, genocide was truly perfected in the twentieth century, and carried to extremes, not only of bloodshed, but also of methodical bureaucratic coolness. It was only in the twentieth century that it came to be a routine method of state control rather than an expression of individual tyranny or religious extremism. Most studies of genocide have focused on these recent tendencies and cases (the main exception, Kiernan 2007, uses a quite different definition of "genocide"; see below). It stands as the twentieth century's most visible contribution to history and to human degradation.

Every genocide is unique, just as every human being and every human act are unique. However, the commonalities greatly outweigh the unique elements. One group massacring another in cold blood, for no reason except that they are different, is common, predictable, and, above all, preventable. We thus reject the usage, still followed by some scholars, that confines the word "genocide" to Hitler's violence, seeing it as unique (Lewy, 2005; Rosenbaum, 2000). Indeed, it was unique in some ways, and deserves recognition as such; the earlier term "holocaust," or *Shoah* in Hebrew, is now usually used for Hitler's campaign as a unique event. But it was, and remains, revealing in the many ways that it resembles other mass-murder episodes.

At the other extreme of specificity, or lack of specificity, there is now a rapidly increasing tendency to use the word "genocide" to refer to any killing based on ethnicity or religion, or even any mass killing of any kind, including ordinary war. Chalk and Jonassohn, for instance, find the classic definition too restrictive, and expand the term to include many wartime massacres of enemies (Chalk and Jonassohn, 1990; Jonassohn and Björnson, 1998). Nicholas Robins and Adam Jones in *Genocides by the Oppressed* (2009) include even slave rebellions that kill small numbers of slave owners and their families (inevitably of a "different race" from the slaves). This seems to us to be a real cheapening of the term. There are obvious and important differences between the considered policies of the entire government of Germany or the USSR or Mao's China and the desperate outbreaks of a few enslaved individuals. Motivations are surely different. Certainly the actions are different: bureaucratized, systematic, methodical extermination versus a tiny, local act in the heat of passion. There are, however, some links, especially the organized hatred that leads people to kill wantonly and often in particularly cruel ways.

More seriously, Ben Kiernan, in his great work *Blood and Soil* (2007), includes almost any war that targets civilians. We depend on Kiernan's book for much that is below, and regard it as one of the great historical classics of all time, but we must respectfully disagree with Dr. Kiernan on the use of the term. Kiernan uses the term "genocide" to cover every case in which victors massacre the vanquished—in which case it becomes a part of every war in history. Moreover, Kiernan not only uses the term "genocide" for all officially invoked massacres, but also for the universal, small-scale killings in which one group takes another's land and kills off the former inhabitants in the process. Again, this would broaden the term to include literally millions of cases.

Kiernan's "model" genocide is not Hitler's but the Roman destruction of Carthage. The Roman ruin of Carthage, however, was not a destruction of helpless civilians by their own government. It was a straightforward destruction of a sworn traditional enemy who would most certainly have done the same to Rome if the tables had turned. Other cases noted by Kiernan include the Crusades, which were exceptionally murderous and unprincipled, but were actual wars against real enemies. All recorded wars, throughout history, have led in the heat of battle to mass murder of innocent civilians, because they are "enemies" or "harboring enemies." The United States has in its history the bombing of Hiroshima and Nagasaki and the My Lai massacre in Vietnam. Horrible and tragic this certainly is, and it certainly deserves a more serious term than "collateral damage" (the current military euphemism), but it is not genocide under Lemkin's definition. The difference is that in Hitler's Germany, Pol Pot's Cambodia, and elsewhere, the government, fully marshaled and under full bureaucratic control and as a matter of deliberately chosen policy, massacred its *own* people when they were either noncombatant or were only feebly able to defend themselves. Moreover, people joined with each other to kill not some faceless alien stranger-group, but their own friends, neighbors, and even family members. This is so different from ordinary war, even Carthage-type massacres, that it demands a different explanation. Wars occur for all sorts of reasons: land, booty, traditional rivalry, outraged honor, or even a soccer game (the Soccer War between El Salvador and Honduras in 1969) or an ear cut off in a brawl (the War of Jenkins' Ear between England and Spain in 1739). Most wars of any significance are multicausal, typically involving both material and political reasons as well as sheer contingent events. Genocides occur under a much narrower and more specific set of circumstances.

In fact, as noted above, it seems to us that such cool murder of one's own people is as much like spouse abuse, or like schoolyard bullying, as like war. Massacring people in the heat of battle in aggressive war calls for quite different emotions. Genocide seems more a cowards' act. It is abuse of the helpless for the purpose of maintaining shaky control—like bullying, and like spouse abuse (Barbara Anderson et al., 2005). It involves suspending normal empathy, as bullies do (Baron-Cohen, 2011). There is more about this below.

This said, many of Kiernan's cases are true genocides, or close enough to genocide to provide insights. This is especially true of his most numerous cases: what we call settler wars. In these, an invading group conquers and exterminates a group whose land they covet. Such campaigns go back to the dawn of time. Even ancient Sumer and Babylon had such local histories. The Hebrew Bible records many instances in which the Israelites exterminated enemy groups whose land the Israelites wanted. (The Lord even occasionally rebuked the Israelis for leaving some survivors, and even for sparing their sheep; see, e.g., 1 Samuel 15.) Many, if not all, of those groups were equally anxious to take the Israelites' property and exterminate them, so we cannot count them as genocides; genocides occur after the land is conquered, when the conquerors want to eliminate all chance that the original owners can take title back. Thus settler campaigns may lead to continued massacres once the former enemies are peaceful and trying hard to be good citizens. Usually, complete peace and full citizenship ends this persecution, but until it does, even the slightest and most trivial "outbreak" can produce retribution on an irrationally large and merciless scale. Here we need Kiernan's insights.

Settler wars can truly confuse the definition of genocide, because they typically grade through gradual evolution into true genocide. In the nature of things, the stronger group eventually conquers and subjugates the weaker one. At some point—and not a point that can be easily specified—what was once a war becomes a murder campaign. The losers become so weak that they can no longer resist, and—this is the most important point—so thoroughly subjugated that they are no longer "enemies" in any meaningful sense, *but are newly acquired subjects of the victors*. They are no longer independent entities, whatever legal fictions may say about "separate nations," but are individual subjects. *The worst situation is one in which they are no longer autonomous but are not citizens of their conquerors either.*

During the eighteenth and nineteenth centuries, the American Indians moved from being frank enemies, often fighting desperately for their land, to being "dependent nations" (see chapter 5). In the latter capacity, they were not citizens of the United States but were fully subject to its government, and less and less able to mount any military threat. It was in this period that real genocide occurred—outright, government-backed extermination campaigns against helpless and innocent noncombatant subjects. Settler wars thus morphed gradually into outright genocidal campaigns. The Cherokees, for instance, mounted credible campaigns against the Anglo-American settlers in the eighteenth century, but they were no longer combatants by the time Andrew Jackson drove them from their homes in a specific attempt at exterminating them as a people. During the late nineteenth century there was a slow but steady decrease in massacres of Native Americans. In 1924, Native Americans in the United States became citizens. Massacres and other genocidal killing (such as deliberately infecting groups with smallpox) ceased altogether.

The same pattern of gradual evolution from genuine fighting to simple murder to eventual peace occurred in Australia, where settler wars between Whites and Australian Aboriginals graded slowly and gradually into genocide, as the Aboriginals were progressively conquered during the nineteenth century. The pattern can also be found in most Latin American countries, in Japan (against the Ainu), in old Russia, and in many other countries. In these cases, we shall consider genocide to occur only when the target group presents no credible threat and when the government has given every appearance of officially deciding to eliminate it completely by extermination and forced assimilation.

Yet another borderline case is presented by the slave trade, which expanded horribly in the sixteenth to eighteenth centuries as sugar plantations developed in the New World (Mintz, 1985). It led directly to the deaths of several million Native Americans and 50 million to 150 million Africans (no one is sure how many). Much of this was through slaving wars, in which a community would be attacked and all its members killed if they could not be enslaved. This, of course, wiped out many entire cultural groups. This cannot quite count as genocide by the usual definitions, but it dwarfs most recent genocides, and it certainly was mass murder. It remains a very difficult case to classify. (Jonassohn and Björnson, [1998: 20–22], for instance, discuss it along with genocide, noting that sometimes people do not massacre prisoners only because it pays better to enslave them; however, their cases involve war against actual enemies, not murder of one's own innocent taxpayers.) Slavery is well addressed by many books, and we will leave it to their care; however, we certainly do not intend to minimize its bloody horror, or the evil of the racism that made it possible. The motive was, of course, economic greed, excused by racism. The latter grew along with the slave trade. Racism was real but minor in the sixteenth century, peaked in the eighteenth and early nineteenth, and declined with slavery in the nineteenth. The most extreme racist writings, however, come from the last decades of the slavery period, when the slaving interests were fighting a rearguard action against the growing antislavery movement.

Significantly, no one in the history of the world—to our knowledge—advocated the abolition of slavery until the eighteenth century. Only then did people conclude that slavery was an absolute moral wrong, and this position remained a minority one until well into the nineteenth century (Davis, 1966, 1971; Pinker, 2011). Today, however, though slavery persists (see Cockburn, 2003, for graphic accounts; Doyle, 2006, for statistics), it is underground and is almost universally rejected as an acceptable social form.

Genocide is genocide even if a war is used to justify it—which, as we shall see, is frequently the case. Often, governments bent on genocide try to provoke target minorities into rebelling or engaging in terrorist acts, then use those as an excuse for genocide. Hitler used the Warsaw ghetto rising to excuse mass murder of Jews. Earlier, in the nineteenth century, the United States and Australia repeatedly broke treaties with indigenous peoples, permitted crimes and corrupt practices to be carried out routinely against them, and then used any retaliation (however meek) as excuse for massacres (Brown, 1971; Kiernan, 2007). This was standard, frequently quite deliberate, practice.

Genocide also merges into colonial and postcolonial wars, which not only may result in genocide but set the stage for later genocides in "independent" former colonies. William Easterly, in *The White Man's Burden* (2006), has provided a scathing and extremely insightful and thorough history of the ways in which colonial and neocolonial policies set up ethnic tensions that resulted in genocides in Congo, Sudan, Iraq, and many other countries. He points out, for instance, how the British diplomat Sir Mark Sykes, and others, set up the Middle East for countless wars by drawing boundaries and establishing regimes (2006: 297). Significantly, the standard history of this dismal operation is titled *A Peace to End All Peace* (Fromkin, 2009; the title is an ironic reference to the claims of diplomats in World War I that it was "a war that would end all war"). Colonial divide-and-rule policies have been widely ascribed a causal role (to varying degrees) in the genocides in Rwanda and Burundi, Indonesia, and several other cases we shall note below.

Genocide, democide, national meltdown ("state failure"), and civil war are closely related, with similar trajectories and correlated factors. All are within-country, not involving international war except as an indirect causal factor. All are usually caused by the same thing: fear and hate breaking out in ethnic, religious, factional, or regional conflict. Tensions between groups defined by these factors build up until they snap. Differences are caused largely by the relative strength of the sides involved.

International wars have been relatively few since World War II (Pinker, 2011), partly because that war sobered many people. Civil wars, however, have abounded (Hironaka, 2005). Niall Ferguson, in a brief but detail-rich newspaper column (2006), noted,

> Of 30 major armed conflicts that are either still going on or have recently ended, only 10 or 11 can be regarded as being in any sense *between* civilizations [or even nations]. But 14 were essentially ethnic conflicts, the worst being the wars that continue to bedevil Central Africa. Moreover, many of those conflicts that have a religious dimension are also ethnic conflicts; in many cases, religious affiliation has more to do with the localized success of missionaries in the past than with long-standing membership of a Christian or Muslim civilization.

The final comment is a depressing commentary on how little is needed to develop groups that hate each other. It is also a very revealing, and again depressing, comment on what some missionaries actually accomplish.

We shall use the following definitions: *A civil war has identifiable sides of roughly equal strength. It is very often a regional conflict. A meltdown, like that of Somalia in recent decades, has no real "sides" with recognized authority and legitimacy, just random or mass violence. A genocide or democide pits a powerful, controlling government against weak or nonexistent opposition.* Obviously, these will often blend into each other, leaving hard-to-classify situations. Civil wars are especially prone to merge into genocides. The line between them is usually impossible to cut sharply, though, as noted above, one can speak of genocide when the government has virtually total power and the "other side" has lost the ability to provide credible threat or deterrence. One source, the University of Michigan list of civil wars, gives an arbitrary cutoff: a civil war occurs when there are one thousand or more dead, and two sides such that at least 5 percent of the deaths are on each side (Collier, 2007: 18). Presumably, if 95 percent or more of the deaths are on one side, we are looking at genocide rather than civil war. We shall use this definition (though it is often impossible to get accurate enough figures to be sure that one is dealing with 95 percent rather than 94.9 percent).

In Guatemala, for instance, "civil war" was alleged in the 1970s and 1980s, but it consisted of the full might of the Guatemalan army deployed against a tiny guerrilla group—and then massacring not the guerrillas themselves but the *civilians* of Maya descent in the areas involved. The *conservative* estimate is that the army was responsible for 97 percent of the two hundred thousand deaths in this civil "war" (see Kiernan, 2007; Stoll, 1993, 1999); other estimates run to 99 percent. Almost all the deaths were of noncombatants, and the army especially targeted teachers, local priests, community aid workers, and other good-doers, so as to wipe out all imaginable progress or success among the Maya communities. This was clearly genocide, not civil war.

Thus Gerald Prunier initially characterized the case of Darfur in Sudan as "ambiguous" (Prunier, 2007). In the 1980s, the military-Islamic government of Sudan gave every appearance of attempting full-scale genocide against the non-Muslim tribes in the south. The tribes fought back, and succeeded in forcing a peace and eventually full independence. In this case one may still talk about genocide, but it was surprisingly unsuccessful, and, indeed, backfired. One looks at the ruthlessness and indiscriminate totality of Sudanese retribution against "rebel" southerners, the targeting of all members of the ethnic group rather than merely rebel combatants and settlements, and the apparent goal of extermination as opposed to mere surrender. More recently, Prunier concluded that outright genocide was occurring (Prunier, 2008)—not so much because of a change in the data as because he accepted Lemkin's original definition of genocide rather than insisting (as he had done) that nearly total extermination is necessary before one speaks of "genocide" (Prunier, 2008: 155–58; as noted above, Lemkin specifically did not use this latter definition, for practical reasons). The government continued, and even expanded, the attacks, while the Darfuri resistance lost most of its power. Major aerial strikes were beyond the Darfuri capacity to resist. (At present, fighting has died down, but troubles continue; meanwhile, in a separate conflict, South Sudan has become independent, and suffered both continued fighting with Sudan and considerable internecine bloodshed.) Prunier's comments on definitions are well worth reading.

Genocide is, in fact, the endpoint of several continua. One continuum is from war between two roughly equal and militarized sides to war between one powerful and militarized side and one helpless and powerless one. Another is a continuum from one-on-one violence to mass violence. A third is from disorganized civil strife—chaos and meltdown—to organized, cool, systematic civil campaigns. Since one can always move varying lengths down a continuum, one can always argue about both the general definition and specific cases.

In short, the term "genocide" is necessarily vague, because it blends into other forms of killing (we will consider another case, structural violence, later). There are, as a result, *boundary phenomena*: situations that are "ambiguous," that can be called either way, and, most importantly perhaps, those that move either insidiously or suddenly from one state to the other. Observers and preventers must be aware of warning signs and of the importance of boundary phenomena in this, as in every other, social definition.

TWO

Paper Tigers

Fear and Hatred

FEAR

In this chapter, we explore factors that may be indirect causes, but do not necessarily result in genocide. These "paper tigers" may correlate or coexist with mass murder, but there are vastly more cases in which these factors exist in society but do not lead to genocide. The paper tigers of fear and hatred are correlates and precursors, yet they are too widespread to be direct or proximate causes of genocide. Indeed, fear and hatred between major neighboring groups seems—most unfortunately—to be the human condition. Few, if any, societies are free from them.

We will, however, begin with them, because they are predisposing variables. To invoke a different metaphor, they are the seeds of genocide. If the seeds find fertile ground, they may grow.

All animals, including humans, when cornered, will defend themselves, their young, and sometimes the group in which they are bonded. Many animals extend this protection to a symbolic level, defending resources they potentially could control or need. Such resources could be mates, food sources, or desired rank within the group. Humans place special emphasis on defending rank or social place, often codified as "honor" or "position."

Young male animals are prone to defensive and aggressive behavior. Biologically, they are more expendable in continuing the species than are fertile females, who have to invest more, physically, in reproduction. Conversely, males have much to gain, in terms of reproductive advantage and rank, by conducting a successful challenge; if a male wins, he can impregnate many females. However, this does not explain *mass* killing, and in fact most species have evolved ways to minimize killing even of male rivals.

Among many species, however, group conflicts do exist. Groups displace each other from prime feeding territories. Humans resemble chimpanzees in this agonistic behavior—fighting to sustain local feuds that defend the group against rival groups. However, we cannot follow any further the "Darwinian" explanations for genocide (on which see Smith, 2009). Humans have the innate capacity to kill, just as they have the innate capacity to be peaceful and to love their neighbors. But we are not programmed for mass murder. Some (shakily) "Darwinian" writers have claimed that murderousness is natural to young males. However, most young male humans spend their time happily partying, chasing girls, and otherwise acting as nonviolent as they possibly can. Their feelings, while strong, tend toward the pursuit of passionate love and sex. Young human males often become aggressive (not merely defensive), but most of them do so only when feeling seriously threatened. A young male human may kill a rival, or—much more often and much more likely—join a group fighting a rival group, but getting them to mass together to kill their *own* people is far more difficult.

Conversely, though young males are the most violent demographic by a large margin, recent experiences with women and older men as soldiers and genociders suggests that these groups can become as aggressive as young males. In previous eras, women rarely participated in combat; their reproductive capacity was desperately needed to make up population losses. However, in current history, women have rapidly moved into the armed forces and into terrorist groups, and have proved as militant as men. We may recall episodes of torture involving a woman as lead perpetrator in the notorious Abu Ghraib prison in Iraq. Much more important is the fact that *mature and older males (and sometimes females) are the leaders and invokers in every case of mass murder—genocide, democide, ordinary war, or anything else.* We can blame young males for barroom brawling, but not for war.

We conclude that aggressiveness and violence are socially controlled and manipulated, rather than some innate and inevitable property of one or another subset of humanity (cf. Geen and Donnerstein, 1998). Arguments that genocide is natural and inevitable can be safely dismissed, and we can work on solutions.

To be sure, people are certainly warlike and always have been (Bowles, 2008, 2009; Guilaine and Zammit, 2001; Keeley, 1996; LeBlanc and Register, 2002), and pleasant tales of the peaceful world of hunter-gatherers or simple farmers are usually pure fiction (Pinker, 2011). Some have held war that began only with civilization, but they acknowledge that a great deal of local feuding and tribal conflict went on before (Kelly, 2000). On the other hand, there are many examples of human societies that have managed to exist and prosper with minimal aggression, and there are some societies (mostly leaderless or stateless ones) that are almost totally non-aggressive clearly disproving the Hobbesian views of humanity (Dentan, 2008; Gusterson, 2007; Robarchek, 1989a, 1989b; Robarchek and Robarchek, 1998; Roscoe, 2007). Above all, even warlike societies spend *most* of their time at peace; otherwise they die out. (There are records of societies so warlike that they were exterminated by neighbors who were pushed too far, but obviously their behavior is self-limiting and is an evolutionary dead end; see Robarchek and Robarchek, 1998.) Evolutionary biologists who view humans as doomed to be endlessly war torn (e.g., Jones, 2008; LeBlanc and Register, 2002) ignore the reality: people are usually peaceful.

Humans evolved under reasonably egalitarian conditions (Boehm, 1999), in spite of the universality of parental and elder authority, and humans are not adapted to vast, faceless, extremely hierarchic systems. Humans are vigilant about all issues of trust, as evolutionary psychologists have demonstrated in recent years (Dunbar, 1993, 2004). They are reactively defensive. But they are not prone to unreasoned aggression on a large scale. Moreover, *hate—especially genocidal group hatred—has little to do with innate aggressiveness*, whatever that is. Some humans are more aggressive than others, because of genes, brain damage, family tradition, or even, according to one questionable theory, low blood sugar. There are even psychopaths, who seem unable to internalize normal human controls against aggression. Group hatred that drives genocide is a different thing, with different correlates. It involves usually peaceful and orderly citizens in mass campaigns against the people with whom they normally interact in peace.

BIOLOGY OF FEAR

Fear is the most dramatic example of human emotion sweeping away reason. Being seriously afraid necessarily takes precedence over everything else. Figuring out where to go for food today may leave time for rational calculation, but figuring out what to do when chased by a lion does not afford that luxury. Thus, fear has evolved to blank out rationality and force an immediate reaction. If one is afraid for life, loved ones, or life-supporting materials, it becomes all consuming, and one acts as soon as possible. It thus may underlie genocide, but cannot explain the methodical, rational, calculated aspects of many genocide campaigns— though some genocides do seem to rest on a sort of collective breakdown of normal rational behavior. (Straus 2006 describes this for Rwanda, and the consensus seems to be that something similar occurred in the Armenian genocide in Turkey in 1915; see below.)

The ability to fear, and to respond to fear, is based in ancient structures of the brain. A focus is the amygdala, buried deep in the brain

(LeDoux, 1996, 2002). Messages of fear from the amygdala project to other areas of the brain, dominating thoughts until one copes with the threat. Since no animal is ever completely safe or secure, fear always has some salience in the brain. Once a real or imagined threat is actually present, reaction is immediate—well before conscious recognition of the threat. The amygdala sends a high priority message to motor cells. Before completely conscious recognition that a long, moving thing is a snake, one has leapt away. Fear, as a human emotion, is dominant, non-rational, and preemptive (Franks, 2006, esp. pp. 56–59; LeDoux, 1996).

The more serious and immediate the fear, the more it animates the back brain—the center of raw animal terror. The front brain, which would only deliberate too long, responds with immediate coordinated action; the back brain takes over with more visceral, immediate reactions. Mental energy shifts from the ventro-medial prefrontal cortex, which integrates emotion and reason, to the peri-aqueductal gray, which just yells "run!" (Mobbs et al., 2007). This explains why people become markedly less rational when they become prey to major fear. Obviously, politics can and does exploit this.

Fear also produces a situation of choice: "fight or flight?" Usually, the decision to fight occurs only if seriously cornered or if the threat seems easy to defeat. Otherwise, flight is the preferred choice, either through physically fleeing or cowering down and hiding. In humans, a continual state of fear can lead to chronic fight-or-flight arousal. Chronic flight may take the form of depression—a human construction of the cowering-down response—or to situation-induced shyness, escapism or other similar responses. Chronic fight response leads to continuous anger and eventually to hatred. For those who hate, mental barriers—personal, cultural, and social—take over and become their world. They see the bars of Max Weber's "iron cage" of society (Weber, 1958), like the caged panther described in a poem by Rainer Maria Rilke, who sees "only a thousand bars, and beyond those thousand no world" (our translation; German in Rilke, 1957: 64).

Humans differ from other animals in the ability to project the future imaginatively. Animals manifest fear of immediate, direct threats. They can invoke a fight/flight response and be done with it. Humans, on the other hand, face continual threats from real or imagined fears, represented by hateful neighbors, job threats, and enemies across the hill or across the world. So humans can live in a state of constant fear and arousal, leading to physical and psychological damage that may shorten or even terminate life. Animals experimentally subjected to chronic fear often die of stress in a relatively short while. People can live with fear for a lifetime, but the fear may lead to early death, or leave little time or emotional energy for anything else. In the face of fear, reason is the first brain function to go and the last to be restored.

Human Nature: Biological Background of Fear and Exclusion

Philosophers from Mencius (1970) to Sidgwick (1907: 53, 501) have pointed out that people are basically "good," in the sense of "social." People want to be liked, to be supported, to be secure in a social place. They need social support and a sense that they are doing well by their families and friends. They need a sense that they are useful—that they are doing something helpful or useful to those others. Unfortunately, the heritage of tribal wars is strong, and the best way to be "useful" may seem to be a suicide bomber (Atran, 2010) or a genocider.

Conformity to social codes and loyalty to the social group are among the strongest behavioral pulls for humans. This makes people sociable, hopeful, trusting, and spontaneously helpful, as Mencius taught. It also makes them defensive, reactive, and prone to group hatreds. Which state dominates depends more on hope and despair than on innate character, though individuals show some differences in innate predispositions toward caring or hating. As the folktale says, "you have a good wolf and a bad wolf within you; the one that wins out is the one you feed."

Are people, then, "bad" or "good"? Thomas Hobbes, in a famous line, saw people as basically evil in the rawest way:

> [D]uring the time men live without a common Power to keep them all in awe, they are in that condition which is called Warre; and such a warre, as is of every man, against every man. . . . In such condition, there is . . . no Knowledge of the face of the Earth; no account of Time; no Arts; no Letters; no Society; and which is worst of all, continuall feare, and danger of violent death; And the life of man, solitary, poore, nasty, brutish, and short. (Hobbes 1950 [1651]: 103–4)

Less known is the thinking that leads up to this conclusion. Hobbes is describing what he thinks is humanity in a state of nature, but not only that; Hobbes thought that everyone regressed to this state when autocratic government was lacking. His evidence was not the state of "savages" in remote lands, about which he knew essentially nothing, but the reality of the English civil war, which was in full swing as he wrote. He could see the effects of government breakdown, and saw its logical conclusion as the imagined state of savagery that ancient writers had alleged for the "wild man" or *homo selvaticus*, the hairy, naked, club-wielding, solitary being that is a literary figure from Enkidu in the Epic of Gilgamesh through all the literary wild men of renaissance Europe (Bernheimer, 1952). *Selvaticus* evolved into our word "savage." Of course, this being is entirely imaginary, and all human groups—as well as chimpanzee and gorilla groups—are highly social. Humans are compulsively social animals, and cannot stand isolation or solitude unless they are remarkably tough.

Hobbes concluded that people would not want "warre," and would create a social contract to put themselves under a leader. Every freshman philosophy student knows that this would not work; a group of wild men would never be able to come together in the first place, let alone trust each other to draw up a contract. Still less would they follow it. Only an already-social animal could have such a concept.

Freud and many modern Darwinists follow Hobbes in seeing humans as implacably selfish and individually competitive. Much modern philosophy and political science is based on this assumption. The idea of "rational self-interest" in economics is based on it: each human is said to be interested, basically, in his or her own immediate material welfare, and regards others solely as potential providers thereof. The economic view is more hopeful than the Hobbesian, however, in that it assumes people will normally find each other useful enough to keep alive and friendly. Other philosophers, of course, have stressed the social, generous, and affiliative side of humanity. The rationalist view of economics and politics, however, does not stand examination (Taylor, 2006).

The western world is not alone in having this debate. In China, it has gone on since the fourth or fifth century BCE. At that time, the Confucian philosopher Mencius stressed the social side of human nature in strikingly modern terms (Mencius, 1970). Mencius's optimistic view was countered in the next century or two by the political philosophers Xunzi (1999) and Han Feizi with views that strikingly paralleled Hobbes.

Let us, then, take a long biological view. The other necessary component of genocide is a high level of social solidarity. The groups must be defined, they must be set against each other, and they must be obedient to their leaders. This is poorly understood in some of the literature, so an extended discussion of the actual nature of human sociability seems necessary here.

Yellow-rumped Warblers breed in the mountains near our home, and winter in large numbers on ENA's university campus. Many a dull and interminable committee meeting was made bearable by a flock of these little birds in a tree at the window.

They are true individualists. They pair off in spring, mate, and are very attentive to their young for a month or so. For the rest of the year, they are without family. Yet they are not antisocial; they like each other's company, and even the company of other species of birds. They eagerly join the large flocks of mixed small birds that forage through the trees and bushes. Here, however, they act not as organizers but as classic free-riders. They are interested in the insect concentrations that these flocks find. They also appear to know that there is safety in numbers. They respond to the alarm notes of more social species. Except for nesting pairs, yellow-rumped warblers do not help each other. They will happily tolerate others feeding with them as long as there is a superabundance, but shortage leads to conflict.

In short, warblers are perfect rational humans. They act exactly as rational-choice theorists (e.g., Olson, 1965) say we act. It is a wonderful comedown for the word "rational"—early sages used it to distinguish us from the brutes; now we know it applies only to some brutes, not to humans.

At the other extreme are the crows that also come to our windows. Compulsively social, they are never alone. They travel in large flocks. All the crows in the community are part of one flock that flies, feeds and sometimes nests together. This flock is composed of family groups, stable over many years. Children of previous years come back to help their parents raise or protect the young. Crows regularly sound the alarm when they see an enemy, and often the whole flock gathers to attack. Individual crows risk their lives this way. It is probably safe to say that such extreme sacrifice is done only for the closest kin, and thus not altruistic from a genetic point of view, but the bird presumably does not calculate gene distributions; he or she simply dies for the family. John Marzluff and Russell Balda, in their study of closely-related pinyon jays, provide a quite moving account and picture of a flock leader sacrificing his life to drive off a goshawk that was threatening his flock (Marzluff and Balda, 1992: 46–47). They draw the appropriate genetic implications, based on their meticulous data about relationships within the flock. ENA has seen crow leaders go up against Cooper's hawks in the same way, and sometimes has later found small piles of crow feathers under the hawk roosts. This is serious business. (ENA is grateful to Drs. Marzluff and Balda for discussion of the above.)

There are bird species in which some populations are social while others are individualistic. The Acorn Woodpecker is an example (Koenig and Mumme, 1987; thanks to Dr. Koenig for discussion). Acorn Woodpeckers are extremely social in California but not in Arizona. California's oak forests provide much food. Woodpecker groups store large numbers of acorns in "granary trees," and help each other defend these stores. Thus, the larger and more solitary the group, the better it does. Arizona's oaks are less productive, and woodpeckers have to space themselves out in pairs. Significantly, the cores of the social groups are groups of closely related males, and these groups fiercely defend their territories and storehouses against other groups.

Clearly, humans are a great deal like crows and California acorn woodpeckers, and not a bit like warblers. As David Hume pointed out in the eighteenth century (Hume, 1969/1740), only an animal that didn't need a basic social contract could form one.

Humans—like crows, dogs and chimpanzees—are instinctively social animals. Chimpanzees are violently aggressive in large groups and against strangers; humans usually are not (see de Waal, 2005). Humans, even perfect strangers, can aggregate in vast herds and swarms without breaking down into total violence. Humans can live in cities, which often present almost endless vistas of densely-packed apartments.

Many early theories of human evolution were based on the assumption that Darwinian selection necessarily produced competitive individualists. This belief, derived from economic theory, is wrong. Humans join a vast group of animals—crows, parrots, wolves, dolphins, monkeys, and even colonial corals and amoebas—in living highly social lives based heavily on cooperation. Individual advantage comes from working with one's society. Social scientists speak loosely of "society" as if it were a single tangible object, but this must not lead us to reify or essentialize society. Society is people—families, friends, foes, and those "other people" our parents were always invoking. ("What will other people say if you wear that shirt?")

Social scientists who take their reification too literally can delude themselves into thinking that individuals react rationally to society, or its institutions, or its principles. Ethnographers know that, in reality, individuals react emotionally to other individuals or to symbols of reference groups. The individuals may be filling social roles to enforce cultural rules, but they are confronting each other person to person, and that is a confrontation that always, necessarily, invokes a total personal response. Social attacks, criticisms, and even small verbal slights are physiologically very stressful, causing major release of stress hormones (Flinn, 2009) and preparation of the body for fight, flight, or depression.

Humans probably evolved in groups of fifty to one hundred fifty (Dunbar, 1993, 2004; Van Vugt et al., 2008; the figure is confirmed by several independent lines of evidence, though it is not uncriticized; see de Ruiter et al., 2011). Robin Dunbar also notes there are expanding circles of close friends within these groups, few people having more than three to five close friends and about thirty to fifty more distant. A group of one hundred fifty would have few more than fifty adults available for friendship, and people seem definitely adapted to such levels of sociability.

This means that we are evolved to think in terms of sharing, being responsible, being protective, and caring within groups of this size. People are not "selfish"; unless traumatized and abused to the point of fearing and hating their own, they will care for their families and friends. But, on the other hand, people are not evolved to take care of the whole world. It becomes harder and harder to care about other people as they get farther and farther from one's immediate reference group. One of the proofs of this is corruption: corrupt officials sometimes look out for themselves, but usually look out for their families and friends, if only because they have to have mutual support. Long experience living in corrupt countries is that the problem is not selfishness but lack of unity above the group level. People are fully participant in their families, friendship groups, villages, and neighborhoods. They just don't feel any real identification or participation with the wider state-level polity. An extreme example is the Mafia, characterized as it is by incredible levels of loyalty and mutual support at family and village or gang level, but a purely predatory attitude toward everything beyond.

However, humans are amazingly comfortable in large groups. Even simple hunter-gatherer societies usually run to about five hundred individuals. *Homo sapiens* naturally lives in a world of expanding social circles that typically run from a very intimate inner circle of three or four to a wide one of perhaps five hundred. These larger groups in turn add up, and people now feel solidarity with much larger groups—nations, religions, even all humanity or all life. The interesting question, clearly, is how "we" and "they" are defined. Threat can bring together warring factions. Humans are individualists as well as social, and this leads to endless reshuffling of groups. Most of us have multiple memberships and roles, and can be mobilized to defend our country, our neighborhood, our profession, or our family, according to whatever threat seems most immediate. Government can be my defender and organizer against invaders one year, but the next year can be the enemy when it tries to build a superhighway over my family land. Much, if not most, of social life is a constant negotiation and renegotiation of threats and priorities for defense.

A critically important point here, one not widely noted and not at all well studied, is the tendency of groups to band together into larger ones and then break down again into very small ones. Most groups (and also crow flocks) can join together or cleave into fragments along kinship lines. This is known as segmentary opposition—the great human truth captured in the Middle Eastern proverb "I against my brother, my brother and I against our cousin, my cousin and brother and I against our village, and our village against the world!" This proverb (cf. Atran, 2010: 256 for an Afghan form) tells more about politics (and about Middle Eastern history) than many a textbook. With the contingencies of alliance, group solidarity may move up the kinship and neighborship system, or break down. Genghis Khan started off uniting his nuclear family and wound up incorporating much of the known world into his united fighting force. After him, the league broke down again, and within three hundred years the Mongol polity was almost back to nuclear families. The relevance of this for genocide becomes clear when one realizes that humans have decoupled it from kinship. We can join or cleave along any lines—"racial," cultural, religious, ideological, anything. One recalls the ways that Christian sects have fought ruthlessly against each other in the past, only to join up again when faced with a common enemy. Communism rapidly cleaved into many splinter ideologies. This human tendency is critical to genocide, which involves setting one part of a (former) social unity against another part.

Social life, including altruism, could have evolved through "kin selection, direct reciprocity, indirect reciprocity, network reciprocity, and group selection" (Nowak, 2006: 1560)—in other words, at first through kin sticking together in families, later through extending networks of reciprocal help and exchange. Such networks could extend farther and farther. Finally, groups held together by such ties could compete with other groups, making some degree of group selection at least theoretically possible (Curry, 2006). It is now very well recognized that humans have an innate moral sense, as philosophers have pointed out since time immemorial and as all modern scientific findings confirm. Even chimpanzees have a little of it (de Waal, 2005), and bonobos rather more. This moral sense is *enough to keep the vast majority of people, the vast majority of the time, from committing violence.* History looks bloody because we like to make it so; we study kings and battles, not the invention of bread, the perfection of the wagon, or the development of herbal medicine. (Historians challenging this claim are invited to look at any school textbook, or to count the number of currently in-print books on war and the number of books on bread.) It is understandable that many scholars of violence, from Roy Baumeister (1997) to Donald Hamburg (2010) and Steven Pinker (2011), follow Thomas Hobbes in seeing humans as inherently violent and bloodthirsty, and follow Richard Wrangham (see, e.g., Hamburg, 2010: 21) in seeing humans as like the savage chimpanzee rather than our equally close relative the pacific, lovemaking bonobo. There is a great deal of violence in history. But if these grave authors had considered how much more common are eating, curing the sick, caring for children, worrying about the rent, and simply lying around doing nothing, they might have been less cynical.

Furthermore, genocide, as we define it, is a rare crime. We are thus studying a phenomenon that, however appallingly common in the modern world, is not an everyday or even every-decade event. It is simply too revolting to too many people. The problem today is that modern political life is messy enough on a world scale to make even a relatively rare crime common enough to be terribly deadly to millions and terribly dangerous to all humanity.

Altruism is very common among humans. We do it all the time, and even enjoy it. Some economists, like high school debaters, take great pleasure in pointing out that people enjoy altruism, therefore it is selfish, and therefore altruism cannot exist. This argument would be beneath notice if it were not so common. The interesting fact is *precisely* that people do good simply because they enjoy helping. They often do it by stealth, without anyone but the helper knowing. Even when they help because they "should," they are being altruistic. Try to explain "should" to a mountain lion, the quintessential loner animal. Crows who go up against a hawk understand "should" perfectly—not in the ear, but in the heart, where it matters. The mountain lion will never understand.

Fairness and egalitarianism also characterize humans, and are also wired in. This makes great sense if we evolved to find and share (and, yes, collectively defend) large patches of food, but no sense if we evolved only to fight. Egalitarianism as opposed to simple selfishness develops between the ages of three and seven in humans (Fehr et al., 2008), if not even earlier. It never develops in chimpanzees, our closest relatives, or in dogs. Dogs can be generous with puppies in their pack, but throw the pack some bones, and selfish competition with even the closest packmates is the rule. This startles us humans when we see it in such an otherwise social animal.

Solidarity and responsibility decline with social distance. This is quite different from hatred, rejection, or prejudice. One may feel nothing but good will toward the people of India, but one usually cannot feel as loving and responsible toward them as toward one's children. On the other hand, genetics is not destiny; for most adopters, their adopted children are as close as their biological ones. This sort of socially-driven distancing and closing are normal and valuable; they are nothing like the deliberate distancing of actually close populations that occurs in genocide.

The debates over human nature have now been resolved beyond reasonable doubt in a stunning series of papers and books by Samuel Bowles and Herbert Gintis. They and their many collaborators have been studying human altruism and competition for years, using an extremely sensitive interfacing of mathematical modeling and field data from all over the world. This adds up to produce a remarkably thoughtful and convincing model of human evolution (based on an idea of Darwin's).

Briefly, they suggest that humans evolved as competing groups, each group with a core of close relatives. A group that wins naturally leaves more descendants than one that loses, and thus hard-fighting, highly solidary groups win out in the evolutionary race. This is supported by evidence from our close relatives the chimpanzees: chimp groups fight over resources. A key difference is that chimp groups have cores of older females, whereas human groups typically have closely related males at the cores—females marry in from outside. Among mammals, males generally do most of the fighting because female reproductive capacity is too valuable to risk. Thus one would expect male-core groups to be particularly combative.

In even the smallest and simplest human societies (and also among crows, ravens, and many other social animals), groups coalesce into bigger ones or break down into smaller ones according to resource abundance and social desires (Bowles and Gintis, 2011: 96). Thus today's enemy can be tomorrow's friend, if there is good reason for alliance, while today's friend is tomorrow's enemy if there is a sudden competition for mates, hunting territory, leadership, or status. All human societies have also figured out how to have conflicts over religion and other intangible matters. War is therefore quite common among almost all human groups, and is more deadly among small traditional societies than among modern states (Bowles and Gintis, 2011: 99–106; Keely, 1996; LeBlanc and Register, 2002; Otterbein, 2003, 2004; Pinker, 2011). Some authors (e.g.,

Ferguson, 2003; Kelly, 2000) deny that such small simpler societies have war, but this is only because "war" is restricted to mean large-scale, formally declared conflict; it is thus absent by definition from the simpler non-state societies. The fact remains that fights to the point of extermination are common among almost all human groups. They appear to have delayed the rise of agriculture (Otterbein, 2011), and evidently many good things since. The few exceptions, such as the Semai of Malaysia, are groups so much smaller than their predatory neighbors that they have no recourse except running in fear. Other societies are so violent internally and externally that they threaten to exterminate themselves, let alone rival groups. Recall, however, that extermination under such circumstances is not genocide by our definition; it is not calm and systematic, and it is part of conflict with genuine enemies, not extermination of one's own innocent people.

Groups of fifty to one hundred fifty must have been able to unite and exterminate smaller groups. Modern *Homo sapiens* appeared in East Africa about two hundred thousand years ago, and very possibly the key adaptation was development of tight, fast-moving, warlike bands of this size that quickly eliminated rivals.

Hatred of rival groups is very often the deepest, most intense, and most involving human feeling. Markers of group membership, such as physical similarity and shared basic ideas and beliefs, evolve into racism and religious bias. Often, the only way to unify a diverse group is to oppose a common enemy (Arrow, 2007; Bowles, 2006; Boyd, 2006; Choi and Bowles, 2007; Nowak, 2006). Bowles thinks that competition over resources in the harsh, fast-fluctuating conditions of Pleistocene Africa would have made this a likely scenario (cf. Potts, 1996; see also Boyd and Richerson, 2005; Cheney and Seyfarth, 2007; Richerson and Boyd, 2005). Leaders manipulate this by targeting hated groups.

The birth of sociability through war explains only our vicious and cruel streak and our sometimes fanatical loyalty. Human sociable goodness, so common in all societies, must have evolved in connection with more beneficial group activities. War by itself would not produce the whole spectrum of "caring and sharing." The arts, usually neglected by students of human evolution, but universal and biologically grounded, must have arisen to communicate deep and usually positive emotion within a wide group.

Fortunately for optimism, human cooperation presumably had something to do with group hunting (Szathmáry, 2011) also, and indeed had a bootstrapping quality that allowed proximal causes (like group hunting) to affect evolutionary contingencies (Leland et al., 2011), thus getting it partially out of the Darwinian trap that predicts any cooperation would break down due to cheating. Humans have exceptionally good cheater-detection abilities (Bowles and Gintis, 2011), but this would not save us if there were not plenty of good Darwinian rewards for cooperation, in the form of more food, more mating options, and so on.

As many others have argued (but with less elaboration), a core bonding mechanism is reciprocity. People pay back favors. Marshall Sahlins showed long ago that reciprocity can be ranked on a scale from generalized reciprocity (pure giving—his example was a mother nursing her child) to balanced reciprocity (fair exchange) to negative reciprocity (cheating, or, at worst, robbery; see Sahlins, 1962). Humans have clearly evolved to spot cheating and to dislike it intensely. As early as they can be tested, human children show a strong preference for fair trade and a strong dislike for cheating and for simply grabbing. This shows up before the children are taught much of anything; it is clearly innate, and comparable phenomena exist among other primates. Altruists are those who engage in generalized reciprocity without thought for the return. Usually, such altruism exists only among close kin, who share enough genes to have a genetic stake in mutual support. Beyond the close kin network, however—and this is absolutely critical—humans are very often far more altruistic and cooperative than hard-headed genetic calculus would suggest. Moreover, people would be expected to show a good deal of generosity, "warning others of danger, acquiring and sharing valuable information, participation in the defense of the group or in predation of others, [and] punishment of those who fail to conform to these group-beneficial behaviors" (Bowles and Gintis, 2011: 113)—and to other behaviors as well. This is exactly what we do find.

However, if groups that live next to each other or mixed with one another are segregated, as by segregated schools and other facilities, they can quickly develop hostility. This can be reversed (all too slowly) by integration, but only if it is genuine and harmonious, not the paper "affirmative action" that does not integrate neighborhoods but does serve to inflame certain types of bigotry. A long history of experiments in classrooms and other places shows that when arbitrary groups are created and given distinguishing marks, rivalry and hostility usually arise; reintegration is fairly easy in such cases, but not automatic. A recent field study shows the expected effects—to a quite dramatic extent—in the real world, specifically in the highly polarized and hatred-torn country of Bosnia-Herzegovina. Marcus Alexander and Fotini Christia (2011) found that two integrated schools (Catholics and Muslims together) showed very considerable altruism and cooperation across religious lines, while two segregated schools drawn from the same populations in the same community (one Catholic and one Muslim school) hosted students that were far less well-disposed toward the "other" religious community.

Not infrequently, concerns with social as well as material reciprocity leads to an obsession with honor, and this in turn to much of the world's conflict (Baumeister, 1997; Pinker, 2011). Honor seems irrational to many a modern urbanite, but in a society without strong state control, being able to enforce one's social rights and just returns is a matter of survival not only for oneself but for one's group. Dying for honor is perfectly reasonable in such cases, especially if one is in a densely populated but genuinely lawless society. Examples range from the montane Middle East to Sicily in early Mafia days and to the American South through much of history.

Thus Bowles and Gintis suggest that "parochial altruism"—mutual support among "us" as created by opposition to "them" (Bowles, 2006, 2008, 2009; Bowles and Gintis, 2011; Choi and Bowles, 2007; De Dreu et al., 2010)—is the easiest and commonest way to unite a society. A society of tolerant altruists would not have enough reason, or selection pressure, to maintain strong altruism and self-sacrifice. A society of bullies—Hobbesian, oppositional and non-altruistic—would quickly destroy itself. Van Vugt et al. (2008) suggest that violent conflict and war create the conditions for this kind of leadership and followership. It is essential that a solid "us versus them" mentality be established, that a community conforms, cooperates, and endorses the violence.

But humans sacrifice their own self-interest for unrelated individuals and even for abstract ideals, making simplistic kin-selection explanations inadequate (Haidt, 2007). They will also kill their own kin, sometimes over ideals, as in the classic "brother against brother" tales of the Civil War—recapitulated, chillingly, in many eyewitness accounts of genocides in Rwanda and elsewhere.

Humans also sacrifice their lives willingly for their social groups, whether kin or no. Not only loyal soldiers, but even punks in street gangs, do this without a second thought. Social solidarity is constructed through religion, songs, folklore, festivals, co-work, shared cultural knowledge, and other ways. These are what we call "culture," in the broad sense, and they define ethnic groups. Such groups naturally feel solidarity, and feel some degree of exclusiveness. They do not usually hate other groups—that takes special effort—but they may easily be led into competing with others. They also form stereotypes, good or ill, that condition their dealing with others (Steele, 2010 gives a particularly good and up-to-date account of stereotyping).

Such devices are increasingly necessary as populations get larger and more "faceless." Even a small group needs some of these social mechanisms, but a nation needs massive investment in them. From media and museums to schools and songs, nations draw on every mechanism they can think of to create "imagined communities" (Benedict Anderson, 1991). The most universal way of constructing "imagined communities" is by making their members into fictive brothers and sisters, or, with some churches, "brethren and sistren." Some such ideology of fictive kin—"we are a band of brothers"—always seems to enter in (see, e.g., Pinker, 2011). Sometimes it is a very small fig-leaf, but often it is all-important, creating genuine supportive communities where there were none.

Humans do take care of their nuclear families, but they are also protective of wider groups. Humans everywhere create levels of fictive kinship, from full adoption at birth to courtesy-aunts. Sacrifice for the wide group is universal and routine.

In fact, human society *depends* on bonds that go far beyond anything that can be maintained by direct reciprocity or any other rational or economic bond (let alone blood relationship). We have to be respectful to perfect strangers, obedient to governments whose leaders we never meet, and faithful to abstract rules and concepts that have no personal embodiment at all. Not even crows and dogs manage this. They will die for their groups, perhaps even for the flag if you condition them to see it as a pack marker, but not for liberty or capitalism. People, by contrast, will sacrifice themselves for symbols of "imagined communities" and for ideological labels as for their own families. As Benedict Anderson points out, this is a double-edged sword: it makes them good subjects but also good soldiers—not least in genocides.

So the sociable view wins, and Hobbes was wrong. However, *it is precisely due to human sociability that humans indulge in group hates*. The Hobbes-Xunzi view of people as basically savage loners is completely without foundation. Human problems are caused by excess of solidarity, not excess of individualism. Original Sin is group hatred, not selfish individualism.

A number of myths about aggression, largely stemming from the individual-against-the-world stereotype, continue to condition modern minds (Nordstrom, 1997). The most dangerous from the point of view of genocide is the idea that individual aggression, committed by "bad" people, is the problem. Actually, group aggression is a different matter; the vast majority of people who commit it are very ordinary, often mild and gentle, folk. The best socialized can sometimes be the worst, since they are conformist and obedient (see below, especially in re Cambodia and Rwanda).

Our noblest and most human trait, our social solidarity, can thus be perverted by fear into the most evil human viciousness. Shakespeare was thinking of something of the sort when he wrote, "Lilies that fester smell much worse than weeds."

Human Infants and Fear

Freudian and neo-Hobbesian theories tell us that we are savage, licentious, and powerful. We are not. Once again: humans are peaceful and sociable the vast majority of the time. Genocide, however coolly invoked by leaders, often appears on the ground as a break in normal pleasantness. It often astonishes no one more than the perpetrators themselves.

Many accounts by ordinary people suggest that they later saw themselves as having gone temporarily out of their minds (see, e.g., Straus, 2006).

At every human's core, deeper than love or hate, deeper than learning or feeling, is fear, based upon a fundamental helpless dependency. Unlike many newborns of other species, human infants are born almost totally helpless with no ability to satisfy needs alone or defend self by running and keeping up with the group. The ability to "keep up" grows initially by utilizing a marvelous and complex ability to solicit attention. Human infants cry under stress, suck the breast for food, move their arms and legs, and use complex eliciting eye contact, but, otherwise, they can do little to protect themselves. The newborn brain is only one-fourth of its final size. Whatever instincts and basic personality structures the infant may have at birth, at least three-fourths of the brain's structure and content comes afterward.

The vast majority of a person's growth and development takes place through interaction with the world—through growth and change, adaptation, conflict, and learning to manage fear. Infants, and indeed all children up to the age of eight or ten, are completely dependent on the people around them for survival. Thus *fear of social abandonment or rejection is necessarily the primary and strongest fear.*

The infant learns quickly. Physical control increases. The infant emerges into a toddler: anxious to please and learn, active and eager, but fearful, often manifested as uncontrollable anger and temper tantrums. These little humans manage fear and develop their individuality relative to their caregivers. They must learn to negotiate sociability, individuality, connection, and resistance within the context of dependency and fear. They are in a position of weakness when they do this. The caregiver's behavior mediates and shapes the child's learning. Most of this learning—language, morals, coping strategies, and the management of fear—is done in early childhood, before the child is capable of adult rational thought. Our basic strategies for dealing with fear are established before we can analyze or evaluate them. It is a rare adult that can completely change early learned ways.

Years pass, and the child becomes an adult—more or less able to control fear and anger, but sometimes beaten and broken by life's vicissitudes. Often, the active, eager enthusiasm and attempts at rationalizing fear are early casualties. No one learns to cope with fear perfectly. People get hurt, learn bad coping strategies, and make mistakes. They may experience harsh judgment, rejection, or mocking criticism: freckles, braces, skin color, and anything else is fair game. Verbal and physical attacks are justified as ways of helping the child to become a functioning adult. However, a young child subjected to abuse or harm is a fearful child. She has little sense of power or recourse except to retreat into a fight or flight pattern, maximizing the fear response.

Throughout it all, the child remains physically and psychologically dependent on others, desperately afraid of aloneness, needing social support and buffering against fear. A child's way of coping is to break down into sobs or temper tantrums. Much "adult" behavior seems little more than a thinly veiled repetition of this early coping mechanism. Coming of age is expected to strengthen people, to make them less fearful; it often does the opposite.

PRIORITIZING FEAR

The need for place in a social group is clearly a priority for surviving and thriving physically and psychologically. Hunters and gatherers, as well as many animal groups, such as zebras, monkeys, and wolves, depend upon the group above all, to stay safe from fearful things: lions, hyenas, huge snakes, and the other natural perils.

Some events are more fearful than others, or at least are perceived to be more fearful, based upon social learning, instinct, and threat to group inclusion. Intentional harm by others, especially by groups, has always been perceived as highly fearful. Next in priority comes actual pain and bodily harm. All primates react with fear to large predatory mammals, lightning storms, and snakes. Such reaction is instant and not very controllable. The slightest detection, out of the corner of an eye, of a long sinuous object sets off a fear reaction. Thus we frequently mistake hoses and sticks for snakes—rarely the other way round. (An exception occurred when one of us [BA] stepped directly on a boa constrictor in a Costa Rican rainforest in the midst of a hurricane. Fortunately, the boa was merely annoyed). Generally, this experience notwithstanding, we are primed to pick out regular patterns from chaotic leaf litter, in part as a way of spotting danger— a camouflaged snake or a leopard in the grass. Ancient Hindu and Buddhist philosophers speak of this fear reaction, using it as an example of confusion about reality—mistaking a stick for a snake—as a foundation for investigating illusion, delusion, and reality.

Fear is grounded in the perception of danger. The more uncontrollable the fearful event, the greater the fear. We are far less worried about driving, even when drunk or on icy roads, than about flying in an airplane. Those rare crashes or hijacks are well-publicized for the very reason that they are rare. Americans are less worried about suicide than murder, although in the United States, suicide is twice as common as murder (see Center for Disease Control figures for 2010, in "Murder Knocked Off List of Top U.S. Killers: CDC, Reuters news online, January 11, 2012). Charging lions, snakes, or people evoke gut-level fear, but the danger of freeway traffic and the danger of chronic illness, while killing literally millions more people than snakes do in the modern world, are frequently ignored.

Americans fear irradiated foods used safely for decades in the rest of the world. Europeans fear genetically modified crops used safely by Americans for years. A few Americans or Europeans are still scared by witchcraft, which still terrifies millions in other parts of the world. Tornadoes are rarer in the southern United States than in the Midwest, but do more damage in the South, because southerners fear them less, considering them in the same manner as Californians who ignore the dangers of earthquakes. While there is great fear of murder by strangers, focuses on the menacing nature of the unknown, almost all murders are committed within the circle of family and friends. In short, as Ulrich Beck (1992) and Mary Douglas and Aaron Wildavsky (1982) have noted, people are poor at rational risk assessment. In general, fear is generated in intensely emotional ways, grounded in instinct and social learning, and replaces cool reason (Lowenstein et al., 2000).

Humans are less afraid of small-scale events than of huge catastrophes (Douglas and Wildavsky, 1982). Terrorist attacks, perceived as catastrophic, are more threatening than food poisoning, considered, until one experiences it, as a minor illness—though in fact food poisoning kills far more people. Of course, this means that people are especially stressed by genocide. Moreover, the sheer malevolent intentionality of genocide is impossible to ignore. People actually wanted vast masses of perfectly innocent fellow citizens to die horribly. This is simply impossible to ignore or forget; it is nothing like a random murder, or violence in the heat of battle. Yet, paradoxically, it is now so familiar that it is accepted in many quarters.

Targeted social messages are frequently aimed at establishing priorities of fear. Recent American examples include messages of fear about Muslim-Americans, Hispanic immigrants, and gay marriage. Such messages assume high salience in an environment of deep and wide-spread social insecurity because they identify a direct, intentional threat but from a controllable, safe, and only slightly scary source, often a social group regarded as a salient minority.

COPING WITH FEAR

Coping with fear can be done by rational search for solutions, but often humans cope through defensive aggression, dependency, withdrawal, and, above all, desperate attempts to regain control. (See Bandura, 1982, 1986; Damasio, 1994; LeDoux, 1996; Satir, 1983; Tashiro, and Mortensen, 2006; also Anderson, 1992.) Most people feel a need for more control of their lives than they can reasonably expect. Some are "control freaks," living their entire lives under heavy and direct perceived threat, because almost everything fails to satisfy fully their needs to have everything secure, controlled, and socially harmonious. They are thus almost permanently scared and angry. We all know such people, and we all know they frequently gravitate to high places, for obvious reasons. They are the last people we want in such places, but they are often the first to try for them. (See Kemper, 2006, who uses "power" for what we call "control.") If rational coping is inadequate, or if people are scared enough for raw emotion to take over, they resort to a hierarchy of more emotional coping strategies.

Most devastating of all are the effects of losing control within society. The psychological effects of being bottom dog include loss of self-efficacy (Bandura, 1982; cf. Glasser, 1981, 1985), learned helplessness (Peterson et al., 1993), anomie and alienation, alcoholism, and despair. All of these interfere with rational choice, and indeed with every aspect of living a normal life. The most available coping mechanism is often violence. "Better feared than despised" seems to be the logic, and if one cannot frighten the big people on top, one can at least frighten those weaker than oneself.

As adults, we can learn to control these and choose rationally which to invoke. This seems usually to require help. Some very effective schools of psychotherapy (Beck et al., 1987; Glasser, 1985) are based on this, as well as some interesting philosophical speculations (Gibbard, 1992). These psychological and philosophical schools should be explored further in dealing with genocide—something outside the scope of the present work, but a major goal for the future.

THREE

From Fear to Hatred

HATRED AND IMAGINED HURT

Hatred, springing from fear, is grounded in some level of actual or imagined hurt, perceived nonconformity, or threat of competition for resources by certain groups within the society. Actual hurts are common enough in the world, but far more common are imagined slights or overreaction. Lifetime friendships and family unity have been broken because of an unkind word, an invitation inadvertently forgotten, or defaming gossip. Nonconformity is widely seen as a direct attack on group cohesiveness. The haters must assume that the nonconformist is deliberately breaking from the fold because of treachery or intransigence. Finally, when resources are perceived as limited and more deserving for certain groups than others, hatred evokes a competitive effort to withhold resources. A current example is the vociferous reaction to providing basic health services for undocumented immigrants, even if they are among the most vulnerable segments of society, for example, pregnant women and infants.

Hitler's *Mein Kampf* (1940) is a veritable museum to fear and imagined hurt. His life, as he saw it, was one long struggle against the dangerous and hurtful Jews. His book has spawned countless imitations and invocations. A wide range of haters and genociders have been inspired by it; his writings were used as a textbook by the Argentine military during the genocidal regime in the 1970s. The best way to feel secure and manage imagined hurt is to get rid of the perceived source of fear. This was the direct factor that led the Turks to massacre the Armenians in World War I and the Germans (not just "Hitler") to exterminate the Jews, Roma, homosexuals, and several other groups when the tides of World War II began to turn against Germany.

Priorities become so distorted by group fear and imagined hurt that they seem genuinely not sane. A survey of the ten biggest concerns of voters, just before the 2006 election, placed "Hispanic immigrant" ninth, and as a major concern to 59 percent of voters. ("Iraq at Forefront," *Seattle Times*, November 3, 2006, p. 3). Tenth was "gay marriage." That dreadful threat to the survival of life on earth was viewed as "very important" to "extremely important" by fully 37 percent of voters. No environmental problems placed at all—not even food safety, global warming, or clean water access. Health care was fourth, but no specific diseases or conditions were mentioned. Conditions that kill tens of thousands of Americans a year were less frightening than the prospect of gay marriage.

Ordinary misperception of risk gives way to outright total irrationality when people displace fears of failure, or poverty, or illness onto completely irrelevant groups. Just as the peoples of the ancient Near East laid their sins on a goat and then ritually sacrificed it, modern people scapegoat their minorities. From long before Freud, psychologists have known that when one wishes to go after one's superiors or equals, but does not have the courage or power, one displaces the aggression to a weaker victim. (Everyone who has been bullied on a schoolyard knows this, too.) Only this can reasonably explain the panics over Hispanic immigrants and over gay marriage, and, especially, the way these panics rose after the financial decline of 2008. The anti-Hispanic concern in particular rose to genuine hysteria, with measures passed in Arizona and then other states (notably Alabama) that targeted all Hispanics, not just immigrants. The potential for genocide suddenly became real and immediate. These panics were stirred up by venal politicians, to be sure, but they could not have fanned a dead fire into the conflagration that actually occurred. People were scared of innocent and well-behaved fractions of the body politic. This could result only from a combination of deep and wide insecurity and need to displace it onto the least threatening people around. Fear is much more manageable if one is worrying about things that provide no objective threat. Indeed, the anti-Hispanic hysteria waned as the economy began to turn around, and some very shamefaced politicians surfaced in Arizona and Alabama; the leader of the hysteria in Arizona (Russell Pearce, a Republican state senator) was recalled in a vote led by his own party. (On emotion in general and fear in particular as political motives, see Marcus, 2002; Westen, 2007.)

PREJUDICE

Prejudice has been the subject of commentary and criticism from ancient times onward. No one has missed the unfortunate tendency of humans to make invidious distinctions between "us" and "them," and attempts to counteract this tendency run through many religious and moral teachings.

A classic work by Gordon Allport, *The Nature of Prejudice* (1954), written in the wake of the Nazi horrors, reviewed the literature of the time, and established what has become more or less accepted wisdom: ingroup, out-group, and reference group; stereotypes and how they form; the roles of projection and other defense mechanisms; and much more. Recent survey works, including Dovidio et al.'s *On the Nature of Prejudice, Fifty Years after Allport* (2005) as well as the American Psychological Association's recent survey publication *The Psychology of Prejudice* (Jackson, 2011), repeat and update the lessons. As usual in this book, we will avoid summarizing this well-covered, easily available terrain, and will look instead at some recent byways and approaches that influence our own conclusions. Prejudice also explains too little: since it is universal in human society, it is only one background factor in genocide—one cannot explain a variable by a constant. The questions are why it sometimes spins out of control and reaches hysterical levels, and why it sometimes becomes the basis for extreme violence. These two eventualities do not necessarily occur together. Quite "ordinary" levels of hate have accompanied systematic genocide (especially politicide), while hysterical hate has very often failed to produce it, especially in democratic societies where checks and balances exist.

A study by P. J. Henry (2009) showed that groups and individuals low in status within their societies are apt to become resentful, and that violence—especially in defense of "honor"—is extremely common in such societies. His main example is Southern United States poorer whites, but he compares ninety-two countries for which reasonably good violence statistics are available. These embittered, resentful bottom dogs are often the main—but, recall, *not* the only—backers of genocidal regimes. In our experience, they are people who feel they are a pariah group *within* their wider society, rather than either a fully accepted part of the wider society or a genuinely different ethnic group held down to low position within the latter. One example was the rise of Pol Pot, Kieu Samphan, and the Khmer Rouge, basically a group of less-than-affluent rural people from a remote part of Cambodia that had traditionally been considered backward (see, e.g., Hinton, 2005). Our experience is, in fact, that genuinely different but disempowered groups often become super-orderly and peaceable. They are model citizens, because they not only have to stay below the radar of their oppressors, but also function and maintain coherence and mutual support as a somewhat separate society. This was our experience with Chinese fishermen in several Asian countries and Maya Indians in Mexico, as well as with immigrants in the United States.

NONCONFORMITY

Humans everywhere notice personal differences and stereotype groups they know if those groups differ on salient characteristics. This seems rooted deeply in human nature, and is expectable from the evolutionary sequences noted (Bowles and Gintis, 2011: 35; Pinker, 2011: 323–24).

Humans hate fold-breakers, "different" people within our own societies (Pinto et al., 2010). These "different" people fall into four categories: the highly emotional ("unreliable"), the deviant ("weird"), those who fundamentally disagree with the basic principles of the mainstream ("nonconformists," religious dissidents, political dissidents) and, above all, those who are politically, ethnically, or religiously marked as a separate group. But any fold-breaker is disliked—even people who are unusual or exceptional by being good, in the sense of conspicuously better than normal by the group's own values (Parks and Stone, 2010). Some readers may recall being tormented as "goody-goodies" (along with every other conceivable label) by schoolyard bullies. Relatively successful but politically vulnerable minorities are routinely targeted for genocide (Jews in Germany and Argentina, Armenians in Turkey, Baha'i in Iran, Vietnamese in Cambodia, Tutsi in Rwanda, Quiche Maya in Guatemala, Chinese in Indonesia, and many other cases). The psychology appears to be the same.

Humans do not usually hate strangers. They are usually quite welcoming and tolerant of strangers and visitors. Strangers, unless clearly inimical, are not a threat; even if a threat, they are not hated, merely resisted. Welcoming strangers and visitors, at least superficially, is globally considered to be good manners and even a social responsibility. What people hate are their own most visible minorities, what might be called "structural opponents." These embody Difference (with a capital D) in its most flagrant form.

People tend to scapegoat groups that are "lower" in the social pyramid. Asian/white mixed-"race" persons are lumped as Asian in the United States, but as white in many Asian countries where outsiders (including whites) are held inferior (Ho et al., 2011).

People everywhere seem particularly prone to scapegoat four types of "others": those weaker than themselves (the poor, the slaves, and so on); those handicapped in some way, especially socially handicapped (autistic persons, and the like); those who are open nonconformists to social ways; and, above all, the visible and salient minorities. A little-known but very important fact is that Hitler's Holocaust started not with the Jews but with the physically and mentally handicapped; he was sending them to mass graves years before he invoked the "Final Solution" to the "Jewish problem." The more basic are the differences displayed by the nonconformists and minorities, the worse for them. Skin color differences are bad enough, language differences are worse, but religious dissent is far worse (over history), because it is really an attack on the most basic guiding ideas of the wider society.

COMPETITION

Hatred requires not only imagined hurt and nonconformity within the society, but also a sense of threat and competition from a particular individual or group—the cold, gut-level fear inspired by a spouse who might cheat on you, a minority member who might be the lover in that case, the poor man who might be willing to do your job for less pay, or the politically emerging group that seems poised to displace you and your "kind." Almost every society has this structural opponent group, a particularly salient group that is singled out as a fearful, nonconformist and competitive. This group may be identified by any single defining variable, gender and ethnicity being common ones.

Steven Pinker's account of human evils (Pinker, 2011: 482ff.) lists predation, dominance, revenge, and sadism as the general motives for violence, adding ideology and groupthink as more cultural matters. All are, more generally, motives for competition, and all are motives abundantly demonstrated in genocide. Pinker is more or less in the Hobbesian camp, assuming that people are individuals in a permanent state of warre, and thus sees this as rather natural, with his "better angels" as very much marked cases. But humans are preeminently social. Their competitiveness is largely for social place and social approbation. People compete for recognition, respect, mates, position goods, and other social markers much more than they compete for actual necessities. This is true even in the simplest and poorest societies, unless they are downright starving.

A key biological need is the need to feel in control of one's life—to feel some degree of self-efficacy (Bandura, 1982, 1986; Langer, 1983; Schulz, 1976). Pinker's "dominance" is only a small part of this. Dominance is only one small aspect of felt control. In a preeminently social animal, far more important and more general is control over one's social situation and position. Challenge to this—to one's honor, reputation, status, social place, social self-regard—is unnerving far beyond any other sort of threat. We are all aware that even a trivial or imagined slight can lead to days of anger or depression among people who cheerfully endure high levels of physical pain or want. The commonest cause of domestic violence is perceived (often imagined) challenge to the perpetrator's sense of authority, honor, and control of his (more rarely her) familial world (Stets, 1988). Genocide recapitulates all this: it is the response of a leader and group to perceived challenge to their control. It is most often (in fact, as far as we can tell, *always*) invoked when the wider situation of a leader or government seems to be spiraling out of control, and a sense of control can be regained by designating and targeting a scapegoat group.

Oddly, given Pinker's Hobbesian mindset, he tends to refer to humans, and to members of a given culture, as if they were homogeneous, though he is not unaware of individual differences. Of course people differ greatly among themselves; people with great differences in aggressiveness and ideology jockey for power within every society. Often a society is split close to 50/50 between relatively well-meaning and relatively ill-meaning individuals, and a very slight contingent happening can result in a "tipping point" (Gladwell, 2002) that leads to enormous differences in behavior. We see this all the time in genocides; a key individual's death, or a minor incursion, can change the situation. The tipping-point concept is important, a fact that should be remembered by those who wish to prevent genocide. Genocides most often occur when unusually horrible people get control of a country—not just a leader, but a whole world of thugs, toughs, ideologues, bigots, and the like. It seems initially surprising to realize that bigotry makes very predictable bedfellows of the zealous and the amoral. A little reflection shows that it is to be expected: these are the two categories of people who have everything to gain and nothing to lose from killing a lot of innocents.

The problem comes not from our mythical Id but from perceived challenges and threats to our very real sociality and sociability. Genocide and domestic violence are extreme overreactions, at different levels of social solidarity, to perceived threats in those areas. Genocide is most likely to take place when there are also quite real threats to economic and physical security.

Pinker's "better angels of our nature" are empathy, self-control, morality, and reason. We can only agree, but must point out that all these depend on the basic social need and social instinct of *Homo sapiens*. Again, try to teach any of them to a mountain lion. Conversely, it is very difficult to teach a dog *not* to feel the animal equivalents of them. It is probably impossible to teach a crow to be a loner, or to be antisocial toward other crows. We are wired to want, above all things, warm, close social relationships. Ironically—as Pinker is aware—our very solidarity is key in war and genocide. When all our empathy, self-control, morality, and reason are marshaled to stand with "our own" against "the others," the result is worse than it would be if mere predation, dominance, revenge and sadism were unleashed. Self-control, for instance, is taught to all soldiers, who must carry out their tasks with a full dose of it. Pinker also realizes at some level that the "ideology" in his evil column and "morality" in his good one are essentially the same thing differently labeled. He uses "ideology" as a pejorative term; by normal social-science usage, his "morality" of democracy, open trade, learning, and restraint is an ideology just as much as Communism is. Pinker recognizes several types of morality, following Haidt (e.g., 2007) and Alan Fiske (Pinker, 2011: 625–27). The latter gives us communal sharing, authority ranking, equality matching, and market-pricing/rational-legal. The last, Pinker recognizes, is less a morality than a modern utilitarian calculus. Of the other three, Pinker sees correctly that the first two moralize genocide and give it purpose. Only the third is a genuine, deep-rooted morality.

Finally, group mentality and morality was famously demonstrated by Stanley Milgram's famous experiments in obedience, in which students gave other students increasingly violent electric shocks, even when the victims appeared to be in great pain. (The experiment was deceptive; the shocks were not really occurring.) A major recent review, discussion, and partial replication by Jerry Burger (2009; replicating in so far as modern review boards would allow) concluded that people do indeed tend to obey. Burger, however, highlights the point—usually missed in accounts of Milgram's experiments—that the more individualist students refused early and dropped out of the experiment, and more and more students refused and dropped out as the shocks got larger. Apparently some people can be trusted to follow orders all the way, but others have varying degrees of independent moral consciences.

GENDER DISCRIMINATION

A useful comparison is with gender discrimination—not a cause of genocide, but a cause of mass loss of life in many cultures (Croll, 2000). Perceived competition along gender lines is particularly fearful and results in group hatred responses. This is revealing of how group tensions form. More, it is related to genocide (Totten, ed: 2008a). A striking number of genocidal governments have also been highly repressive of women, and have taken uncontrolled female sexuality as a deadly danger. This was true of the Nazis, and it is true again today in Iran, Sudan, and many other genocidal countries. Sexual repressiveness must therefore be explored briefly. One observes visceral responses to same-sex marriage, the changing roles of women, and women's role in society. The American presidential election of 2008 spotlighted this issue; the first viable female candidate for president, Hilary Clinton, evoked enormous outrage and fear on the right about the role of a politically experienced woman to lead the nation. (Interestingly, at the same time, considerably less politically experienced women, Sarah Palin and Michelle Bachmann, were presented by the same right-wingers as candidates for top national leadership.)

The gender connection between fear and hatred is conspicuous in intimate partner violence, and also in sadomasochism, repressive gender codes, gay-bashing, and obsessive religious focus on sexual repression. Part of this may derive from the biologically rooted fear of losing control over one's reproductive space. Ultimately it often ends up seriously damaging reproductive potential. For instance, a woman beaten to death by her partner or murdered in an "honor killing" by her brothers is not going to help anyone's reproductive advantage (see B. Anderson, 2005;

Stets, 1988). However, there are countless social factors as well, most conspicuous of which is displaced aggression. Women who are physically weaker and often socially, disenfranchised become the target of insecure and bullying persons—not necessarily by male persons, either.

Likewise, messages about fear, nonconformity, competition in relation to gender roles can have devastating psychological effects. One of the authors (BA) poignantly remembers such messages of fear about gender roles from her natal family, including messages to achieve through education but to be careful about not being competitive with men in the workplace. On one occasion, she was admonished by a family member for holding professorial rank in a university when her brother, also doctoral prepared, could not find a position. She was told, "We raised you to be a good mother, not to keep your brother from getting a job. We don't approve of this women's lib stuff." The illogic of the situation was that she was being accused of usurping her brother's rightful role as a male in the workplace. (He was in a crowded field in the humanities, she was in a health profession with serious person-power shortages, and neither she nor her brother could do each other's jobs!) Fear was manifest in imagined hurt, nonconformity to expected roles, and perceived competition for scarce resources.

In actual practice, ideologues often fear that women's rampant, uncontrolled sexuality will lead to constant adultery, promiscuity, and other social ills. It appears to the ideologues that men must keep women firmly under control, in subordinate and highly unpleasant settings. This causes a high rate of maternal and child deaths in societies where it is a dominant ideology, and so carries a high social cost; but this cost is willingly borne, at least by the dominant males. In much of Asia today, the sex ratio of children is 1.3 males to 1 female (Croll, 2000).

Women do not seem to be a cause of war, at least since Helen of Troy's time, but they certainly have suffered from hatred deaths: female infanticide and killing-by-neglect. These are insidious, even invisible, but the sheer scope of them is appalling, and ranks with genocide.

This all goes with strong taboos around sex, and double standards for men and women. Cross-cultural studies reveal that the more women are given unequal treatment, the more the sexual taboos and extreme practices. Sex and love are about psychological support and bonding, consolation, friendship, and almost every other interpersonal good, as well as children.

With all this, it is not surprising that women suffer horribly in and after genocide (Totten, 2008a), and that their plight often gets little consideration or attention. The extremely striking similarities of abuse of women within dysfunctional families, within dysfunctional traditional societies (such as parts of northwest India), and dysfunctional genocidal regimes is particularly significant. Comparing Jan Stets's classic monograph on partner abuse (1988) with Samuel Totten's collection of studies done on women in genocide (Totten, 2008a), one sees so many chilling similarities that it is hard to believe they are not writing about the same phenomenon. Maintaining control of women and "different" people, and quickly defaulting to violence when control is threatened, seems more or less the same whether done by one person or by a government. Simply substituting "regime" for "male partner" in the relevant literatures can be a revealing activity.

INDIVIDUAL VERSUS GROUP HATRED

The psychology of hate, as analyzed by Roy Baumeister (1997, 2005), Aaron Beck (1999), Robert and Karin Sternberg (2008), and others, often fails to distinguish group hate from individual hate, and therefore limits the value of this literature in understanding genocide. However, they provide enough insights to be foundational for understanding the underlying hatred that fuels genocide.

Beck takes a cognitive approach, acknowledging that hate is a basic emotion, but looking more at the forms it takes, the justifications raised, and the targets selected. He reminds us, for instance, of the long and terrible civil war between rival sports teams, the "Blues" and the "Greens," in the Byzantine Empire (Beck, 1999: 144; see also Gibbon, 1995). These started out as fan clubs for rival chariot teams, and grew into rival gangs that indulged in mass crime and thuggery. They tore Constantinople apart for centuries. One is reminded of the football hooliganism of Europe and the "Soccer War" of 1969 between El Salvador and Honduras. Even the silliest and most ridiculous matters become excuses for group hate.

Robert and Karin Sternberg (2008) provide a long discussion of types and levels of hate, based on their work in individual psychology, but applied to group hate as well. They provide a number of "stories"—an anthropologist might say "cultural models"—including "impure other," "enemy of God," "barbarian," "greedy enemy," and related images (pp. 84, ff.). These are exploited by leaders when the latter want to mobilize hate. They also compare hate with interpersonal violence and with ignoring people in distress; these seem to us to have less to do with group hate, being more directly motivated by immediate personal situations.

They see hatred as having three components (Sternberg and Sternberg, 2008: 59–60): repulsion and disgust, the opposite of intimacy; anger and fear, the opposite of affection or passionate love; and devaluation and diminution, the opposite of commitment or solidarity with those one cares for. These characterize both individual and group hate. Up to a point, hate is hate, and studies of individual hatred can be used to understand group hate. However, group hate is a far more widespread, serious, and deadly thing than individual anger or hate. Most of us hate somebody—the schoolyard bully, the irresponsible boss, the betraying lover—but we get along, and usually get over it. This sort of individual hatred is a strong emotion but a surprisingly non-dangerous one. Murder is rare. The notoriously murderous United States peaked at about forty thousand a year, only twice the lowest estimate of the number of people killed in tiny Serbia by the genocide of the 1990s. The US rate has declined since, and is now a mere seventeen thousand or so.

Group hatred is more salient, motivating, and important to people than their individual angers and concerns, especially if the people in question believe humans to be a bad lot (see, e.g., Jost et al., 2003; Jost, 2006). Among experts on hate and mass killing, only Erwin Staub (1989, 2003) has focused more on group hate, and on him we draw for much of what follows. Group hate is more violent, more intense, more able to be manipulated, and more irrational than individual hate. It is a different manifestation of the emotion. Recall its Darwinian roots in defense of one's band against the enemy bands next door.

Staub finds correlation of group hate with hard times (usually both economic troubles and ongoing war or violence), extreme loyalty to the group or cause, and zealot ideology that prefers ideals over real people. He makes it clear that democracy is no absolute protection (though it usually protects fairly well); that cultural tradition is relevant but not determinative (Germans no longer kill); that almost anyone, anywhere, can become a genocider, but it takes a lot of systemic work; and that the violence feeds on itself in a vicious cycle. It does appear from his accounts that one needs psychopaths, or something close, to lead and inspire genocide. The vast majority of people are just followers, often secretly very unwilling.

"Pluralism" is protective. So is real morality, based on experience of helping people. Staub reports much evidence, experimental and ethnographic, for this. In all cases, also, Staub concludes that any real organized resistance had an effect, often a major effect—though often not enough to save the group being attacked.

The human animal is easily made monstrous. Staub strongly advises nipping that feedback process in the bud. On the other hand, the human animal is also made nice with even greater ease.

Eidelson and Eidelson (2003) list five particularly psychological traits that very commonly accompany group hate: superiority, injustice (to the hating group), vulnerability, distrust, and helplessness. It seems odd to find the hating group feeling itself vulnerable and helpless; its members certainly think that of the target groups, but they feel vulnerable themselves. This is part of the association of genocide with chaotic or downwardly mobile times. It also brings us back to the threatened control that unites spouse abusers and genocidal regimes.

FROM GROUP HATE TOWARD GROUP KILLING

Intergroup aggression is notably more violent than ordinary interpersonal violence (Wildschut et al., 2003). Typically, the same individual who avoids barroom fights, or pulls his punches when he does fight, becomes a far more savage being when animated by group conflict (again, see Atran, 2010; Straus, 2006). The individual hater may have no personal experience of hurt connected to the hated structural-opponent group; many people really mean that proverbial "some of my best friends" line. Indeed, the hater may even have personal acquaintance or like individual members of that group. Second, rather than being based on actual hurtful behavior (bullying, irresponsibility, etc.), the hater may base his or her beliefs on widespread negative stereotypes, often in defiance of his or her own actual experience. It seems easy to convince people of the innate impurity and vileness of a particular group (Kiernan, 2007). The structural opponent is defined in an all-or-none kind of way. Crudely obvious salient features—skin color, religion, language—become definitive, and are often marks of "impurity."

Targeted group hatred is more salient, motivating, and important to people than their individual angers and concerns (see, e.g., Jost et al., 2003; Jost, 2006). Many white Americans dislike and fear African Americans more than any other minorities (Kaiser and Pratt-Hyatt, 2009). Other more liberal Americans may embrace African Americans, and even claim to be "tolerant" in general, but state that they hate "Republicans" or "conservatives." Status-conscious persons are more prone to use terminology of "hate," reflective of their fear for security in their position (Kaiser and Pratt-Hyatt, 2009).

Amartya Sen, in *Identity and Violence* (2006), describes the coupling of hate and identity—hating persons for having a single identity and categorizing a person basically by that one identity, for example, Muslim, African American, woman, or gay male. The resulting language places the emphasis on the defined identity rather than the broader definition of an individual. (Examples include "the *black* teacher," "the *woman* (or '*lady*') doctor," "the *queer* neighbor," "those *Muslim* students"). This one-dimensional view, failing to see the teacher who is a father, the doctor who is a talented musician, the kindly neighbor, or the talented student, singles out the individual by an identity that has devalued social meaning. Such language results in the repulsion and devaluation that define hatred (Sternberg and Sternberg, 2008).

Sen's view is conditioned by his own experience with single-identity Muslim-Hindu violence in India. In this, Sen is oversimplifying the problem. Hatred may extend to many groups. The great genociders of history have been highly eclectic. They see many problem groups, and hate them all. Hitler, Stalin, Mao, Pol Pot, and the butchers of Guatemala all killed along religious, ethnic, regional, lifestyle, political, gender-identity, and even aesthetic lines. Hitler killed "modern artists," Pol Pot exterminated traditional dancers. They were aware of the multiplicity of identities involved. Even the Rwanda genociders killed a range of individuals, not just Tutsi. At a more basic level, all of us know bigots who hate a broad spectrum of political and ethnic groups. Talk-show hosts adeptly move their denunciations from one identity group to another, using a scorched earth approach with dazzling speed.

Defense of one's group is clearly a basic human trait, a key part of human nature, very deeply rooted in the human brain. Even the "love hormone" oxytoxin plays a role, though a relatively benign one: it not only causes or encourages bonding and affection, it also encourages and motivates closing ranks and organizing for mutual defense within a group (De Dreu et al., 2010). It does not, however, cause aggression or hate toward the outgroup.

The more directly aggressive, hateful pattern of response is a standard coping mechanism not only of powerful groups that feel challenged, but also of groups who have little power or hope and are not an immediate focus of threat (Bandura, 1986). If the scapegoated group does actually represent a threat, especially if it is upwardly mobile, the situation rapidly becomes worse. History reveals countless cases in which a major crisis has been dealt with by genocidal attacks on the most salient minority. In the bubonic plague epidemics in medieval Europe, the first recourse was to kill the Jews, or whatever other minority was locally salient. Today, economic downturns lead to sharp rises in anti-immigrant feeling, as we have witnessed in the United States since 2008. When resources are perceived as limited and more deserving for certain groups than others, hatred evokes a competitive effort to withhold resources. A current example is the vociferous reaction to providing basic health services for undocumented persons, even if they are among the most vulnerable segments of society.

Targeted social messages are frequently delivered by religious groups and may serve as a positive force to managing fear (Harvey, 2006: 15, citing Stewart Guthrie). An example is the thematic approach by Dr. Martin Luther King Jr. in leading the civil rights movement in United States. Unfortunately, religion is at least as often a polarizing force, exacerbating fear around political or religious issues that are perceived as threatening to the dictates of their own group. It can potently play into fear and raise ingroup-outgroup tensions (Hinde, 2007).

Unbridled fear can lead to over-defensiveness, necessary to the development of hatred. Group fear is a powerful ingredient of group hatred, sowing the deadly seeds that will poison the soil, creating the conditions for genocide (see discussions in Appadurai, 2006; Staub, 1989, 2003; and indeed most of the cited literature in the present book).

The Twin Towers tragedy of 9/11 revealed attitudes toward Islam, even though the attackers were a tiny band of religiously non-observant

Muslims. Hysteria resulted. The religion was portrayed in every possible unflattering way, often by recycling, sometimes word-for-word, crusaders' propaganda from the Middle Ages. Yet the vast majority of Muslim clerics condemned the attack and the Al-Qaeda agenda. Meanwhile, individuals with other agendas have generated a range of conspiracy theories blaming 9/11 on other groups, from Israel to the United States itself. Earlier, the Oklahoma City bombing by Tim McVeigh was initially ascribed to structural opponents—African American or Middle Eastern terrorists—until proven otherwise. When it was confirmed to have been the work of unstable white Americans, this terrorist atrocity was never considered evidence that all white Americans are united in evil, or even that one should be wary of the extralegal right-wing militias that spawned McVeigh and others. The structural opponent is almost always identified with a minority within the society, often defined in terms of ethnicity or gender. Majority-member killers are individuals and exceptions; killers from a minority are taken as representatives of that minority.

Individual hatred is often manifested with high emotion and hysteria, especially in scapegoating. While it is too dangerous for one's social position to get hysterically angry at an irresponsible boss, it is easy to project hysteria about "those people." Hate can make even the most peaceful and ordinary of humans into a madman, contorted with rage upon mention of the structural-opponent group.

Conversely, and always surprisingly, the emotion may be very mild, and yet may lead to horrific torture as well as murder. Recall again the notorious "good Germans" who were often "just doing a job." Hannah Arendt's famous book about Eichmann, *The Banality of Evil* (1964), has made proverbial the fact that genocidal evil can seem very mundane and dull when seen in the person of a mundane, dull, emotionally limited man. Philip Gourevitch (1998) and Scott Straus (2006) recount the horrors of Rwanda in the 1990s: the vast majority of killers in the genocidal strife of those days were ordinary people, some married to "the enemy," who simply followed the directions of a small clique that had seized power. Perfectly ordinary individuals who had liked and gotten along well with Tutsi, or with Hutu, turned on their neighbors and even their spouses (Gourevitch, 1998). Both Gourevitch and Straus blame it on a tradition of obedience to government rather than on widespread hate. Hinton (2005) reports the same from Cambodia, and we have heard the same from refugees; under the Khmer Rouge, many individuals murdered their own families.

Almost all recent accounts of genocide describe people who were totally mystified by their own behavior. Sometimes the change was permanent; sometimes it went away and later seemed like a nightmare. Naturally, both rabid hatred and cool banality can be combined. Much Nazi propaganda, and plenty of talk-show rhetoric in the modern United States, combines both. Talk-show rants reach appalling levels of hysteria, but are written by cool-headed paid writers just doing a job. The same is reported for many propaganda mills that accompanied genocides.

The hated group is defined in an all-or-none kind of way. Crudely obvious salient features—skin color, religion, language—define it. Group hatred differs from the prejudicial individual hatred fueled by stereotypes. Raving speech and threatening acts by individuals often lead to requests for law enforcement. Group hatred may be sanctioned by law enforcement. It is easy to point out examples from Nazi Germany; yet witness how law enforcement agencies in the United States once assisted at lynchings, and now sometimes ignore requests for protection from minority individuals or from legally sanctioned providers of reproductive health care, sometimes culminating in direct attacks upon the health care providers themselves or the women they care for in reproductive crisis situations. Group hatred is deliberately and thoughtfully developed. For instance, hate for one's tribal enemies are taught to children, often praised as ardent patriotism. As one of us has written elsewhere, "a child has to be taught, very carefully taught, to hate" (B. Anderson, 1995: 141).

Development of unified group hatred toward a nonconforming group perceived as hurtful and competitive exemplifies the steps of community organization, as described by Saul Alinsky (1971), but in a pathological cause. Alinsky's brilliant work in community organization outlines the necessity of general discontent before a charismatic leader can articulate focus to the discontent and offer solutions. Dr. Martin Luther King's community organization for civil rights closely emulated Alinsky's teachings. Unfortunately, it is at least as easy for evil but charismatic persons to use the same techniques in a horrific service.

Articulating focus through group hate is a tool that cynical and evil leaders use to give shape to widespread fear. Unlike an individual sputtering fear and hate, group hate sows the deadly seeds of genocide. As the soil is poisoned and the seeds of genocide sprout, there is generally silence, a stunning lack of negative social sanctions even when the targeted group has not historically been hated by the larger community.

Much of the genocide literature focuses on cases in which a long-hated or long-attacked minority was victimized: Jews in Germany, Armenians in Turkey, Native Americans in the United States. However, some of the worst examples of genocide are very different. Group hatred has often been unleashed on groups previously ignored or even admired. The Guatemalan military in the 1980s sought out teachers and local development workers. Stalin often turned on groups he had previously supported. Mao not only attacked elites, who might have suffered from some class conflict, but also attacked most vehemently the most universally admired groups in China: scholars, religious leaders, and grassroots community development workers. Mao was able to get ordinary Chinese to change, within two years, from adulating such figures to killing them.

Political purges in eastern Europe and Chile also operated through whipping up previously tolerant populations into haters of groups they had previously admired. In short, group hate is more serious, more violent, more intense, more able to be manipulated, and more irrational than individual hate. It is a different manifestation.

Its elaboration in the twentieth century is a more complicated story. Group hatred is common historically, wars with neighbors and traditional enemies are common historically, but the progression to genocide—mass murder of one's *own* people—is rare. While the paper tigers of fear and individual hate expose the vulnerable, weak side of humanity, group hatred sows the deadly seeds that poison the soil. The seeds sprout quickly, group hatred leads to dehumanizing, diminishing and ascribing evil intentions to the targeted group. Hitler, with the support of many (though far from all) Germans, moved rapidly from incited group hatred of the Jews to condemning "Jew science" (including modern physics), "Jew art," and everything else he believed to be related to Jewish humanity.

In most, if not all, cultures, group hate is far less negatively regarded than is individual hatred. Hate for one's tribal enemies is or was worldwide, and usually praised as necessary and desirable. Hate for unpopular minorities and structural-opponent groups carries that emotion, and the positive evaluation of it, into modern times. Raving speech and threatening acts in an individual hating another individual would often lead to calling the police (at the very least), and would be socially unacceptable almost everywhere. In group hatred, by contrast, books, TV talk shows, and even newspaper columns get away with murder—or at least calls for it. Consider the incendiary talk radio of the United States, with its constant dire warnings to immigrants, political opponents, and other groups. All this is closely related to the stunning lack of negative sanctions on genocide, a point we shall raise below.

When culture constructs this, pathological defensiveness becomes the norm, taught to all. A culture with a long history of conflict and social hierarchies will show this at its worst. This sort of culture is often developed, quite cynically, by politicians who exploit emotions to get and keep power (Westen, 2007).

Of all political considerations, the most serious, basic, and vitally important is defining "friend" and "enemy." Capable politicians and opinion makers know this, and work hard on it. Demagogues represent the hatreds of their constituencies; statesmen and stateswomen focus the popular will against genuine enemies. Careful experimental studies (Bernhard et al., 2006) establish that people in areas as diverse as Switzerland and Papua-New Guinea are more altruistic to their fellow ethnic group members, according to their own definition of what their primary or reference ethnic group is. They are notably more punitive toward structural opponents. Group hatred is so universal and accepted that we tend to condemn "selfish greed" more, because it is more unusual. If group hatred were not stronger, it could not be used—as it routinely is—to sell greed. Greed policies are very often politically defended by appealing to deeper levels of hatred. Even more commonly, corrupt officials get away with their games, when caught out, by redirecting public attention to structural-opponent minorities.

One revealing tendency is the widespread condemnation of the poor. The rich and middle class, everywhere, tend to regard low-status and non-affluent persons as not only vile, but evil and undeserving. This sort of condemnation can only come from fear. Oddly, the rich and powerful seem genuinely afraid of the poor, even when revolution is not a conceivable threat. Guilty conscience may be a factor. Another is a sense of escape: "there but for the grace of God go I." In our experience, this seems especially true in "self-made men" and women, who can add "in fact I *did* go there, without much grace from God or anyone else." As researchers, we have often found either warm sympathy for the poor or vicious hatred of them among persons who had escaped poverty. In our experience, the former were those who had solid, supportive families, and rose through mutual aid and hard work. The latter were those that had felt alienated and rejected. Some had worked hard, but alone and unsupported. Others had clawed their way up by amoral means or outright violence. Either way, they carried a Hobbesian sense of the world.

People may suddenly come to tolerate a formerly hated group. This famously happens when they unite against a common enemy, but sometimes time alone does the job, and sometimes changing political winds change the opposition structure. The British have learned to live with the Scots (more or less), the Dutch, the French, and other traditional hates. Most white Americans have learned to tolerate Asians, and often Blacks and Hispanics as well. Every nation whose history is known reveals some changes of group hatred over time, as conditions of conflict and cooperation shifted.

Over time and space, genuine enmity (especially traditional warfare or oppression over real issues like land) is naturally one cause of structural opponent group hatred. This feeds on itself. Hated groups respond—by attack if they can, by everything from petty theft to foot-dragging otherwise (Scott, 1985)—and thus get themselves even more hated. This feedback loop can go on for centuries, as in the cases of England and France or China and Tibet. At least, the former of those shows that things can change eventually. England and France found too many common interests in the twentieth century, and could not keep up the warring. They united against a common enemy—Germany, in this case. Once again, and the point does need repeating, *the most important thing to recognize is that humans do not usually hate strangers; they hate their own minority or structural-opponent groups*. In fact, when individuals hate other individuals, they often hate their wives, sons, parents, neighbors. Above all, they hate the most visible minority in their own society.

The most salient minority is always the target of particular hatred and stereotyping. An odd thing about humanity is that stereotypes of "inferior" structural opponent groups are remarkably uniform: they are dirty, violent, hypersexual, musical, athletic, and emotional, with poor impulse control. This is the racist stereotype of Blacks in the United States, Roma in much of Europe, Koreans and Burakumin in Japan, scheduled castes in India, outcaste groups in Arabia, Native Americans in Canada and much of South America, Irish in England, fisherfolk in South China. It seems to be a human universal. In fact, evil itself—the whole tendency of humans to do each other wrong for no good reason—is universal enough to be considered "normal" by some (Bartlett, 2005).

In genocide, minorities are identified in a highly essentialized way. They are seen as *totally* different when most people realize, at some level, that the difference is not really great. This leads to a type of cognitive dissonance that can make hatred worse, as appears to be the case in Rwanda and other areas where closely linked and intermarried groups killed each other.

RELIGION: THE BEDROCK SOCIAL INSTITUTION

Genocidal regimes are not caused just by one man's madness. They are large-scale operations supported by systematic social infrastructure (see esp. Staub, 1989, 2003). They generally target historical hatred (Hinton, 2002, Hinton [ed.], 2002; Kuper, 1983) and build upon existing social institutions. By sharply defining historical group hatred, genocidal regimes create extreme differences that cannot be wiped out by admixture. With well-defined, existing infrastructure, social institutions in society can turn deadly, poisoning and strangling everyone, victims and perpetrators alike.

Religion can work for good: in the United States, both the antislavery movement (originally started by the Quakers in England and America; Davis, 1966) and the civil rights movements were heavily religious in origin and orientation, using morality and solidarity as their guiding principles. But, unfortunately, because religion holds high moral power, has strong systematic infrastructure, and appeals to solidarity, it can be divisive, and it can be subverted to vicious, destructive purposes. History is full of examples of religion as the mobilizing force for murderous intolerance, not only of rival faiths but also of "heresy" within. Heresy is, indeed, particularly threatening, because it seems like a deadly form of treachery within what is, for many people, the most trusted and important community. Hence the passion in an apparently silly cause that so puzzled Edward Gibbon as he contemplated Christianity torn by wars over *homoousia* versus *homoiousia* (Gibbon, 1995: vol. 1, p. 787) and later over leavened vs. unleavened communion wafers.

Religion, as a social institution, has been subverted in genocidal regimes throughout recent history (Bartov and Mack, 2001; Juergensmeyer, 2003). Hitler's "final solution" is, of course, the most flagrant case (Bartov and Mack, 2001, focuses on this), but other cases include Ottoman persecution of Armenians and other Christians; Christian persecution of Jews in Europe; and the meltdown of Yugoslavia into warring religious camps, with Serbian Orthodox and Croatian Catholics fighting each other while both tried to eliminate Muslims. Stalin to some extent and Mao Zidong to an extreme degree tried to repress all religions. Today, Islam is the most visible source, being more polarized than ever before into Shi'a versus Sunni and, within those, into various subsects and legal interpretations. Christianity is widely used to justify terror in parts of Africa and increasingly as a threat (increasingly acted on) in the United States. Over historic time and over the world, religion is the worst hate-maker and violence-maker. Those who thought we had gone beyond this or come to the end of history have learned bitter recent lessons in Afghanistan, Iran, Iraq, and the United States.

Recently, hate-based forms of religion have been called "fundamentalist," but this is a strange term for them. Islam, for instance, explicitly forbids murder of innocents, and explicitly forbids killing fellow Muslims unless they commit capital crimes or are involved in such (including rebellion). It also takes a dim view of suicide. Yet mass murder of innocent noncombatants, Muslim and non-Muslim, often by suicide bombing, is now routine among Wahhabist and extreme Shi'a Islamic states and terrorist groups.

Hate ideologies have attached themselves, like cancers, to the most merciful and tolerant of religions. Christianity begat the Spanish Inquisition. Islam, *contra* modern stereotypes, was a highly tolerant religion over historic time, protecting its Christian, Jewish, and other minorities in medieval times when few regimes were so forbearing; things have sadly changed, thanks especially to the rise of Wahhabism and its promulgation by Saudi Arabia and its oil money. Even the religiously tolerant Chinese Empire had grim moments, especially in the Chinese Muslim (Hui) "rebellions" of the mid-nineteenth century. Most of these rebellions were ordinary civil wars, but some degenerated into genocide (see, e.g., Gillette, 2000, 2008). Even atheism, as a religion-based conviction, can also turn deadly, as we note from Stalin's, Mao's, and Pol Pot's murderous attacks on all religious groups. The various defenders of atheism (e.g. Dawkins 2006) would do well to remember this.

Juergensmeyer (2003) describes how religion can be manipulated into hate ideology. He describes a Belfast Protestant group that "attacked an innocent Catholic working man. . . . The Catholic was stripped naked, tied, and ritually carved as a sculptor would carve a block of wood. Still alive after having received 147 wounds over his body, the hapless victim was suspended from a beam by a slowly tightening noose, where he eventually died of strangulation. His mutilated corpse was then put on display for Catholics and Protestants alike to see" (Juergensmeyer, 2003: 122), and this was in a time of (relative) peace, not genocide. (The Northern Ireland "troubles" lasted for decades and are not totally resolved yet; see Feldman, 1991.) Juergensmeyer concludes that hate and subsequent violence perpetrated in the name of religion followed from a distortion of the religion's belief of "a world gone awry . . . a cosmic war" (Juergensmeyer, 2003: 188). Religious convictions of any sort can be manipulated to become lethal.

The social check on intolerance among religious leaders is weaker than for political leaders. A religious leader is not managing a secular government and may have less accountability within the religious organization than a political figure might. Leadership may be structured on the ability to maneuver within the religion's infrastructure, to hide unacceptable behavior, or to build up a charismatic support base. A religious leader usually wins from extremism; it makes him seem a true zealot, a true warrior for the faith. Conversely, a political leader must deliver at least some actual benefits to be credible, and must usually be somewhat moderate and tolerant to deliver them.

Also, speaking under the mantle of religion, a religious leader is given social credence and respect, even when violence is defended. An example from "fundamentalist" Christianity occurred when James Dobson of "Focus on the Family" roundly denounced a House of Representatives bill barring gender-based hate crimes. He maintained that this law was counter to the Christian view of homosexuality as sin (reported on National Public Radio, May 3, 2007, and in *Seattle Times,* May 4, 2007, p. A3). The bill explicitly did *not* outlaw hate speech (let alone ordinary religious rhetoric); it merely adding the penalty for "hate crimes" to regular civil penalties for violent personal attacks. Dobson took particular offense that the bill was passed on a "Day of Prayer." A secular leader making such a naked call for violent brutality against an inoffensive minority group, in a time of peace, would have had his career ruined; Dobson went on from strength to strength in right-wing politics.

Thus, religion has three things going for it: First, it teaches solidarity. Second, it is not accountable in the way secular regimes are. Third, majority religion is usually (if not always) "politically correct," above criticism. The world has repeatedly seen that organized religion can escape criticism not only for organized and systematic genocide, but for ongoing sexual violence and abuse. Most recently, the Catholic church has recovered almost unscathed (except for trivial fines) from long-running practices of child molestation in schools and other facilities around the world. Political attacks on gays and interracial couples have also gone without major challenges, in many countries, because they are "religious."

Thus, we learn without surprise that true genocide developed and was perfected in the service of religion: the Albigensian crusade, the wars of religion in the early modern period, the persecutions of Muslims in Qing China and non-Muslims in the Ottoman Empire, and on up to Hitler's Holocaust and the Iranian ayatollahs. However, it must be emphasized that *the vast majority of twentieth-century genocides were not about religion*. Most were invoked by Communist or fascist regimes defending and consolidating their positions; many were explicitly atheist, and religious people of all persuasions were specifically targeted by Mao's genocides in the 1960s. There are those who have held (largely informally) that Communism and fascism are religions themselves; they are about belief rather than reason, they have mythologies, and so on. This seems to us a shaky extension of the word "religion." However, the requirement of passionate belief in a fixed dogma links extremists in religious, Communist, and fascist regimes, and is clearly a problem. It allows leaders to insist on extreme commitment to the dogma. They can add heresy and doubt to other difference markers such as ethnicity, politics, skin color, food habits, and politics.

Yet religion, in spite of being probably the commonest excuse for genocide over time, is a thin excuse for genocide. Christianity, Buddhism, Hinduism, and Jainism explicitly teach peace. Chinese religions teach tolerance, and detachment for brutality. Islam teaches justice, including— quite explicitly—sparing innocent noncombatants even in war with unbelievers. Islam explicitly forbids killing Muslims unless they commit capital crimes; these can include rebellion or unprovoked war on other Muslims, but there is no license for mass murder of innocents. The modern regimes that use Islam to justify genocide—as in Iran, Iraq, and Pakistan—operate in flagrant defiance of the Shari'a. It is thus not surprising to find that many Islamic terrorists, including the perpetrators of 9/11, were very lax Muslims (see Atran, 2010). Atran has found that terrorists die for their friends and relatives, not for hope of heaven. Remarks like Pinker's claim that they died for a mythical "posthumous Playboy Mansion" (Pinker, 2011: 356) merely show ignorance and religious bigotry.

MAKING HARMLESS PEOPLE INTO KILLERS

Paul Roscoe (2007) presents an overwhelming amount of evidence, showing that people do not like to kill other humans, and have to be induced to do it, through dehumanization, intense propaganda, or outright threats (cf. also *The March of Folly*, Tuchman, 1984). Roscoe maintains that humans kill only when it pays, politically or economically, enough to overcome this aversion. However, this is true only if the payoff is social conformity or social approval—because those are the motives for the vast majority of genocidal killing. Scott Atran (2010), a leading authority on terrorism, has shown how individuals have to go through long indoctrination programs, involving enormous peer pressure, to make them into terrorists. The fact is that humans are not deeply murderous or aggressive animals. They will defend themselves, and they will fight bravely when attacked, but a great deal of effort is required to make them into the killing machines that characterize genocide. The effort is generally along the lines of making them conform to what seems to be the will of the group (see Baumeister, 1997; Staub, 1989).

Leadership is another concern that evolved, again in connection with war as well as foraging. An excellent discussion by Van Vugt, Hogan, and Kaiser (2008—note the third name!) finds the origin of leadership and hierarchy in tribal warfare and its need for rapid, organized dealing with any emergency. We agree, though these authors exaggerate both the extent of the warfare and its monolithic role. Leadership surely involved defense against predatory animals, organization of foraging and food-sharing, care for the long-helpless human infants, eldership in kingroups, and ordinary dispute-resolution, as well as actual war-leading. As we shall see later, genocide requires a leader, and usually stops if that leader is deposed (Pinker, 2011: 332, and below).

These authors also emphasize followership: people have to have a strong capacity to put themselves under an elder or leader. This would follow naturally from our long childhood under parental supervision, but it does go well beyond that. Nothing could be further from Hobbes's "savage" in a "warre of each against all" than the human animal docilely following a warchief, boss, or priest. The human problem—control over life versus sociability—here takes the form of maintaining a balance of power, with conformity but with full accountability and recourse, in hierarchic situations.

Thanks to Emmy Werner and others (Werner, 1989; Werner and Smith, 1982), we now know something of what produces the difference in "which wolf you feed." Good people are raised in warm, supportive social environments, and—of course—positively reinforced for good behavior, negatively for bad. Everybody knows this, but somehow we never think much about how to apply it. Bad people are raised abusively; bullies are almost always beaten by their parents, and criminals come from criminal families. One can always point to exceptions, but Werner and her group showed that even the exceptions are only partial. They are usually broadly predictable from the same basic variables.

However, one salient point that emerges from close studies of genocide and terrorism is that a vast range of people is swept up in the process, such that most of the perpetrators are ordinary humans. Thus Scott Straus said about Rwanda, "I find that the profile of Rwanda's perpetrators strongly resembles the profile of adult men in the country. Rwanda's perpetrators were not especially mad, sadistic, hateful, poor, uneducated, ideologically committed, or young" (Straus, 2006: 10). Hitler's perpetrators included countless "good Germans." A list of American settlers who massacred Native Americans in pre-1900 America would be a very long list, and the exceptions would be relatively few: people whose highly rigorous religion or heightened sense of common humanity made them think that "Indians" deserved to live. In a related note, Scott Atran (2010) found from a very long and detailed investigation that terrorists and suicide bombers are a wide and not especially skewed sample of modern Islamic society; they are not even necessarily very religious. We found the same thing interviewing Cambodians and Cambodian refugees and interviewing in China and Ethiopia. The same is reported for the Indonesia genocide of 1965–1966. Everyone got caught up in the nightmare somehow, and the perpetrators—though not the leaders—were a cross-section of society. The authors of this book were raised in parts of the country where the Ku Klux Klan and pro-Hitler groups had been strong within living memory. Some of the members of those groups were nothing but thugs, but by all accounts (and our own experience of surviving members of those groups) many of the participants were the sort who described themselves—without undue dishonesty—as "ordinary, decent, law-abiding citizens." Under exceptional circumstances, especially terrifying and chaotic ones, people will suddenly or rapidly turn to hatred, and from hatred to killing. Pinker, in his more hopeful moments, sees genocide as committed largely by thugs and bizarre local gangsters (see Pinker, 2011: 311–12, 331–32), but he is wrong—dangerously wrong. All major genocides involve countless ordinary people.

A truly Machiavellian leader, like Osama bin Laden, may take advantage of his enemies' blundering by getting them to seem opposed to a huge group rather than to a tiny band. Bin Laden openly admitted that Al Qaeda's 2001 attack on the United States was deliberately calculated to make the Bush administration incautiously blame "Islam" or "the Islamic world" rather than a tiny, ragged band of not-very-Muslim fanatics. Bush played into this, talking of a "crusade" and letting his stalwart backers rant about a "clash of civilizations" and other wild-eyed matters. The result was that a group that would have ordinarily been written off as mad managed to get all Islam to see the United States as their collective enemy. Also, Osama boasted that his small raid led to a state of fear in the United States that led to huge economic losses through wars, security expenditures, foregone travel, and the like (estimated at "half a trillion dollars"; Pinker, 2011: 346).

What matters in this story is that it shows that humans have to be stirred up to feel truly threatened by a structural-opponent group, but that it is generally easy to stir them up, and once they are stirred up their enmity often gets out of control and becomes all-dominant and implacable.

The question, then, is what precipitates this: what changes ordinary human solidarity and conformity from a source of good and desirable sociability to a rush to mass murder.

FOUR

Animating Tigers

Dehumanization, Justified Violence, and Paper Tigers

[A] savage who was no more account than a grain of sand in a black Sahara.
—*Heart of Darkness*, Joseph Conrad, 1905, p. 111

DEHUMANIZING

The paper tigers of fear and individual hatred are not, in themselves, causative for genocide, but when society allows them to be unrestrained and offers no solution for their management, they may lead to unbridled behaviors and to dehumanizing a targeted group. It becomes essential to re-categorize and redefine the hated group so that it ceases to have the characteristics and the rights of the community.

Dehumanization is a strangely equivocal word. It is and is not involved in genocide. Social haters generally have a lively sense of the full humanity of the targeted group, and hate them all the more for it. This sense of humanity of the "other" is invariably tinged with stark fear, usually quite obvious: "they're taking our jobs," "they're raping our women." The term "dehumanizing" is often used for such behavior, but Roy Baumeister points out that it is often an incorrect and misleading term (Baumeister, 1997). When put into a category of humanity that is hated and feared, the targeted group is still seen as human. Most soldiers, in the heat of battle, while forced to see the "other" as enemy, still see the humanity of their foe. This is one of the most confusing and frightening events of warfare. Soldiers do what they have to do but they do not necessarily hate the enemy nor see them as non-humans.

A recent book by David Livingstone Smith, *Less Than Human* (2011), undermines its own case. It tells of countless cases of dehumanizing rhetoric, from ancient times until today, and even some "othering" by chimpanzees. Humans compare their victims to rats, cockroaches, pigs, and so on. The problem is that this is invariably an excuse or pretext to torture and abuse of a sort that no one ever wastes on rats, cockroaches, or pigs. With a few exceptions that are clearly displaced aggression against fellow humans, people kill such animals as quickly and cleanly as possible. The idea is to get rid of them. With other humans, the idea is to make them suffer as much as possible. As Baumeister points out, *one must be exquisitely empathetic to do this—one must know exactly what will hurt, humiliate, and abuse those people the most*. This is made clear in countless cases in Smith's book. One does not bother screaming insults at a rat or making a cockroach wear demeaning clothes. One does not deliberately torture a farm animal being killed for food.

In fact, one can go farther: *every case documented by Smith resembles family and neighborhood violence and does not in the least resemble animal control*. All the horrible acts Smith recounts are exactly what abusers do to their wives, children, and neighbors (see, as always, Baumeister's 1997 classic). Exterminators do not keep rats in prison for weeks to torment and control them. Genociders do. So do the various other kinds of oppressors—slavers, small-scale warriors, bullies—that Smith describes.

Another fascinating close study of dehumanizing is Hugh Raffles's brilliant and stark essay on the Nazi equation of Jews with lice (Raffles, 2010). This case is more vexed, because the Germans apparently had something close to a phobia of lice, and thus the attempt to dehumanize the Jews was accompanied by a louse obsession that almost reached the stage of seeing actual lice as demons. Yet, even then, no one wanted to torture actual lice. They were exterminated as quickly as possible, without the horrible torments to which the Jews were subjected by the Third Reich. "Lice" were a trope for disgustingness.

And one recalls the irony that many Nazi leaders, including Himmler, made a show (not, perhaps, very credible) of protection and love for animals (higher ones than lice, to be sure). It was only humans—including many of their own German Christians, not just "others"—that they hated.

In short, dehumanizing is a rhetoric that distances other people just enough to make them abusable. It is the rhetoric, the name-calling that barroom brawlers use when starting a fight. One does not call a male dog "you son of a bitch," though it is the literal truth. Quite the reverse: "You son of a bitch" is a term reserved for humans. It, like all such animalistic rhetoric, is calculated to express and arouse contempt and disgust—*not* to dehumanize. In fact, cases of serious animal abuse, like genocide, tend to look a great deal like family violence. Everyone knows cases of men or women who are abused by superiors and take it out on the dog or the horse. So, instead of abuse of humans being a case of dehumanization, animal abuse may very well be a case of humanizing animals.

Torture, rape, mock trials, and such things make no sense unless the full humanity of the victims is taken into account and used in the most cruel fashion. Evelin Lindner (2009) has provided a particularly insightful discussion of the overwhelming desire of genociders to humiliate their victims. To repeat Baumeister's point, one must see the full humanity of one's victims if one is to humiliate them deeply.

The relationship is complex; people seem able to see enemies as human yet not of their group, and thus somehow not counting as "really" human. At worst, they are human, yet so evil that they do not deserve normal human consideration. One recalls how many languages refer to their speakers as "real people" as opposed to the rest of humanity. The Eskimos of southwest Alaska, for instance, call themselves Yup'ik, from *yua* "person" and *p'ik* "true." The Tojolabal Maya are also the "real humans" as opposed to the rest (Lenkersdorf, 1996). This needs much more study than it has received; simplistic views have tended to dominate.

In short, what has been called "dehumanization" is really a process of developing and consolidating group rejection or barriers, and ultimately developing actual group hate. The opposite is not seeing common humanity, but seeing what religious scholars call communitas: unbarriered sight of common humanity. Ordinarily, sight of others is clouded by barriers of prejudicial labeling and stereotyping.

On the other hand, structural violence—as opposed to genocide—often *does* involve extreme dehumanization. Humans notoriously deaden themselves when faced with mass disasters. It is impossible to multiply pity and compassion enough to empathize with millions, but people go further, deliberately blinding themselves to suffering when it is too great for them to relieve or meaningfully alleviate (Cameron and Payne, 2011).

Dehumanization requires a concerted effort to blind oneself to the humanity of the targeted group. Psychologists note that dehumanization may be the opposite of anthropomorphization. The latter involves desire to understand animals, and desire for social contact and affiliation (Epley et al., 2007), while dehumanization involves both the desire to prevent oneself from understanding and the desire to avoid affiliation. Paul Slovic (2007) has noted that people have extreme difficulty thinking in terms of thousands or millions of sufferers. (This fact, interestingly, runs against the equally well demonstrated fact we noted above: huge but rare disasters disproportionately concern and scare people, relative to much commoner but individually small disasters. It appears that ongoing mass disasters deaden people through "compassion fatigue," while rare disasters arouse concern; but there is serious need for further research.) Surely emotional overload plays a part but there also the denial of the essential humanity of the hated group, thus minimizing or ignoring violence. Slovic speaks mostly about a kind of passive, complacent apathy rather than active stalking of prey.

The process of dehumanization, or rather group alienation, follows deliberate efforts at mobilizing group hatred. It comes at a critical juncture where community, as defined by trust and harmony, begins to deteriorate. Since we are really dealing with members of our own species, it takes considerable energy to hate and to teach others to hate.

Both genocidal group hate and dehumanization propagate through a "follow the leader" mentality. This appears in all sources cited herein. Emulation of condemnation follows observation of condemnation. Condemning persons simply because they have been condemned by others is common from school playgrounds to international politics. Many people will despise and hate anyone they see being despised and hated by leaders in their community. This type of rejection can take three forms. First is hatred of the targeted group for an identified reason—they are "enemies," "heathen," "heretics," "slaves." Second is hating them from mob psychology, passively going along with the mob for social approval. A superb account of this is provided by Straus in his study of the Rwandan genocide (2006). Imitating the successful leadership is rational, up to a point. It pays for the young of any species to emulate their most successful elders. However, if the powerful are cruel and divisive, emulation of them moves toward evil.

Third, and most deadly, is the process of dehumanization that occurs as one internalizes group hatred to justify acquiescence to powerful leaders. People are not usually passive or rational about such things. If a dog has a reputation for being vicious, a history of biting will be invented, and people will talk themselves into believing that the dog is bad. If a targeted group is slandered, stories, caricatures and events will be fabricated or exaggerated to create a living legend. Restructuring the category from human to de-human involves enormous energy, spinning tales, creating images. This is attested in all accounts of genocide (as well as in David Smith's book). No one expends such effort when killing rats or other actual nonhumans.

Once people are convinced that the targeted group is indeed inherently bad, they can rationalize not caring if the group is victimized. They can then be led, progressively with patience and manipulation, to commit extreme acts of violence. This invariably happens in wars. Even if most soldiers follow international rules, at least some individual soldiers act with brutality toward enemies, or even civilians caught in the crossfire, for example, the My Lai massacre in the Vietnam war, and the Abu Ghraib and Blackwater scandals in Iraq.

Personal challenges are bad enough, but challenges to one's reference group are far worse (Atran, 2003). At the broadest level, genocide, criminal gangs, terrorism, ordinary uncontrolled soldiering, and religious extremism wind up more or less the same: mass killing and looting without any compunction. The victims are not so much dehumanized as de-group-ized. They are outside one's own group, however defined. This can lead to people doing everything to predict their local animals and plants while murdering neighboring humans without a second thought. The same individuals who carefully watch over their flocks in Afghanistan or their salmon in Haida Gwaii can, or could, be utterly ruthless toward neighboring human groups.

Dehumanization, or, rather, constructed hatred, tends to displace hatred downward in the social hierarchy. This may go back to ancestral primates. The authors have often watched baboons chase each other in the African bush. Usually the smaller one saves himself by finding an even smaller baboon for both of them to chase. This is fun to watch, and rarely results in anyone getting hurt. Small baboons are very agile and can run up trees, leaping onto small branches where the big ones cannot follow. They are not ostracized from the group, only stratified into lower social status until they grow bigger. In humans, there is rarely such a simple escape. Bullying is bad enough when individuals do it, but worse when whole groups do it with the avowed purpose of creating a target of hate.

In short, we are looking at the social construction of hate and the social construction of hated groups—not dehumanization in any simplistic or essentialized sense.

Genuine dehumanization is, however, characteristic of one form of mass killing: structural violence. This term refers to mass murder by neglect, such that easily preventable hunger, disease, and similar problems kill vast numbers of people. Structural violence is, thus, not really violent; it is the art of killing people while seeming innocent and unstained. Structural violence may kill a large segment of the population of a country. It may occur in the most innocuous-seeming situations, far from the battle front or from any thought of war. In fact, it is more characteristic of such situations than of actual violent genocide. We have repeatedly observed dehumanization in action in calm, quiet boardrooms where people with what appear to be the best of intentions condemn thousands without even thinking of the matter. As with civil war, the line between unfair "aid" and genocide is a vague one that is easily crossed.

The mass murders committed by the Dergue in Ethiopia in the 1970s and by Somalian extremists in 2011, in each case through denying food aid to large segments of starving people, are usually classed as genocide or at least as large-scale deliberate killing. However, the current policies of world trade, which support heavily subsidized firms from the rich nations but enforce supposed "free market" terms on poorer nations (Anderson, 2010), are equally fatal, but do not come under similar judgments. One wonders if future historians will class current World Trade Organization policies with Hitler's and Mao's ideologies rather than with economists'. In short, the dividing line between structural violence and genocide, like the dividing line between civil war and genocide, is a vague one. They grade into each other.

Thus, as we have done with civil war and with gender bias above, and will do with settler wars further along, we will devote some consideration to the phenomenon of "structural violence" as a way of understanding genocide through examining closely related forms of group damage.

"Structural readjustment" is a well known term in development circles that basically means "tightening the belt" to stabilize economic meltdowns. The belt tightening is almost always displaced downwards, from the elites to the ordinary people, especially the poor. It takes the form of denial of essential services. This leads to an increase in class divisions. Structural readjustment often grades into structural violence.

Structural violence includes such things as refusal to provide public health (cf. Farmer, 2004), and refusal to resettle populations displaced by building large dams (Scudder, 2005). Other examples are deforestation that displaces local people, mining with bare-faced defiance of environmental regulations and concerns (see e.g., Kirsch, 2006), and the hundreds of other ways that rulers kill the defenseless by indirect means. World Bank projects, and much of international "aid" and "development" projects, even some funded by the most charitable of NGOs, have often been concocted with little consideration of the poor (Dichter, 2003; Easterly, 2006; Ellerman, 2005; Hancock, 1991; Stiglitz, 2003). Meanwhile, world trade policies set by the World Trade Organization have theoretically increased "free trade," but actually set enormously subsidized, government-backed, or government-run First World interests against unprotected enterprises in the less affluent nations (Collier, 2007). Perhaps commonest of all is refusal to relieve famine. The Ethiopian Dergue's denial of aid, which involved blocking foreign aid, has been counted as outright genocide (Rummel, 1994, 1998). Many more projects should be. Kim Jung Il's seventeen-year reign in North Korea involved the death of "about two million people, almost 10 percent of his country's population" (Demick, 2011), in spite of the facts that international food aid was available and that reasonable economic reforms would have eliminated the problem in the first place. This certainly counts as deliberate democide.

Denying health care or food to a specific minority group or other segment of the population can be as effective as any other genocidal technique. It happens to some degree in almost all countries except full civil democracies—and even in many of them (Farmer, 2004; Sen, 1992, 1999). Killers can appear perfectly calm, cool, rational, and non-murderous. All they are doing is shutting down the health clinics that serve poor or minority neighborhoods. Leaders typically invoke economic policies that they know will benefit the rich but lead to widespread starvation among the poor. Above all, the giant international agencies—the World Bank, International Monetary Fund, World Trade Organization—routinely do this, and they are not accountable to anyone, public or private. Leaders of such agencies protest that are not directly killing anyone. The precise, reasonable language of economic policy can be very chilling in such situations.

Famine is a governmental choice, rendered possible by lack of accountability, rather than a natural disaster. Famine shares a very important characteristic with genocide: As Amartya Sen points out,

> no major famine has ever occurred in a functioning democracy with regular elections, opposition parties, basic freedom of speech and a relatively free media (even when the country is very poor and in a seriously adverse food situation). . . . There remains, however, the problem that a ruthless majority that has no compunction in eliminating minority rights would tend to make the society face a hard choice between honouring majority rule and guaranteeing minority rights. The formation of tolerant values is thus quite central to the smooth functioning of a democratic system. (Sen, 2009: 342, 352)

All this could, of course, be said of genocide. Sometimes, it is clear that mass starvation is deliberately invoked to exterminate groups (Jonassohn and Björnson, 1998: 25ff, cite many cases throughout history; we will briefly consider below the cases of Ethiopia and China).

Today, we could easily eliminate most infectious disease and *all* hunger. Where we do not, it is because governments and international agencies have made the conscious choice that certain populations do not deserve to live (Sen, 1992). Thus, for instance, cases in which ethnic groups find themselves unwilling hosts to the toxic waste dumps or polluting chemical factories of a nation teach us something about why governments kill large numbers of peaceful, docile subjects (E. Anderson, 2010).

The rise of such oppression is really a much bigger story of post–1900 life than the rise of the information economy or the spread of American culture. A part of this has been the rise of propaganda, disinformation, and other public lies, so brilliantly chronicled by George Orwell in *1984* (1949) and *Animal Farm* (1945). Hitler's Nazi propaganda expert, Josef Goebbels, developed the idea of the "Big Lie" in the 1930s; all too many, including more than a few US politicians and talk show hosts, have learned from him. The idea of the Big Lie is not always to convince. Often, a blatantly dishonest claim is deployed with full government backing, simply to convince people that truth is up for grabs and is determined by power, or to make the point that the government is going to act no matter what the truth is. One recalls, from recent years, the denial of global warming by certain governments that clearly knew better, and the widespread denial of the AIDS threat. Often, also, an extreme position is taken solely for the purpose of shifting the center of debate—the old bargainer's trick of starting with a ridiculously low price and working up to a reasonable middle ground.

One could regard structural violence as morally viler than genocide. At least Hitler had the courage to admit what he was doing. The faceless bankers and "developers" who invoke structural violence do it with smiling faces and the excuse of "development." Yet they may kill more than genocide and democide ever did.

We have talked with globally connected economists on the front lines of planning structural adjustment programs. Frequently they genuinely seem to ignore the poor, failing to see them as members of the human community. When queried about policies of structural readjustment leading to social divisiveness, dehumanization, and excess deaths among the poor, some economists freely admit these outcomes. They argue, often without apparent emotion, that draconian economic measures are necessary so that the more economically productive members of society can flourish. This dehumanizing approach is couched in cliques such as "a rising tide floats all boats" or, "the trickle-down effect." The poor, as Amartya Sen concluded (Sen, 1992), are unseen and simply do not matter.

Mohammed Yunus (1999), founder of the Grameen Bank, challenged this dehumanizing approach to economic development. We were most privileged to visit his work in Bangladesh as well as to participate in replications of the Grameen Bank principles in southeast Asia and Africa. Profound social changes have resulted from the seminal works of Sen and Yunus. Similarly, we have interfaced with environmentalists and observed first-hand, most specifically in our work in Madagascar and India, where dehumanization and displacement can occur in the effort to save lemurs or tigers. In Madagascar, for instance, we studied a project in which lemurs were saved but the complex direct and indirect effects on local humans were not even considered until too late (cf. Harper, 2002). While we are highly in favor of programs to save natural resources, including lemurs and tigers, the programs that are most impressive are those that improve the economics of the poor because they, themselves, are protecting their natural environment. Madagascar once had, and Costa Rica still has, stunning small enterprise development projects exemplifying this principle, preventing the dehumanization and group targeting that can occur when the poor are unseen or redefined as social objects of hate.

Structural violence appears to be replacing genocide as the preferred way for contemporary governments to get rid of undesired elements of the population. China, for instance, has shifted from outright mass murder under Mao Zidong to massive environmental pollution and degradation, cutbacks in health services, and economic policies that disadvantage the poor. It appears that China has found structural violence preferable to open violence. The results may, in the end, be worse.

Structural violence is typically under the radar; Steven Pinker, for instance, does not consider it in his book about the decline of violence in the modern world (Pinker, 2011). Yet it is killing millions, in peculiarly horrible ways, while the world focuses its attention on terrorist acts which—while horrific and absolutely inexcusable—kill at most a few hundred. Unlike the forms of violence chronicled by Pinker, it appears to be increasing.

The main difference in epidemiology between genocide and structural violence seems to be that genocide is invoked to destroy minorities that are in a position to act in their own interest; they are well-to-do, or armed, or were once militarily or politically powerful, or in charge of local regions, or have political defenders. Structural violence is directed against the poorest of the poor, who have no conceivable way of doing anything about it, even in the minds of paranoid leaders.

JUSTIFYING VIOLENCE AND CONFLICT

Individuals sometimes fight and kill each other, but ordinary homicides are dwarfed into insignificance by the numbers killed in group-against-group conflicts. Sometimes the group perpetrating the violence is so large that no amount of kin selection, reciprocity, cheater avoidance, or other simple Darwinian mechanisms can possibly explain the loyalty and self-sacrifice so universally demonstrated—often in a cause that no one could reasonably justify if in cool mind.

Peter Turchin (2006), among others, has shown that justified violence culminating in conflict, war, or empire building is grounded in social loyalty and solidarity. Theories of human evolution do not well explain positive examples of sociability and solidarity, notably cooperation. Simulations that model the evolution of high levels of cooperation and sociability among humans suggest that conflict is only one, among many methods, employed in promoting solidarity (Bowles, 2006; Hall and Turchin, 2007). In fact high levels of violence and conflict quickly become counterproductive, resulting in anarchy and self-destruction.

The problem of evil that results in genocide arises from unmanaged fear, targeted hatred, dehumanization, and finally justified targeted violence.

Fear and Hate May Lead Elsewhere: Some Noncauses of Genocide

A range of very shaky causal explanations for genocide is found in the literature. One is the concept that warlike societies are genocidal. Often, nations that committed genocide and democide were also aggressively warlike, starting the twentieth century's wars: Germany, Japan, Sudan, and so on. The United States was an aggressive twentieth-century war-maker, however, without committing further massacres of Native Americans, and many countries were genocidal without starting wars.

The correlation is poor. Countries with genocidal histories often go on to commit more (Pinker, 2011: 341). One thinks of Brazil, Indonesia, Nigeria, Rwanda, and a few other cases. But most genocides seem to be one-shot affairs. Moreover, countries can change dramatically—as Germany most certainly has, to say nothing of the United States.

Even availability of guns is not necessarily important; the genocides in Rwanda and Cambodia involved mass killing with machetes, rocks, and even shovels. Far more deadly than antiquity, agrarianism, or even guns are declining economic conditions leading to erosion of hope.

In the 1960s, partly as a reaction to the student radicalism of the time, a strange belief arose that any strongly held ideology, even democratic and libertarian ideologies, led automatically to genocide (Hoffer, 1963; oddly, Pinker buys into this view; Pinker, 2011: 328ff.). Hitler and Stalin were the poster children for this belief. Model ideologues like Jefferson, Lincoln and Gandhi were forgotten. Fortunately for idealists, the delusion did not survive. A flood of corrupt dictators, singularly lacking in any ideology except hate and greed, arose around the world, from Haiti to Burma and from Congo to Serbia. They were anticipated by equally ideology-free murderers in the past; Qin Shi Huang Di—so idolized by Mao—and Zhu Yuanzhang were perfectly open about caring about nothing but power. It was realized that most dictators who play the ideology card are total hypocrites; they care no more about their stated ideals than they do about the people they kill. Genocide became more and more clearly the natural reflex of totalitarian government, with or without ideology, and democracy—necessarily ideological, and typically pitting conflicting ideologies against each other—emerged, more and more clearly, as the only hope for prevention (Rummel, 1998). Thus Straus (2006: 11) dismisses "utopian" ideologies as relevant. After all, the ideal of a peaceful, democratic regime with freedom and security is an ideology too, and a very strong and compelling one. No genocide has ever occurred in the name of that ideology, except when it was invoked in a totally hypocritical way (as, for instance, by Mao Zidong when talking to the more gullible westerner listeners).

However, there are important exceptions. In addition to religion, there are the religion-like but hatred-based ideologies. Of these, the most important has been Marxism-Leninism (not just Marxism in general; it has peaceful variants). It explicitly calls for elimination of dissidents. The other highly important one is Hitlerian fascism. Fascism, originally defined by Benito Mussolini, was autocracy plus cooperation within big industrial firms. It was not particularly murderous or anti-Semitic. Fascism turned brutal even under Mussolini, but what really made it genocidal was the whole poisonous soup of dictatorship, industry, ethnic hatred, anti-intellectualism, anti-woman and anti-gay attitudes, and general bigotry that Hitler put together. It is far more widely influential and widely copied than most people realize; it lay behind several post-Hitler genocides, notably those in Argentina, Chile, Guatemala, and other Latin American countries. It has been influential to varying degrees on almost every military dictatorship.

Similarly, ethnic diversity does not cause genocide. All countries are diverse, yet not all kill. Traditional rivalries do lead to genocide on occasion, but usually do not. The Jews were massacred over and over again in Europe, from the medieval period onward, and this fed directly into Hitler's genocide; some of the episodes were as murderous on a local scale as Hitler's continent-wide massacres. But only Hitler and his henchmen carried out systematic, cold-blooded searches and massacres, over years, with the goal of exterminating all Jews totally. Even the less systematic and coldly bureaucratized genocides, such as those in Darfur and Cambodia, were qualitatively different from local massacres and mob actions. They involved high-level bureaucratic decisions and operations. This goes beyond traditional hate.

Samuel Huntington's "clash of civilizations" (Huntington, 1996) is similarly irrelevant. Civilizations are analytical abstractions; they cannot clash. (Huntington's in particular are very dubiously meaningful entities—so far as the authors of the present book can determine, they do not exist in any meaningful or verifiable way.) Only human beings can actually clash. And humans are not motivated by imaginary "civilizations," but by beliefs in actual imminent threats and prospects. Modern bureaucratic genocide is a western invention that has spread with westernized global culture; we repeatedly find dictators reading *Mein Kampf* or Lenin and Stalin, and buying arms and torture techniques from "developed" countries. Mass murder, as a more general type of butchery, is as old and universal as warfare, and needs no explanation beyond human combativeness; in fact, even chimpanzees do it (Smith, 2009). But genocide, by our definition, is far more limited and recent.

Chirot and McCauley (2006) find four frequent themes in genocide: convenience (clearing people off the land to get rid of them), revenge, fear, and pollution. These are, however, genociders' excuses, rather than actual risk factors. The degree to which they are actual motives (as opposed to purely dishonest excuses) remains to be seen. Our examination of the evidence does not disclose any correlation between revenge and genocide. Genocide is, by definition, slaughter of the innocent. If mass killing is done in revenge, it must, again by definition, be in a combat situation in return for prior mass killing. The line can be a fine one, but it is real.

Pollution (Chirot and McCauley, 2006; Kiernan, 2007) is another rather shaky issue, unless defined very widely. People want to eliminate the structural opponents not because they really pollute but because they are a salient minority; pollution is alleged of them only *after* they have been selected for hatred. One might say the Jews were polluting the Christian fold with their heretical ideas, or that the Native Americans were polluting a continent that the European settlers needed, but such claims are excuses, not reasons, for hatred. This seems to stretch Chirot and McCauley's point. Minorities are routinely called "dirty" and in India are often held to be genuinely polluting in a ritual sense, but this, again, all seems only part of a wider and pre-existing negative ideological stereotype. It does not usually lead to genocide. Convenience was a factor in the settlement-related clearings of the nineteenth century, but seems an odd thing to allege about, say, the Nazi murders or Mao's campaigns, which were anything but convenient. Mao's campaigns paralyzed China for years, setting back development by two decades. Fear is, of course, universal, but too general to be a "cause" by itself.

Some theorists have proposed that genocide is not so much a crime of hate, but a crime of social cognition (Sternberg and Sternberg, 2008; Waller, 2002). Hannah Arendt's famous book about Eichmann, *The Banality of Evil* (1964), makes the case that genocide can seem very mundane, dull, and even normal in a dull and emotionally limited man. Still, this is not usually sufficient unto itself. Eichmann was following orders of higher-ups who were truly exceptional in many ways, including the levels of their hatred. And Eichmann was operating in exceptional times. It seems awfully difficult to believe that genocide is not about hate; the social cognition follows, rather than drives, the agenda.

Pinker holds that "genocides can emerge from toxic reactions among human nature (including essentialism, moralization, and intuitive economics), Hobbesian security dilemmas, millennial ideologies, and the opportunities available to leaders" (Pinker, 2011: 332). Indeed, but not very often, and certainly not predictably. No one of those factors is even remotely adequate, and the combination in the quoted sentence is too much a grab-bag to be useful. We must be more specific.

AGRARIANISM: AN IDEOLOGICAL PAPER TIGER

Ben Kiernan's great work states its thesis in its title: *Blood and Soil* (2007). Heredity is the stigma, and gaining or holding land is a goal. These are excuses for killing in general. As noted above, they are not directly associated with genocide by our definition. Most of Kiernan's mass murders are settler wars or other wars over land, but these involve killing of actual enemy groups, not killing of one's own people. And, if one is killing one's own, blood is either not a factor at all (as in politicide, to say nothing of extermination of gays or educated people or modern artists) or a suspiciously thin one.

Kiernan's explanation of genocide, in *Blood and Soil* (2007), is that politicians and political movements become obsessed with "race, antiquity, agriculture, and expansion" (2007: 605). "Race" is unproblematic, since "race"—here meaning ethnicity—is often the defining concern of genocide. Racial, religious, or ideological purity is always invoked, since without it the whole enterprise seems merely silly (in a macabre way). However, it is clearly not a cause in itself, since "racial" (ethnic) hatreds are virtually universal among humans, existing within all societies. Expansion is a concern only in settler wars; genocides by our definition do not involve expanding territory, though they may involve taking land from victim groups (as in Darfur and Rwanda). This leaves us with antiquity and agrarian virtues as concerns to address.

Kiernan has established that such rhetoric accompanies many mass murders. Kiernan is also aware of a well-known point, made by Adam Smith, Karl Marx, and other political economists, that trade and commerce go with modernizing or progressive ideologies, while farmers and agrarian regions tend to be conservative and rigid, if not downright reactionary. Kiernan's own views were also shaped by his focus on the Cambodian genocide, which did indeed invoke his four stated ideals.

The problem is that appeals to the good old days and agrarian bliss accompany not only hateful politics but almost all politics, especially in agricultural areas. In our childhood in the Midwest and South, no politician could avoid appealing to the Founding Fathers, America's glorious past, and the stalwart farmers with their wonderful, virtue-creating family farms. (We understand that this remains true today.) Henry Wallace, the champion of the democratic left in the Midwest in our childhood, was as sure of this as the most reactionary Republicans. So was Aldo Leopold, the liberal environmentalist. So were Helen and Scott Nearing, radicals and pacifists who inspired the 1960s back-to-the-land movements. It is also clear that the world has little to fear from Wendell Berry or the Audubon Society, in spite of their idealization of the good old days and the agrarian ideal.

Today, the tradition is as lively as ever. Nostalgia for the great past and idealization of the farm is typical of the entire spectrum of American politics, and is widespread everywhere else as well. Political thinkers who have sung the praises of agrarian society range from Voltaire to Jefferson, from the anarchist Pyotr Kropotkin to the socialist utopians of nineteenth-century America, and from Abraham Lincoln to Gandhi; hardly a genocidal lot.

Conversely, many genocidal regimes have been closely connected to "progress" and industry. Kiernan is rather quiet on the entire industrial component of fascism—originally a political philosophy of government-industry cooperation to bring industrial progress. There has never been a more ardent apostle of industry, technology, and mechanical progress than Benito Mussolini, whose famous accomplishment was making the trains run on time. Hitler certainly spoke much about the virtues of rural life, but his actual economic agenda was largely focused on mutual support arrangements between the Nazis and Krupp, I. G. Farben, and dozens of other big firms. The other European fascist regimes were also overtly industrial. So was Japan's. So are Latin American, African, and Asian imitators, including most of the oil regimes of the Middle East. It would be hard for the Saudi government to be very agrarian. On the left-wing side, Communism idealizes progress, industry, and forced marches to the future. Mao carried out his mass murders with some vague comments about rural virtues, but a great deal of far more serious talk about industrializing China rapidly and bringing it into modern prosperity through heavy industry. In direct contradiction to Kiernan's point, Mao wanted to bring agriculture into the glorious future by the most direct and brutal means, turning it into an industrial production system with forward technology, and turning the peasants into proletarians.

On a more general level, Kiernan shows a true historian's fondness for explaining everything by high ideals, rather than by such grubby matters as hate and greed. Even when dealing with the most naked land grabs, such as the Spanish conquest of the Americas, though he cannot totally deny bare-faced greed, he quotes the high agrarian ideals of the land-grabbers as if these were actual motives rather than threadbare excuses. Almost two centuries after Marx, it still seems simply beyond the ken of historians that humans are motivated by anything other than noble words. In fact, the sort of politicians that invoke genocide are not motivated by high ideals, agrarian or otherwise. They invoke high ideals only when reduced to extremes of hypocrisy. The people who actually *hold* the high agrarian ideals—people like Thoreau, Leopold, and Wendell Berry—are among the least offensive and most democratic of humankind.

There are at least three different reasons for invoking agrarian bliss: First, because one actually believes it; second, as a purely cynical way of getting the farm vote; and third, as an even more cynical excuse for killing other people to take their land. Kiernan does not differentiate these. The last one clearly motivates mass killing (though largely in ordinary war, not in genocide). The former two do not. Kiernan ends his book thusly: "The cure and prevention of the crime of genocide must lie, at least in part, in the diagnosis of its recurring causes and symptoms" (Kiernan, 2007: 606). Alas, we must rule out race, antiquity, and agrarianism as causes, and regard expansion as only a very limited causal agent.

Returning to Kiernan's defining case of genocide (recall that it was not a genocide by our definition), the Roman extermination of Carthage and the Carthaginians, brings up a point that seems to us to be critical. Kiernan writes of Cato, the conservative Roman most responsible for the extermination campaign: "Cato's alleged hypocrisy is less important than his romanticization of peasants in opposition to merchants" (Kiernan, 2007: 54). We see things exactly the other way round. Cato's hypocrisy— his actual life as an urban slave owner rather than farmer, and as an abusive and treacherous politician rather than a moral model—seems to us to be exactly the problem. His ideology, like the nostalgic ideologies of other mass killers, seems merely a part of the hypocrisy—mere paint to cover the viler and far more effective material beneath.

In fact, genocide does not go with agrarianism; it is far more typically coupled with a deliberate effort to establish *an economy based on centrally organized primary production*, be it agribusiness, mining, oil, or logging. The key difference between Thomas Jefferson, Aldo Leopold, and Wendell Berry, on the one hand, and Hitler, Stalin, Mao, and Pol Pot on the other, is that *the former idealized the stalwart independent farmer, whereas the latter idealized the state-run enterprise*—the fascist bureaucracy, the commune, the collective farm. Whether the government is "capitalist," "socialist," or "Communist" appears to make little difference in such cases. Geography also means little. Appeals to antiquity mean little.

Back-to-the-farm economic ideology can be dangerous, but only when coupled with severe rural poverty, centralized economic control of agrarian life, and targeted hatred. The manipulation of the economic infrastructure along with hate messages foster the conditions for genocide.

In short, war, ideology, cognition, pollution, and agrarianism are not explanatory factors. They are part of generic hate and fear, but do not lead to genocide unless there are direct factors turning hatred into action.

FIVE

The Tiger Stalks

The Steps of Genocide

> The world is a dangerous place to live—not because of the people who are evil but because of the people who don't do anything about it.
> —Albert Einstein (www.famousquotesandauthors.com)

CREATING A CULTURE OF HATE

Using religion is one way to overcome a more general problem: the worldwide value on civility. Every culture has extremely elaborate and tightly—but informally—enforced politeness and etiquette codes grounded in the cultural worldview. "Being nice" (in whatever culturally appropriate form) is extremely important, though often difficult for individuals and communities. The most respected people in any society are those who are competent at conveying cultural values and handling social relationships. They can de-fang a conflict, or marshal the troops if de-fanging fails. Genocidal leaders must not only neutralize such tendencies; they must actually take over the job of defining cultural values. They must have a firm grasp on the prevalent worldview, utilizing it in order to create the cultural conditions for genocide.

One way of subverting civility is to co-opt it, often by comparing the best values of one's own culture with the worst practices that can be alleged of the target "enemy." Every nation has a history, and a "story" within the history. The story usually speaks to a noble and brave people, forbearing, strong, and true to their ancient principles. The enemy is cowardly yet "fanatical," unprincipled yet merciless, and so on. The same behavior that is "heroic self-sacrifice" when done by one of "ours" becomes "fanatical terrorist suicide bombing" when done by one of the "others." The same dogmatism is "being true to principles" on one side, "hidebound inflexibility" on the other. Also, stories of hatred may be targeted toward fold breakers, deviants, or minorities who are perceived to interfere with or oppose the established cultural world view. Often, the stories promulgate and build upon stereotypes. The fact that the fold breakers also have a story to tell is frequently neglected.

A trivial, mild example of the subtle growth of nasty stereotyping is the classic modernist attitude toward the Middle Ages. (It is relevant to our story because of its use by Pinker; see chapter 7.) We moderns value peace, harmony, cleanliness, and kindness to animals, while the medieval people, so we are told, practiced wars, burned people at the stake, did not wash, and beat their animals. In fact only the lowest citizenry of the Middle Ages lived the uncouth lives of modern fiction. The modern world's worst citizens are not notably different. On the whole, medieval times were harsher than today, but not by a huge margin. In fact, the comparison is made in reverse by more than a few Society of Creative Anachronism hobbyists; they hold the Middle Ages to have been a civil and honorable time.

This trivial but familiar example shows how even a world perfectly irrelevant to ours—not our enemy in any way—can be stereotyped negatively if it is not in a position to defend itself. We can extend such observations to the more extreme comparisons made by the Nazis, who set the finest of "Aryan" behavior against imagined horrors of Jewish, Slavic, and Mediterranean life.

ECONOMIC DECLINE AND GENOCIDE

In spite of much ink spilled to the contrary (e.g., Hamburg, 2010: 28ff on "harsh conditions"), it is conclusively established that poverty by itself is not a risk factor for genocide (Pinker, 2011, esp. p. 341). Neither is bad or inept government per se.

The clearest counterevidence is the genocides that occurred in peaceful and/or prosperous countries with strong, capable, modern governments. The most visible recent cases are Argentina and Chile in the 1970s, but also the greatest genocides of all—those under Hitler, Stalin, and Mao—took place in relatively well-off and secure states (once China was consolidated and on a path of economic development). Serbia under Milosevitch was not a "failed state." By contrast, many truly needy states, from Bhutan to Mali and from Bolivia to Tanzania, have not come even remotely close to genocide (see appendices). Particularly noteworthy is the lack of genocide in South Africa, in spite of racism and political upheavals (see Hamburg, 2010: 72–96 for a particularly good discussion of this case). South Africa had relative economic security, world support, and at least some degree of democracy going for it. That was all that was needed, though the statesmanship of Nelson Mandela and others mattered too.

Julian Borger, in a long analytic piece in *The Guardian* (online, April 28, 2007), argues that climate change bears some of the guilt for the Darfur war. Global warming created desperate poverty in this area by reducing rainfall drastically. The same could probably be postulated for the enormous rash of wars and meltdowns all over northeast Africa in recent decades. However, Declan Butler (2007) and Gérard Prunier (2007) point out that Sudan's murderous regime has been engaging in genocidal attacks on its own people for decades, and that climate change has not altered this policy one way or another; nor has the same drought managed to bring genocide to impoverished, climate-affected, but politically stable Mali or Senegal. We must exonerate climate change and return to human evil.

A short but excellent article by Lydia Polgreen in *The New York Times* (Polgreen 2007) confirms this, and quotes Alex de Waal: "an environmental catastrophe cannot become a violent cataclysm without a powerful human hand to guide it in that direction." She adds that policies of the World Bank and the International Monetary Fund had at least as much to do with devastating Sudan's environment and people as any natural causes did, and that "the government exploited tensions over water and land to achieve its own aims," including especially the suppression of non-Arab groups and of the poor in general. So conflict over resources, defined by group and class hatreds, is the problem, not resource shortage per se. Sudan's oil, and the need of China and other nations for it, has led to Sudan being protected from sanctions or intrusion. China in particular has emerged as a powerful ally of Sudan, and thus a powerful facilitator of genocide; China's own policies toward its minorities, especially the Tibetans, are highly relevant here.

One of us (ENA) took up the study of genocide partly to investigate this very issue, in the full expectation that the "resource squeeze" would be explanatory. Our findings have been totally opposite to this. Never has a hypothesis wilted faster under the sun of truth. It is always interesting to see oneself convinced by the evidence that one's conviction was totally wrong! A long enquiry by many authors into this issue was collected in the volume *The Coming Age of Scarcity*, edited by Michael Dibkowski and Isidor Wellimann (1998). All possible sides of the debate are taken by someone somewhere in this large collection, but the sensible and fact-based articles generally conclude that the relationship is tenuous at best (see e.g., Smith, 1998). One need only consider the particularly horrific genocides that have taken place in relatively prosperous, resource-rich countries, starting, of course, with Germany itself. David Victor, debating a number of people who claim that "resource wars" are the order of the day, points out that they are actually rare, and today's wars and genocides have more complex causes, including shaky or failing governments (Victor et al., 2008). Finally, in an evolution similar to ENA's, Wendy Barnaby sought for "water wars" and found that—as of 2009, at least—nations did not go to war over water (Barnaby, 2009). They argue, negotiate, compromise, or in some cases simply suffer helplessly as more powerful upstream nations appropriate a disproportionate share of critical river resources. (There is a large literature on these matters, but it seems tedious to review a vast literature that comes to essentially negative conclusions.)

Too much can be made of environmental decline (Homer-Dixon, 1999, and in dialogue with Victor in Victor et al., 2008, for instance, is overly simplistic; see Victor's commentary). There is no denying that many countries with dense and impoverished rural populations experienced genocide or mass killing. Burundi, Cambodia, China, El Salvador, Equatorial Guinea, Ethiopia, Guatemala, Indonesia, Nigeria, Pakistan, Philippines, Rwanda, Sudan, and a dozen other countries fit the model. (On Sudan, see the balanced account in United Nations Environment Programme, 2007, as well as Prunier, 2008.) There is a genuinely critical observation here: the poor nations that have seen genocide were largely ones that were *actually exceedingly rich in resources; the poverty and the genocide were both caused by bad government*—government bad enough to squander sometimes incredible wealth. In addition to the Sudan, cases include China (under Mao), Congo, Ethiopia, Guatemala, Indonesia, Nigeria, and others—indeed, most of the genocidal countries of the past forty years.

Rural hierarchic society can breed the sort of racism that can come out in genocide. The Dutch in the Netherlands and the Afrikanders in South Africa were the same people in the seventeenth century, but by the late twentieth they had certainly diverged in practice, in spite of still sharing a common religion and language (with some dialect differentiation). Trade in the Netherlands prospered; South Africa's Afrikanders became, under the British, an oppressed minority threatened by an even more oppressed black majority, and later a dominant, extremely oppressive, racist elite. This seems to be about as perfect a comparison case as one could wish. Yet—and this is really significant—the expected civil wars in South Africa never came, and the place became a rare African success story; Chirot and McCauley (2006) and Hamburg (2010) point out and discuss this in the context of genocide.

Moreover, genocide in poor nations may not be a function of poverty. Even in Rwanda, where desperate poverty, dense population, conflict over land, deforestation, and ecological devastation produced one of the worst economic scenarios in the world (Diamond, 2005), all sources who were actually on the ground agree that genocide was due to the aftereffects of colonialism and to ongoing political conflicts rather than to ecology. Contrary to the thesis that Rwanda fell apart for Malthusian reasons (Diamond, 2005), there was a *negative* correlation between local poverty and genocide. This was because the Hutu hardliners had most power in the capital city (the least poor and bare part of the country, of course) and least in the remote outback (Straus, 2006; see esp. pp. 55–62). Many truly remote and economically flat parts of Rwanda were so far from the center that they had no significant killings.

Yet poverty is not wholly exonerated as a contributing factor. Poverty strongly predicts civil war (Collier, 2007: 17–37): the poorer and the less upwardly mobile the country, the higher the chance of civil war. This does affect the genocide equation, because civil war so often leads to genocide. As Collier describes (2007), deteriorating economic and ecological situations make historical rivalries worse; fighting breaks out; hatreds arise, and the government uses the conflict as an excuse to exterminate a group. So civil war is made more likely by economic deprivation (Collier, 2003; Collier and Bannon, 2003; Collier and Sambanis, 2005). Not just poverty, but stagnation or decline, is often the problem; the civil war brings economic chaos. Civil war is also made more likely by having many young men on hand (Juergensmeyer, 2003), but, as we have seen, genocide is different; it is ordered by older leaders. Easily extractable and portable resources like oil and diamonds are correlated with civil war: "Diamonds are a guerrilla's best friends" (Paul Collier, quoted Ferguson, 2007: 60). They are also frequently correlated with genocide and democide, and indeed much of what Collier calls "civil war" would be "genocide" or "democide" under Rummel's definition (Pinker, 2011, discusses these points at length, citing largely to Collier but adding some perceptive commentary).

African, Latin American, and Asian countries involved in genocide have often been ones that are ecologically devastated. A problem with analyzing this is measuring ecological devastation: erosion, deforestation, depletion of groundwater, depletion of fisheries if any. No one, however, could reasonably question the extreme level of degradation in Rwanda, Ethiopia, Indonesia, Guatemala, El Salvador, or other cases. But this should not be exaggerated. Most genociding countries are not particularly devastated compared to countries that did not suffer mass killing. What protected Mali, Senegal, Ghana, Kenya, Tanzania, Zambia, and so on?

Poverty and ecological degradation make people desperate and remove incentives to stay peaceful. They can make people indifferent to living or dying (Baumeister, 2005). However, rural poverty does not by itself cause rebellion, war, or conflict. Some deeper hatred or insult must occur. Perceived social injustice *resulting* in poverty might make people rebel (Scott, 1976, 1985), but in this case the key ingredient is the perceived injustice; the regime loses legitimacy in the eyes of the people. Even an extremely incompetent and irresponsible government can last for decades without major outbreaks, as happened often in the old days of agrarian empires from Turkey to China.

However, once injustice becomes unbearable, a small outbreak may cause an extreme governmental response, such that a minor civil unrest quickly escalates into a major genocide. This happened in Guatemala in the 1970s and 1980s, and in Sudan's Darfur in the 2000s. Also, at least as dangerous, declining economic and personal security really constitutes a major risk factor. A prosperous, formerly stable society that lapses into decline can quickly turn genocidal; this is certainly part of the story in Hitler's Germany, and later in Argentina, Serbia, and several other cases.

A trade-based society has a strong incentive not to engage in killing a large percentage of its productive citizens. It also has a strong incentive to practice tolerance. As noted above, trading communities have often had notably tolerant religious practices: the Jews in mid-twentieth-century United States and Europe, the Parsis in India—in general, diaspora communities almost everywhere. When the Jews acquired a nation-state and were no longer a diaspora trade-based community, they slowly but surely became more and more oppressive toward their most visible minority (the Palestinians).

On the other hand, elites making their money from primary production, and *magna forte* from the giant international extractive firms (with cooperation from these firms' representatives such as the World Bank), have every temptation to garner resources and repress segments of their people, by genocide if necessary (Brainard and Chollet, 2007; Bunker and Ciccantell, 2005; Collier, 2007). The direct link between centralized extractive industry and genocide is well recorded in recent history, for example, Chile, Colombia, Iran, Iraq, Nigeria, and Sudan. Significant in this regard are the more local killings, not reaching genocidal levels but similar in their targeting of innocent citizens, associated with primary production in Brazil, Congo (Brazzaville), Ecuador, and many other countries. Oil is especially involved (Anderson, 2010; Juhasz, 2008). Collier (2007) speaks of bloody oil in Nigeria, blood diamonds in Sierra Leone, and both bloody oil and bloody diamonds in Angola. Dictatorship and corruption notoriously follow Big Oil (Bunker and Ciccantell, 2005). So does extremist religious totalitarianism (Iran, Saudi Arabia, and other Gulf states).

Centrally or externally controlled plantation agriculture, like Big Oil, eventually results in reactionary economic policies that can easily break into genocide. El Salvador, Guatemala, Honduras, Haiti, and several of the African countries are classic "banana republics." The term originally referred to United Fruit's activities in Honduras and neighboring countries, and, indeed, banana companies were still installing dictators (directly or indirectly) through most of the twentieth century.

Recall Benjamin Friedman's point (2005) that an economic downturn is generally followed by the emergence of a more conservative and intolerant society. The United States in the 1930s was an exception because the country still had hope; this pattern emerged again in the United States in the 2009 crash, but when the Obama administration stumbled, the extremist right wing took over, confirming Friedman's general point. Friedman also shows that economic growth is protective (2005). The caveat is that the growth must be real, that is, it must benefit a significant share of the people rather than being captured by a tiny elite. The latter sort of "growth" did not help Diaz's Mexico or Marcos's Philippines, and is not helping Iran or militarized Pakistan.

Economic endeavors heavily subsidized by the World Bank or first-world governments have stripped less affluent nations of the ability to defend themselves or to play a viable role in the global economy. The "global south" has lost any chance to control its economy or its destiny. It has become increasingly a playground for giant multinational interests (Bunker and Ciccantell, 2005; Wedel, 2010).The results have included widespread emergence of intolerance, targeted hatred, and genocide. Angola, Burma, Colombia, Indonesia, Iran, Nigeria, and Sudan exemplify this pattern. One of us has detailed at great length, elsewhere, the shady dealings of multinational corporations, including coup attempts and other actions that led directly to mass murder (Anderson, 2010).

Rapid population growth requires rapid increase in government services and control, which makes dictatorship very much more likely. There is a close correlation between tyranny and population increase rates, worldwide. Yet much of this is actually due to the fact that tyranny causes population growth. The two biggest preventers of population explosion are education for girls and public health—including (but not limited to) birth control availability. Tyrants hate education because educated people threaten their position, and tyrants are very often religious bigots to boot, opposed to both girls' schools and birth control. Thus a feedback loop is established: more tyranny leads to even faster population increase. All this explains why the fastest population growth is generally in the poorest countries, while the most developed ones have the slowest. This link is indirect. It is merely one factor predisposing a country to dictatorship. And dictatorship is merely one factor, albeit a very major one, predisposing a country to genocide. So the correlation of population growth rate and genocide is not high.

This is an area where observations of civil war can be useful. A volume edited by Brainard and Chollet (2007) shows that poverty, especially the extreme poverty that characterizes today's Africa, is closely correlated with civil war and meltdown. The authors give varying degrees of importance to rapid population growth as a problem, but usually discount it, since it does not correlate well with war. They give more attention to foreign interference by oil, diamond, and other extractive interests, and use the concept of the "honey pot": an impoverished, poorly controlled area with rich "lootable" resources, which becomes an irresistible temptation to international looters from oil corporations to simple thugs. Indeed, such areas are invariably ill-governed—the corporations see to that—and almost invariably war torn. However, they do not always commit genocide. Nor are genociders always in such countries; certainly Hitler was not. Most recent genocides are in countries identified as impoverished and unstable. Most of them have experienced some violence, ranging from mobs and revolts to outright civil war. Yet, the vast majority of those countries have not seen a genocide or democide. Conversely, the huge wave of genocides and democides in the mid-twentieth century, from Hitler to Stalin to Mao, took place in developed or semi-developed countries.

Chirot and McCauley (2006) demolish the idea that trade, capitalism, or a merchant society is totally preventive. They point to Germany, Serbia and several other countries. They could have mentioned Guatemala, El Salvador, Indonesia, and a dozen other cases. They argue that "convenience"—profit, basically—has been a motive for genocide, notably in the Americas and Australia. And we all remember Marx's charge that "primitive capital accumulation" is a bloody process. Still, at least greed restrains hate when there is more money to be made by keeping people alive than by killing them. Greed and hate united, however, make the deadliest of deadly combinations.

One economic theory of mass murder, mooted informally, is that "we don't need workers anymore because we have machines." This line at least predicts that genocide would be a child of the machine age. However, it would also lead us to expect that genocide would occur in industrialized countries, whereas in fact it usually occurs in the most impoverished and rural ones.

We can expect to see much more trouble as more and more countries face resource limits. As of 2003, at least fifty-four countries were worse off economically than they were in 1990 (*TIME*, August 18, 2003); one assumes the number is much higher since the economic meltdown of 2008–2009. Many of the rest, including all the largest countries, are facing major problems that may make them genocidal or democidal. In a typical scenario, a deteriorating economic and ecological situation makes ethnic rivalries worse; fighting breaks out; the government uses it as an excuse to exterminate a group.

Overall, genocide does not pay. It shores up leaders for a brief time, but usually dooms their regimes. Settler wars may open up land for the invaders, but at a price: the local people and all their skills, knowledge, and ability to manage the land are gone. This has certainly cost America and Australia countless billions of dollars in foregone income, to say nothing of the far greater but less tangible human losses. Otherwise, genocide usually accomplishes nothing beyond exterminating groups that are almost always among the most productive in the society in question. The genociders in Serbia and Rwanda seem to have genuinely believed that they could take over land and loot, but we believe that few genociders seriously expect their actions to pay in terms of actual socioeconomic benefits. They are acting out of extreme political attitudes. Fear and hate, not economic motives, are paramount. Political emotion, not resource shortage, drives the tiger to attack.

Benjamin Friedman (2005) has shown at length that economic growth creates more expansive, tolerant, hopeful, and inclusive politics, while economic decline usually produces the opposite.

To qualify Friedman, it may take a doubly downward situation to poison the soil: military and social humiliation, the stripping of power and respect *combined with* economic hurt, creates hopelessness, vulnerability and victimizing. Once again, the process is strikingly similar to what often occurs in cases of family and intimate partner violence; the psychological similarities should repay further research.

A classic example is the contrast between the United States and Germany in the 1930s as opposed to the post–2008 years. In the 1930s, the United States was still united enough, with enough loyalty, to meet the challenge of the Depression—though not without a great deal of trouble and debate. France, Switzerland, and Scandinavia also stayed largely away from fascism, at least at first. Germany, being much harder hit by losing World War I and then by the Depression years, went fascist. The key difference is linked to hope (cf. Baumeister, 2005). With some exceptions, the countries that stayed free were the winners in World War I; the fascist countries either lost the war and then faced economic downturns on top of that, or backed the winning side but were then devastated economically. A third possibility was realized in Russia, which was on the winning side, but went Bolshevik during a particularly bleak period in World War I when they were doing poorly in the fighting. There, alliance with Hitler broke up early, but Stalin invoked Hitler-like policies.

Conversely, after 2008, Germany looked forward to more successes, and coped ably and responsibly with the recession. The United States, exhausted by wars, political fights, economic decline, and above all the vast and increasing gap between rich and poor, developed a huge nativist and conservative movement (the Tea Party being the most visible manifestation), and in 2010 moved far to the right politically. Certain business interests benefited from this, because they could whip up hatreds (see also Anderson, 2010). Broadly similar dynamics are visible in the declining Roman Empire, the decline phases of Chinese and Near Eastern dynasties, and other cyclic declines in history. Such downturns not only bring out the worst in the worst people, they send the best into escapism. Well-meaning people in rising cycles can work for the common good; well-meaning people in declining times often escape into mystical religion, eremitism, and the like.

In short, poverty by itself does not cause genocide; correlations of mass killing and poverty are generally due to the fact that both are caused by bad government *and, above all, by economic decline and by the machinations of foreign extractive corporations.* And, on the personal level, *genocide results when deeply cherished coping mechanisms are challenged in such a way that they invoke further coping mechanisms that are extreme, damaging, and savage developments from the immature, weak, and frightened responses of childhood.* This grows worse in proportion to how much of one's life, career, and inner self is tied up in the coping mechanism. Again, genocide seems to be domestic violence writ large.

DOWNWARD BOUND

At what point and under what conditions does the stalking tiger of genocide replace the paper tigers of fear and hatred? We consider here the immediate risk factors in the development of full-blown genocide. The predatory nature of genocide could be stopped at any point, if the relevant phases could be defused by social stability and hope.

Barbara Harff (2005, 2008; see also Pinker, 2011: 341–42) found genocide most likely in countries with previous histories of genocide and of governmental instability. This is a notably broad framework (it would, among other things, doom the United States to endless genocide). She also found that leaders of genocide often came from ethnic minorities; this seems to be a sampling error, since it most certainly is not true of our own sample (which is as close to a "sample of the whole" as we can make it). She found more specifically that autocracy, closed borders to two-way trade, and exclusionary ideology were important. These are clearly important as background factors, though not actual precipitating factors. (The "trade" issue is also shaky, because so many authorities define "free trade" as "trade advantageous to multinational extractive corporations," under which definition such flagrantly genocidal countries as Equatorial Guinea, Nigeria, and Sudan, are economic models.)

Autocracy is the most important point here, and is universally found to be a key risk factor. The clearest correlate of genocide is dictatorship (Rummel, 1994, 1998). Most genocides have been in governments that were either dictatorships or paper democracies in which strongmen had monopolized the real power (as in Colombia, El Salvador, Guatemala, and some other cases we shall address). However, there is one conspicuous exception: democracies are as prone to murder *noncitizens* as dictatorships are. Until American Indians and Australian Aborigines were granted citizenship, they were fair game, and were often hunted down like animals by government troops (see below). A much rarer, but still real, exception is genocide by a genuinely democratic government that is pushed beyond tolerance by economic woes and civil war. Sri Lanka is the major case; over decades, during the war with the radical Tamil Eelam movement, democratically elected governments routinely committed genocidal excesses. This, however, seems to be without parallel in recent history. Other recent genocides have all been under totalitarian governments (cf. Pinker, 2011: 337). Even very partial, compromised democracies, that kill some dissidents or allow goon squads to do so, are not usually extremely murderous (Guatemala in the 1980s is the major exception). Pinker (2011) uses the term "anocracy" for such compromised democracies; they have higher risks of international and civil war than ironclad dictatorships do, but lower risks of genocide. (One wonders if "anocracy" — presumably from the Greek for "without government," thus close to "anarchy" — is a deliberate pun on a Latin-Greek mix.)

What we have done is isolate the actual precipitating factors that make genocide specifically predictable in real time. After socially constructed and politically manipulated hatred, which we have discussed above, the first of these is declining hope, most likely to occur when there is downward mobility or a sense of internal or external threat. A depression often causes the former; a war that turns increasingly sour is often the cause of the latter. In these cases, absoluteness often becomes part of social values and norms. More common and dangerous as a prelude to genocide is facing the prospect of losing or doing poorly in a war, as we have noted above. This is probably the clearest danger sign for genocide, as noted by several authors (e.g. Midlarsky, 2005; Shaw, 2003; Straus, 2006). In the European case, of course, depression merged into World War II, and that war unleashed genocide, primarily after the tides of war turned clearly against the Germans.

The second is the emergence of strong but threatened leadership, articulating the feelings of hopelessness and offering non-inclusive solutions which muster hatred and dehumanize targeted groups. This leads to the critical step of widespread complicity with the hate messages, allowing the abdication of power to this kind of leadership and the stalking of targeted groups. Last, through this complicity and desensitization, genocide is unleashed, creating violent but acceptable normative practices. A new reality is created.

THE RISE OF RUTHLESS LEADERSHIP

Once hopelessness, political anarchy, or political weakness brings a ruthless leader to power, the practice of killing becomes a powerful tool in the hands of a totalitarian government attempting to consolidate that power (as observed long ago by Edward Gibbon, 1995 [1776–1788]). When democracy flounders, a coup brings totalitarian leaders to power, or when civil unrest provides instability and a sense of hopelessness, the conditions for genocide are in place. Very often, no more is needed; the victor methodically exterminates his opponents, and often even his former allies. This occurs primarily when the leader is in the process of installing a new regime that makes a sharp break with preceding ones. This is the sole visible cause of many of the great mass killings in history, including such long-lasting and dreadful campaigns as the consolidation of the Qin Dynasty by Qin Shi Huang Di in the third century BC, and the consolidation of the Ming Dynasty by Zhu Yuanzhang in the fourteenth century AD (Mote, 1999). Most notable among recent cases are the Communist takeovers in Eastern Europe and eastern Asia in the twentieth century. All of these were quickly followed by mass murders (Rummel, 1998), and are summarized in our appendices.

Consolidation of power by a new and shakily established regime is explicitly flagged by Straus (2006) for Rwanda, and was conspicuous in Argentina, Cambodia, Ethiopia, Iran, Serbia, Turkey (1915), and many other cases. In fact, there are very few twentieth-century genocides that did *not* have this as a factor, and most of those few were among the most notable cases of war risk.

Two rare, significant, and closely related exceptions are Stalin's USSR and Mao's China. As long as Stalin and Mao were in power, killings went on and on. The killings stopped short when these leaders died. These two leaders seem to have been either genuinely psychopathic or, at the very least, habituated to mass-murder campaigns as the best and most immediate way to do business. Zhu Yuanzhang, Tamerlane, and some other leaders also seem to have been truly unstable; they killed indiscriminately when it might well seem to any unbiased observer that they were only undermining their position, and the killing got worse and worse over time, rather than stopping when their positions were consolidated and all real threat was over.

To succeed in starting a new regime, a strong leader must usually mobilize the support of the dominant population. This is most easily done by mobilizing them against some entrenched group, especially if it has already been demonized or dehumanized. Hitler capitalized upon hundreds of years of anti-Jewish history in Europe (but recall that he killed many other populations). The Rwandan genocide built on a shorter tradition: the Belgian colonial regime had used a divide-and-rule strategy of setting Hutu against Tutsi (Straus, 2006; Taylor, 2010). The Khmer Rouge were outsiders mobilizing Cambodians against educated, foreign-influenced elites. Milosevich in Serbia attacked religious "enemies" that had been on shaky terms with the Serbs for centuries.

Often, history is rewritten to serve the purpose. Hitler's *Mein Kampf* chronicled a vast litany of imaginary assaults by the Jews on the world in general and Hitler in particular. The radical class hatred mobilized by Mao Zidong and Pol Pot involved rewriting history (Hinton, 2005; Kiernan, 2007). The Hutu genociders in Rwanda developed their own history. Such rewriting by strong, coercive, charismatic leadership is a dangerous sign. It is a part of the systematic development of hatred by politicians.

The next sign is often the development of a whole subculture of hatred, usually involving specific hate-based political factions, gangs, militia, or army units. The Know-Nothing Party in America is one example (see below; and the later Ku Klux Klan came very close to provoking genocide). Organizing youth is very often seen by hate-based movements as a vital step. The Nazis developed Hitler Youth, an elite corps with its own customs, rites, and subculture. Mao's Red Guards and Cambodia's Khmer Rouge were similar. The Guatemalan military developed a longstanding organization for terror. Hutu militia were encouraged to murder the Tutsis through the power and repetition of music. They chanted, "We will finish them. We will finish them soon. They are about to vanish" (Kidder, 2009: 135). However, these gangs are not always present in genocides, and never do much killing unless they can get a great deal of the general population to go along with them (*pace* Steven Pinker's occasional comments that gangs of thugs do, or did, all the killing in certain African cases; see below). Serious genocide occurs only when a huge number of ordinary people are marshaled, whether through fear or threat or genuine belief or collective hysteria, to kill their neighbors.

To create solidarity, strong leaders and their henchmen must work diligently, devoting themselves to cultivating violence, hate-mongering, and subduing of petty, individual rivalries and tensions among their followers. Bullying tactics and carefully crafted social messaging allow no differences of opinion, no fold-breakers, no challenge to the evolving order. This kind of leadership has little time for a domestic agenda or the pragmatic business of day-to-day governance. They often seek out and favor the personality type that deals with personal weakness by adulating the brutal and powerful (a type familiar on many a high school campus). A major study of such a person is Joachim Köhler's depiction of Friedrich Nietzsche (Köhler, 1998); it is very close to our concerns, since the Nazis claimed Nietzsche as their intellectual father, for both his adulation of power and his extreme anti-Jewish ideology. Köhler meticulously traces the links between these two traits. There are more liberal readings of Nietzsche, but, alas, they were not the ones that mattered in history.

Whether the resulting leaders are gray apparatchiki or powerful military figures, they come to resemble schoolyard bullies. Picking on the weak is a remarkably uniform strategy at all levels. Bullying often wins because cowering down works for a short time. This leads to a feedback loop that makes things steadily worse. Folk wisdom has it that "bullies are cowards," and cowards lead by bravado rather than rational, inclusive conversation. Bullies are perhaps easier for scared and hopeless people to identify with than with those truly brave souls whose leadership may be steady, inclusive and less flamboyant. In a world of fear and hopelessness, the bully appears brave and noble; using violence may seem the noble and capable way to solve problems

Those who are, by nature, less violent or apathetic tend to conform, seeking inclusion and the avoidance of criticism. The leader pulls them into the fold. The typical genocidal leader, motivated by personal fanaticism, obsessed with power and greed, and savvy with their bullying techniques, is not a typical example of humanity. His first followers are often marginal: actual bullies, unemployed youths, economically unsuccessful groups within society, small farmers risking dispossession, and disgruntled elements of all kinds. The vast mass of later followers, however, are usually typical—quite ordinary humans.

Autocrats who are secure on their thrones rarely commit genocide. It is the resort of shaky governments. As Straus (2006: 11) puts it, "the compromised and fractured power of the hardliners drove the violence . . . the decision to foment violence was intimately connected to war and, more specifically, to fighting a defensive war from a position of eroded power."

COMPLICITY

Why do people participate in genocide? Almost all the recent accounts of genocide describe those who complied and survived as being largely normal, ordinary people. As noted above, many are totally mystified by their own behavior. They do not fit any stereotype or definite profile. Yet, when they are coerced or cajoled into supporting genocide, ordinary people often go beyond "following orders" (Baumeister, 1997) and actively compete to emulate the bullying leaders. In Rwanda, perfectly ordinary individuals who had gotten along well with their Tutsi or Hutu spouses and neighbors turned murderous (Gourevitch, 1998; Straus, 2006; Taylor, 2010). Hinton (2005) reports the same from Cambodia. Chinese who killed in the mass campaigns of Mao's later years tell similar stories (we have heard many during our work in China). As targeted hatred becomes normative, people cave in, despise what they are doing, and do it anyway. It is clear that, given the right set of circumstances, we are all capable of complicity with genocide, even if we do not like it at the time or later.

Adler et al. (2008) demonstrated that ordinary people who had joined in the killings in Rwanda showed motives of fear, hate, complicity, confusion and greed (they often wanted the land and goods of their victims). Many killed in self-defense; otherwise they would have been perceived as traitors, and killed themselves. These low-level killers accepted the official ideologies of the "need" to exterminate the structural-opponent group to "protect" the rest. This recapitulates the infamous "good Germans just following orders." Hate propaganda works. Genocide literature agrees that a small number of genuine haters influence a larger number of those who accept the ideology without feeling the virulent bigotry. What matters is that the meek—those who do not deeply hate, but who do comply out of fear or mindless conformity—carry out the will of hateful leaders. They will, as ordered, stoke the gas ovens, shoot the rifles, and pack human beings into concentration camps and re-education centers (Hinton, 2005).

Beah (2007) speaks from his own traumatic experiences as a child soldier in Sierra Leone about the use of potent hallucinogenic drugs to ensure that children would be compliant in performing genocidal actions. One of the authors (BA) heard many accounts of similar coercion of children to perform genocide by the Khmer Rouge in Cambodia. Another (ENA) has heard many accounts of ordinary peaceable people getting caught up in the campaigns of Mao's Cultural Revolution; they acted largely from fear that they would be targets otherwise, but also from peer pressure and a sort of mass hysteria.

Complicity of even wider social circles is usually essential to unleashed the stalking tiger. Genocide is usually not a single historical act of compliance but rather a carefully crafted strategy built deeply upon the traditions and cultures of the people. In ancient China, elites used to killing became aware too late that Qin Shi Huang Di and Zhu Yuanzhang had gotten out of hand. In Europe, Jews were massacred over and over, creating precedents for Hitler's genocide. Some historical attacks against the Jewish population were as murderous on a local scale as Hitler's continent-wide massacres. This long tradition of anti-Semitism lay behind the lack of initial opposition to Hitler, and, according to many sources, behind the failure of free nations to act to take in Jewish refugees in the late 1930s. This allowed Hitler and his henchmen to carry out a systematic, cold-blooded policy of genocide, stretched over years, ignored or approved by millions of Germans and by millions of citizens of countries conquered by the Germans. Even the less systematically bureaucratized genocides, such as those in Darfur, Uganda, and Cambodia, were qualitatively different from local massacres and mob actions. They involved high-level bureaucratic decisions and operations by bully leaders depending upon the complicity of the dominant population, including, especially, the people who become the bureaucrats and executioners.

The chief problem in many social problems, such as resource management, is failure of solidarity. The problem in the case of genocide and other mass violence is the opposite: *too much* solidarity. Capitalizing on the insecurity manifested in absoluteness, coercive leadership offers a vision of a world that would be better once the targeted group is exterminated. Eric Weitz (2003) argued that this is a critical step in genocide (see also Kiernan, 2007).

As the new social reality of genocide becomes normative, it becomes an expected part of life. In the end, this new reality, a genocidal society, created by bully leaders and a compliant population, kills the hated group but strangles the potential of everyone in the society. A new and terrifying reality has been created from which none can escape unscathed.

SIX

Excursions into History

Kill 'em all, let God sort 'em out.
—Arnaud Amaury, Abbot of Citeaux, 1209 AD

RELIGIOUS WARS

Béziers, France, 1209: The Cathar heresy had attracted too much attention to ignore. The Pope wanted it exterminated. The French wanted Languedoc, where the Catharists centered. Combining the needs of holy intolerance and secular greed was inevitable, and the Albigensian Crusade swept down on the land. The first city to offer significant resistance was Béziers, which fell to the brilliant general Simon de Montfort. He reportedly asked the religious leader of the crusade, Arnold Amaury, how one could tell the heretics—to be killed; from the faithful Catholics—to be spared. Amaury made the famous answer that has been quoted millions of times since, and is quoted here once more: "Kill 'em all, let God sort 'em out" (the French, modernized, is *Tuez les tous, Dieu reconnaîtra les siens*). This is a horribly out-of-context allusion to the Biblical passages Numbers 16:5 or II Timothy 2:19, both of which use the line in a positive way, to say that the Lord will know his own in the sense of blessing and protecting them rather than sorting their souls after a mass murder.

The line apparently first occurs in a German chronicle a few years later, by one Cesarius of Heisterbach. It may be a bit touched up. But if Amaury did not say exactly that, he most certainly said something very similar, for that is exactly what happened, not only in Béziers but in other situations where Amaury had the call (O'Shea, 2002, esp. p. 269; Roux-Perino and Brenon, 2006, esp. p. 136). Most of the campaigns were less bloody and merciless than Béziers (the first major one of the crusade), but in the end the Cathars were exterminated, the last "Perfect" dying in 1321.

The systematic extermination of the Cathars was an early genocide in the western world—a cold, calculated, bureaucratized attempt to exterminate an entire group of the country's own reasonably law-abiding citizens. But it was not the first; it consciously looked back to the Roman persecutions of Christians in the second and third centuries. (Gibbon, 1995, and for a more recent and concise source see Jonassohn and Björnson, 1998: 191–95). The Romans tried repeatedly to eliminate all Christians; in fact the word "religion"—and its working definition as an exclusive, legal, institutionalized form separate from "secular" life—is Roman, and has much to do with this specific situation.

Amaury and his successors exterminated not just the Cathars but everyone who protected them or was related to them. There had been many exterminations of local tribes before, but these were done in the heat of battle, not by a systematic bureaucracy working in peacetime over an entire century. It was followed by many religious exterminations, especially in the wars of religion that tore Europe into shreds in the sixteenth and seventeenth centuries. These are worthy of record but outside our scope herein.

All the techniques of modern genocide—torture, terrorization, murder of any number of innocents to get one guilty one, creating a climate of betrayal—were perfected in the Inquisition, which arose to eliminate the Cathar heresy and then propagated throughout centuries. Its other major genocide was the Spanish and Portuguese elimination of the Jews and Muslims (including even converts—always suspect), who were either killed or driven into exile between 1492 and the early seventeenth century. Interestingly, the Inquisition was prohibited early on from going after Native Americans—it was too brutal! Given what the Spanish did *without* the Inquisition to those unfortunate people (Las Casas, 1992), this is a truly telling comment on the Inquisition.

Other religions have done their share. Muslims will appear in many accounts below, and this has its history. The Ottomans not only fought without notable mercy, but, more to the point here, massacred not only some non-Muslims but also Muslim dissidents and rebels in the eighteenth and nineteenth centuries; for instance, they put down the Celali rebellions of the eighteenth century by killing so many people that large parts of Anatolia were almost depopulated for years (Faroqhi, 2006). Other religions have similar records. Even the peaceable Hindus massacred Jains (e.g., Jonassohn and Björnson, 1998: 219) and Muslims, and the Chinese, theoretically believers in a tolerant and broad faith, massacred Muslims in the nineteenth century. All these religious campaigns stand as precursors and oft-invoked examples for genocide.

Genocide on a small scale goes back even earlier, often being a matter of exterminating weak groups within one's society so as to free up land, satisfy vengeance, or simply deal with a constant problem of feuding and rebellion. For instance, even the tiny and peaceable island of Tikopia, a Polynesian stronghold with only a couple of thousand people at most, has an oral tradition of the systematic extermination of one or two clans after a long history of squabbles over land and other matters (Firth 1961). Such tiny genocides probably occurred rarely, but not extremely rarely, throughout human history.

Settler Wars and Territorial Conquest

Looking over mass murder in history, there is something of a continuum. Mass murder seems to have started in tribal wars; the winners of such local wars often exterminate the enemy (LeBlanc and Register, 2002). With the rise of the state, warfare actually declined, but total extermination of losing enemy tribes or small states continued to be a standard tactic. Even Xenophon, arch-moralist of Plato's students, writes with a strategist's detachment of how many years it took for a region to recover after soldiers went through, and writes with cheerful equanimity of his soldiers raiding the locals for sex slaves as the Greeks marched through Anatolia (Xenophon, 1998).

Throughout all human prehistory and history, migrants and settlers routinely exterminate any people who get in their way. Few if any of these conflicts qualify as genocide. Even the infamous Mongols generally killed only actual enemies, and spared anyone worth sparing, not only women and children but also crafts persons and learned individuals (Buell, 2008). The exaggerated accounts of Mongol slaughter in the history books owe a great deal to Mongol propaganda (Buell, 2008; Weatherford, 2004). The Mongols greatly exaggerated their ferocity in a frequently successful attempt to scare cities into submission. Thus the Mongols are by and large innocent of genocide (Buell, 2008), at least by usual definitions, though they did occasionally go to extreme lengths in dealing with rebellions.

Conquest wars grade into genocide when they lead to purges by new governments of supposed opponents and rebels. These campaigns differ from wars in being systematic, bureaucratic, long-continued, and thorough: the defining characteristics of genocide (or politicide) as opposed to ordinary warfare. They are most clearly genocidal when pursued by paranoid leaders, whose killing can get out of control and extend far beyond reasonable definitions of "opponents." Such would be, for instance, Zhu Yuanzhang, the founder of the Ming Dynasty (Mote, 1999), who apparently declined into true paranoia as he aged, and ordered the execution of thousands of his supporters. A very few other Chinese rulers, from Qin Shi Huang Di in the third century BCE onward, acted similarly, and the contrast of these individuals with more normal Chinese emperors is instructive. Elsewhere in the world, rulers from Tamerlane of Central Asia to Jahangir of Mughal India killed well beyond any rational level of fear or threat. Many of these purges of potential internal enemies and their families could qualify as genocide, or at least politicide, by our definition. They lack only the systematic bureaucratic propaganda and Big Lies as well as coolly routinized killing.

This sort of killing continued in the twentieth century, blending into the genocides conducted by such leaders as Mao Zidong in China, Idi Amin of Uganda, Efrain Rios Montt of Guatemala, and Stalin of the USSR.

We have noted above the relationship of settler wars to genocide, and must here diverge into some history. We rely heavily on the work of Ben Kiernan, who, the reader will recall, includes settler wars and other all-out wars in his broad definition of genocide. As he states, "Genocide has been associated with expanding colonialism, shrinking empires, religious communalism, atheistic dictatorships, unfettered capitalism, National Socialism, Communist revolution, post-Communist nationalism, Nation Security militarism, and Islamist terror. A few genocidists have even been elected" (Kiernan, 2007: 37). However, Kiernan's explanation is that genociders want purity of blood and unlimited access to soil—hence his book's title. This diagnosis clearly applies to settler wars much better than to what we are calling genocide in this book.

The age-old policy of exterminating a conquered people to take their land shows no correlation with new government, or revolt, or downward mobility of the general population. It is, however, often an accompaniment of weak and corrupt rule. It is correlated with revolt in that resistance by the victims usually brought extermination, but *non*resistance usually did also. Settler wars very often blended into outright genocide, as shall appear below, and as appears also in the excellent reviews found in *Genocide of Indigenous Peoples,* edited by Samuel Totten and Robert Hitchcock (2011).

Kiernan begins his magisterial historical account with the ancient Near East, including the many local slayings in the early books of the Bible (Kiernan, 2007: 2–3). The Lord required the Israelites to kill all enemy men and enslave the women and children (Deuteronomy 20:17). On occasion, God even reprimanded the Israelites for being too merciful, sparing some of the enemy (e.g., Kings 1 20:41–42; 1 Samuel 15). Deuteronomy even tells the Israelites to kill the trees as well as the people: "cut down their groves" (Deuteronomy 7:5 and elsewhere). Deuteronomy 20:19 makes the sensible qualification that fruit trees are not to be cut down, "for thou mayest eat of them"; the trees get better treatment than the humans. (Even so, Israel in recent years has made a major point of cutting down Palestinian olive groves and orchards.)

The most murderous series of settler wars in history was the long-running displacement of Native Americans by Europeans. The Native Americans had done their share of land-taking, with the usual fatal results, before the Europeans entered the picture. The difference was the scale of the European enterprise. The elimination of Native Americans from the New World started in 1492. By 1900, Native American population had been reduced 90 to 95 percent, largely through disease, but very often through deliberate massacre (Brown, 1971; Kiernan, 2007). Indigenous population has since substantially recovered in some areas, but the indigenous peoples have lost almost all their land and resources. The main agenda of the conquerors was simply theft of land. Ethnicity and "race" provided mere pretexts.

In Latin America, Las Casas's (1992) account of initial Spanish settlement in the New World, once dismissed as exaggerated but now known to be accurate, provided grim details of massacres on a vast scale. Far too little has changed since (see, e.g., Hemming, 1978). Pedro Alvarado engaged in wholesale massacres in what was to be Guatemala (Kiernan, 2007: 94); Guatemala's history has been bloody ever since. Alvarado began (or perhaps merely continued from the Maya warlords) a policy of mass killing that remained almost a constant since, though Guatemala's recent history owes much also to the Nazi sympathies of its German settlers and their role in developing and training the Guatemalan army in the 1930s and early 1940s (before they were deported; see Stoll, 1993, 1999). In 1951, a left-of-center government was elected in Guatemala, which led to the United States engineering a coup. The American secretary of state at the time, John Foster Dulles, came from the family that founded United Fruit, which had major interests in Guatemala, and protection of "American" and family interests were paramount. (This is one of the sources of the term "banana republic.") Escalating right-wing repression led to a small guerrilla movement, which was violently repressed from the 1960s onward. A climax of genocide occurred during the presidency of Efrain Rios Montt, who invoked frankly fascist techniques. Some two hundred thousand people, mostly Maya and virtually all innocent of any civil strife, were killed (Stoll, 1999; Totten, 2011b). The civil climate of Guatemala remains poisoned, with "strong men" often elected at all levels. One result is the rapid increase in the power of Mexican drug gangs; resisting these has involved a suspiciously trivial and superficial effort on the part of the army, especially in comparison with the effort expended on a tiny handful of ineffectual guerrillas.

Genocides, though generally smaller and less organized ones, have been endemic in Brazil (Hemming, 1978) and have occurred in most other Latin American countries. Canada has had far less bloody a past, but is not without its own incidents (Woolford and Thomas, 2011).

We shall, however, focus on the United States. Here, "manifest destiny" was the call and Native Americans were in the way. The results were targeted hatred, frequent massacre, and occasional genocide. Dee Brown, in *Bury My Heart at Wounded Knee: An Indian History of the American West* (1971), responds to distortions of history. He recalls the glory portrayed in defeating the Indians in "cowboy and Indian" films. A chance remark by a Native American child, when Brown, himself, was a child, began to unravel the lie. The main agenda of the conquerors was simply theft of land; the justification was often no more than the line "the only good Indian is a dead Indian" (cited in Brown, 1971, and most other relevant works; the line is ascribed to various nineteenth-century figures, but is probably older than any of them). If there is one thing that both authors learned as adults, it is that we had been lied to as children about this and many other aspects of world history.

The resulting campaigns are interesting not only to show the United States has its own genocide problems, but also because examining small, "simple" cases is often a good way to get insight into bigger ones. The United States contributed its share to the evolution of genocide by systematically exterminating several Native American groups in the nineteenth century (Rensink, 2011; Rensink provides a valuable bibliography of recent sources). Rarely did the government officially decide to eliminate whole groups, so most of the massacres do not come under our definition of genocide. Some outright genocides occurred, however, including the "Trail of Tears" that followed Andrew Jackson's murderous expulsion of the Cherokees from their homes. In a campaign reminiscent of the Turkish massacre of Armenians in 1915, the Jackson administration first expelled the Cherokee from their homes, then harassed them, allowed local militias to massacre them, and denied them food and shelter on their trail to Oklahoma, with the result that most of the Cherokee were eliminated. The extermination of the Yuki and neighboring northern California Native peoples in the 1850s was another clear case of genocide, with the government actively colluding with local forces (Miller, 1979). It was explicitly backed by the state government (especially during the "Know-Nothing" government in the early 1850s). In 1851, Governor Peter Burnett "called for a 'war of extermination' to continue 'until the Indian race becomes extinct'" (Rensink, 2011: 20). Sometimes the United States Government joined the attacks. Several other California tribes, from the Yahi to the Wiyot, underwent similar extermination campaigns (Heizer and Kroeber, 1979). These took place largely in the 1850s, in connection with mine expansion. Many miners were southerners, caught up in the racist violence that was soon to lead to the Civil War. Not far away was an even clearer case of deliberate government genocide: the United States Army eliminated the Bear River Shoshone tribe at the Bear River Massacre in Idaho on January 29, 1863 (Fleisher, 2004).

Surviving Native people of northern California today often kept their groups alive by retreating to the mountains and refusing to submit; in some cases (as along the Klamath River) they had to fight armed extralegal militias to a draw. Today, their descendents "point out the particular evil of state-sanctioned attempts to exterminate outright all Indian people in northern California. Doing so, they hope to establish a firm legal connection between what happened there, between 1950 and 1865, and widely and legally acknowledged modern genocide in places like Nazi Europe or, more recently, Rwanda and former Yugoslavia" (Buckley, 2002: 9).

Miners and settlers of the Rogue River Valley and neighboring areas in southwestern Oregon attempted in the 1850s to exterminate all Native Americans in the region (Beckham, 1996; Schwartz, 1997; Youst and Seaburg, 2002). This occurred after a long spell of Anglo-American killings and Native counter-killings, the latter providing the excuse to call in the troops. The army was less desirous of outright extermination, but strong Native American resistance led to runaway killings, and eventually real genocide, as massacres of peaceful noncombatants, as well as hostile bands, got completely out of control. Interestingly, the coastal people in the last successful resistance phase of the war were led by a Canadian *métis*, Enos, who had come with the fur trappers (Beckham, 1996; Youst and Seaburg, 2002). Of course this resistance was hopeless, and was followed by extermination or exile to northern Oregon. Only the heroism of a few Indian agents and settlers, including the Applegate family, preserved the Takelma and the Rogue River and Upper Umpqua River Athapaskans from extinction. The death toll was only a couple of thousand (again, exact figures do not exist), but in terms of sheer effectiveness it ranks high. The Rogue River "War" is a boundary case; it lies on the border between war and genocide. The final phase of it, however, when the Indians were defeated and subjugated, was outright genocide.

Overall, the Indian "wars" of the nineteenth-century United States offer a whole spectrum of cases. The Plains Indians in particular fought hard, with many victories (Custer's Last Stand, among others), and did not go meekly into submission. They even had local successes in driving back the settler tide; the Comanches, in a bitter and long war with little quarter asked and none given on either side, held much of Texas for decades (Gwynne, 2010). Most of the Native American tribes avoided extermination, and some presidents and generals worked to save them. Defining these cases as genocide is hard to defend, even though federal troops did carry out wholesale massacres of Plains Indians, based on ethnicity alone. A classic, still unsurpassed account of the Plains tragedies is James Mooney's great book *The Ghost-Dance Religion and the Sioux Outbreak of 1890* (1991, orig. 1896). Another case of briefly successful defiance was the Nez Perce war (Cozzens, 2002), and again the Nez Perce survived.

Even in California, most groups survived. The Modoc War was a close case. The Modocs were promised their own reservation; the promise was broken and the Modocs were forced to live on the reservation of their enemies the Klamaths. After harsh treatment by both Klamaths and whites, a "hostile" band of Modocs under Captain Jack broke out, took to the lava beds in northern California, and held off a thousand federal troops (as well as local settlers) for six months, until winter and hunger drove them to surrender. They were executed or sent to a de facto death camp in Oklahoma; a few survived to return, many years later. But even here, no genocide was attempted, in spite of repeated calls for it by local settlers. Much of the credit for this goes to the local Indian agent William Meacham and, above all, the incredibly heroic interpreter, Winema, a Modoc woman married to a local white settler; her coolness and bravery under fire deserve immortality, but have been little recognized. This war is particularly interesting in that we have stories from all parties, making this unique in that it is documented from every point of view—rare indeed for a near-genocide. (The story would make the Great American Movie. It is documented from all points of view. It is properly dramatic. It took place in some of the most magnificent scenery in the world. For the best history, see *Burnt-out Fires* by Richard Dillon, 1973; for Meacham's self-serving but broadly accurate story, the best source for settler attitudes, Meacham, 1875; for Winema's story, see her son's chronicle, Riddle, 1974; basic documents are in Cozzens, 2002.)

In retrospect, most of the truly genocidal campaigns against American Indians took place in three periods: the 1820s under Jackson, the 1870s (and into the 1880s) during the height of the Indian wars, and above all the 1850s. The pronounced clustering is important and significant. The particularly bloody genocides of the 1850s took place during the unsettled period of weak government and escalating local violence that led to the American Civil War. During this period, racism was at its height, slavery expanded to include Native Americans as well as African Americans, and random murder and massacre along racial and political lines ran well beyond Native American communities. California briefly elected a Know-Nothing Party government (it fell apart within two years), and it was during that period that the worst genocides in West Coast history took place.

Generals who had served in the Civil War—men like General William Sherman and General Philip Sheridan—had learned the art and science of war against their own people; they had little moral concern for enemies who were not citizens and were not even "white." They were willing to accommodate settler pleas to get the Indians out of the way and off the land, by any means possible; the Plains and Modoc massacres resulted (Brown, 1971). The "heroism" of the Cavalry against the savages was the prevailing "story" for many generations of American children. In fact the Native Americans showed tremendous leadership, rarely mentioned in those days.

The president for most of the 1870s was Ulysses Grant, who genuinely tried to stop the murders, but who was a weak leader overseeing a country with rampant corruption. Massacres tailed off through the 1880s and 1890s as stronger governments gradually extended power, but deliberate and malignant neglect—structural violence—continued (the best accounts are contemporary ones, e.g., Mooney 1991 [1896]; Russell, 1908).

Native Americans today hold in contempt the "vanishing Red Man" idea of the late nineteenth century, but they do not realize how near a thing it was. Native American populations in 1900 were approximately 5 percent of what they were in 1492, and had, in many or most areas, still been declining through the 1890s. After 1900 the curve sharply reversed, and populations rose again (see, e.g., Boyd, 1999; Dobyns, 1983). Most of the deaths were due to introduced diseases or random killing rather than to genocide, but genocide was common. Moreover, much of the disease came from such things as providing smallpox-infected blankets, refusing medical care to prisoners, and allowing tuberculosis to spread unchecked on reservations. By the late nineteenth century, tuberculosis was the leading infectious killer of Indigenous Americans, and it was *not* a newly introduced disease; its horrific death toll was due to conditions of starvation, poor clothing and housing, poor medical care, and other "structural" matters on reservations, prison camps, and other venues to which Native Americans were confined. Such malign neglect would indeed have essentially eliminated the Native Americans in time.

Fortunately, by the late nineteenth century, change was coming. A newer generation of generals were more inspired by the ethnically tolerant policies of Lincoln and Grant. This new generation included men like General George Crook, who advocated for Native Americans not only as humans but also fellow Americans, and the early ethnographers Col. Garrick Mallery and army surgeon Washington Matthews, who were strongly pro-Indian. Outright massacres stopped in the 1890s, but de facto genocide by virtual imprisonment on reservations and denial of food and medical care continued until citizenship allowed Native Americans recourse through voting and legal actions. The cessation of genocidal policies and the granting of full citizenship to Native Americans in 1924 coincided too perfectly in timing to be mere coincidence—a point of extreme importance for dealing with genocide. Rummel (1994, 1998) contended that genocide does not take place in democracies. It does—but almost exclusively when the victims are not citizens. We shall see this pattern again in Australia.

Sometimes there were surprises: the Cherokee survived Andrew Jackson's genocidal campaigns, thanks to heroic resistance. The Apache resisted the United States for a generation and received enormous, rich reservations, while the Pima who were the real strike-force for the United States against the Apache saw their lands taken or ravaged; see the classic, dramatic, thorough account in Frank Russell (1908). The Yaqui, in what must be a unique case of "the mouse that roared," not only survived the Mexican government's attempts to exterminate them in the late nineteenth and early twentieth centuries; they went on to serve as a core part of the army of General Alvaro Obregon, with which he conquered Mexico in 1921, ending the Mexican Revolution.

Australia exterminated many of its Aboriginal groups (Kiernan, 2007; Tatz, 2011) and tried to destroy Aboriginal culture by forced removal of children from their homes. Recall that this forced removal, and education in an alien culture, is explicitly part of the United Nations definition of genocide. In the orphanages and concentration camps miscalled "schools," sexual abuse and death from tuberculosis were more common than successful integration into the white world (Elder, 2003; Kiernan, 2007, 2008; Moses, 2004). This story was poignantly told in an excellent Australian film, *Rabbit-Proof Fence* (based on a true story; see new edition, Pilkington and Garimara, 1996). Kiernan (2008) estimated a decline from 750,000 Aborigines in 1700 (a very low estimate) to 31,000 identifiable Aborigines shortly after 1900. This Australian story indicates that genocide can rest on the most paranoid imaginings of a threat. There were a few murders of settlers by Aborigines, mostly in revenge for massacres and massive thefts, but no one seriously thought the Aborigines were a genuine threat to white society. Rather, they were in the way. They were simply cleared off the land. In an ultimate dehumanization, they were not even legally human beings under the law, until a referendum in 1967 and a judicial decision in 1973 allowed them to be both human and Australian citizens.

The extermination of the Tasmanians was less systematic, but no less effective, though only a few thousand died. Now the Australian "story" includes the Aboriginal history, including their brilliant art, and we personally witnessed the widespread historical revisionism in campaigns of apology in the early 2000s.

Other settler societies have similar records. Russian expansion into Siberia and the Caucasus resulted in displacement, decimation, and local mass murder. For example, several small Caucasus groups were exterminated (except for refugees in Turkey; Colarusso, 2002). Russia's murderous policy toward the Kamchatkan indigenous groups in the eighteenth century was incisively documented in Georg Steller's eyewitness account (Steller, 2003/1774). For European expansion in Asia, we have Fernao Mendes Pinto's (Mendes Pinto, 1990) fictionalized but fact-based account of Portuguese expansion in the Age of Discovery. Colonial powers like the Portuguese were remarkably bloody, but rarely committed actual genocide; they contented themselves with exterminating actual enemies.

Colonial powers, however, resorted to the classic Roman strategy of *divide et impera*, divide and rule, and this sometimes led to mass murders by either the colonial powers or the groups that the colonialists set against each other. The British used this technique in Ireland, setting Protestants against Catholics from the late sixteenth century onward. By the twentieth century, it was a routine tactic of colonial powers. The civil wars and genocides of the late twentieth century typically occur in countries where the divide-and-rule strategy was systematically invoked, from Indonesia to Rwanda and from Cambodia to Sudan.

Actual genocide in settler wars seems to occur when a long history of back-and-forth fighting has made the settler group particularly hostile, *and* when the government is openly racist. This occurred, for instance, in the United States in the 1850s, in Australia (locally) in the nineteenth and early twentieth centuries, and in Brazil at intervals throughout its history. The more social hate is mobilized against such groups, the more the danger.

It also occurred when Lothar Von Trotha and his troops massacred the Herero in southwest Africa, and arguably set off the modern escalating spiral of genocide. This, the first twentieth-century genocide, was also one of the last of the settler wars. In this case, the Herero tried to resist German conquest. The Germans eventually concluded that only extermination of the Herero people could solve the problem. Some sixty thousand Herero and ten thousand Nama were killed (Schaller, 2011: 37), almost ending the Herero as a people. (An odd but good source for this war is Thomas Pynchon's novel *Gravity's Rainbow*, 1973. For more soberly factual accounts, see Chirot and McCauley, 2006, and, as usual, Kiernan, 2007; also Schaller, 2011.) Several men who would become leading Nazis, including Heinrich Himmler, got their start in the Herero campaigns (Kiernan, 2007: 35ff.), which in fact became a precursor, if not an outright training ground, for Nazi genocide (Jonassohn and Björnson, 1998: 65–69). This took place against a background of ongoing murder and local genocide in southern Africa, lasting from the seventeenth century almost into the twenty-first, and very often targeting the small, defenseless and vulnerable Khoekhoe and San ("Hottentot" and "Bushmen") peoples (Hitchcock and Babchuk, 2011).

MODERN GENOCIDES

Within the last forty years, mass murder (genocide or politicide) has been state policy for varying lengths of time in Afghanistan (under the Taliban), Argentina, Brazil, Colombia, Chile, El Salvador, Ethiopia, Guatemala, Iran, Iraq (under Saddam), Liberia, Myanmar (Burma), Nigeria, Pakistan/Bangladesh (in the civil war that led to Bangladeshi independence), Somalia, Sierra Leone, Sri Lanka, and other countries.

Modern genocides are so well covered in many histories that we need only cite a few bare references, except in the cases of one or two debates not well covered in some of the older genocide literature. (See sources cited throughout this work, and also Browning, 1995; Chalk and Jonassohn, 1990; Charny, 1994; Charny and Berger, 1991; Jones, 2004; Kolin, 2008; Kuper, 1983; Levene, 2005; Midlarsky, 2005; Rittner et al., 2002; Roth, 2005; Semelis, 2007; Totten et al., 1997. The German case is, of course, the subject of literally thousands of books and major articles.)

One of the debates concerns the first really large-scale modern genocide, Turkey's elimination of the Armenians. Armenian nationalism and local rebellion became problems for the Turkish Empire from the 1870s onward. The Turkish Empire's response to rebellion had always been decimation or extermination of the rebel populations. This was attempted in the wake of Armenian independence activity, in 1895, with large massacres but nothing close to total elimination. Many Armenians fled from their east Anatolian homeland to other parts of the Turkish Empire, and farther afield to Europe, America, and Russia. Far more serious massacres occurred during World War I. The Young Turks took over, the Empire collapsed, war seriously impacted the Turkish state, and the Armenians worked and sometimes fought for an independent state. (They ultimately achieved it, with Soviet help, but independent Armenia wound up small and resource-poor, and has not greatly thrived.)

From 1915 to 1923 between seven hundred thousand and one and a half million Armenians died. The former figure is the Turkish government's estimate, held by virtually everyone else to be far too low. Religion, ethnicity, and local rebellion were the causes, with the last serving as an excuse for extermination based on the first two. German advisors promoting direct elimination of the "problem" had a major role (see Kiernan, 2007: 395). Some have blamed them for the genocide and seen a forerunner of Nazi atrocities; most see the Germans as merely one small part of the picture, but their advocacy was ominous.

There is still disagreement on how much of the genocide was deliberately planned by the government, how much was spontaneous local action, and how much was simple wartime killing in the context of WWI and its aftermath. Certainly all three were involved. An "apologetic" literature (apologetic for the Young Turks' government) holds that the government merely allowed massacres to happen, doing nothing to prevent them. However, eyewitnesses also reported government soldiers taking active part in much of the killing. In a work that will remain a major landmark for a long time, Taner Akçam (2012) has analyzed recently released records which show that the Young Turks encouraged and supported the murderers, and also the expulsion of Greeks, in a systematic and long-continued attempt to drive out Christians from Turkey. They managed military campaigns to maximize the damage. As Akçam points out, the Turks still hold officially (and, on the whole, popularly) to a view that the Christians were serving as agents of great-power efforts to dismantle Turkey, while the minorities in question—as well as independent scholarship in general—focuses on the genocide. Disagreement on this subject is still so intense that lawsuits, arrests, and the ruin of careers occur in Turkey and elsewhere over the matter. (For various views, see Bloxham, 2005, and Kiernan, 2007, siding with the Armenians; G. Balakian, 2009, for a recently published eyewitness Armenian account; his great-nephew P. Balakian, 2003, for further Armenian views; Akçam,

2012, and Lewis, 1961, for more balanced views; McCarthy et al., 2006, for the pro-Turkish position; Stone 2007 for a general quick overview; and, finally, Lewy, 2005, considers the Holocaust unique and thus does not consider the Armenian massacre a genocide, in spite of the fact that Lemkin explicitly used it in his initial definition.)

The most famous case of genocide, of course, is the Holocaust—Hitler's massacre of six million Jews, Roma, Slavs, homosexuals, handicapped people, political dissidents, modernist artists, and others. It was an attempt to "purify" the German people, by eliminating anyone perceived as different or disruptive. This is by far the best-known case of genocide, being the subject of literally tens of thousands of studies. It thus needs no discussion here (see cited sources in the bibliography), except to remind the reader that it went far beyond mere anti-Jewish sentiment. Attempts to deal with it or understand it as simple anti-Semitism are hopelessly inadequate.

Fascism is not synonymous with anti-Semitism; Benito Mussolini, the inventor of the term and concept, was not particularly anti-Semitic. Franco in Spain actually protected the Spanish Jews from Hitler. Fascism correctly applies to a political-economic system involving a strong, autocratic central government that is intensely and systematically involved with large business firms, especially heavy industry and armaments. This political-economic order has propagated greatly since the 1920s, and is very commonly associated with genocides.

The Nazi worldview was based on a concept of power—physical strength, political power, force of will—as the basic good. The worldview was strongly idealist in the Platonic sense: the world consisted of ideas constructed by the will, not material goods produced from natural resources. This worldview produced an extreme skepticism toward reality and the reality of categories; the will made everything, as in Leni Riefenstahl's propaganda film *Triumph des Willens* ("The Triumph of the Will," her film of the Nazi Party Congress in 1934, shortly after Hitler took power in Germany). Hitler and his group, and most of the Nazi troopers, were anti-intellectual; "when I hear the word 'culture' I reach for my gun," said Hitler's propaganda minister Joseph Goebbels. The jackbooted troops marched in lockstep through Riefenstahl's film and through the streets of Europe.

Intellectuals joined the program, in spite of the Nazis' general hatred and distrust of intellectuals and "culture." The Nazi philosopher Martin Heidegger's idealization of the Self, the will, and the individual Experience developed a mystical individualism based on emotion and reflection (Bourdieu, 1991; Heidegger, 1962). The general worldview that animated the Nazi high command was, of course, rather less subtle than Heidegger's thought, but he remained pro-Nazi till his death. The philosopher and literary critic Paul de Man was another devoted Nazi. The brilliant French writer and thinker Paul Ricoeur sympathized strongly with the

Nazis until he was captured in World War II and saw Nazism close up in a prison camp.

The Nazi ideology ran far beyond mere anti-Semitism. The Nazis also idealized the natural, but only what they saw as natural: a world of brute force, of violence, of domination, and of might making right—Tennyson's "nature red in tooth and claw." They scorned all that was "weak" or "unnatural" by this standard; hence the targeting of gays, mentally and physically handicapped persons, and assorted "degenerates," such as modernist artists, along with Jews and Roma. The leaders—especially Hitler and Goebbels, as well as Riefenstahl—were brilliant in their ability to use this worldview to construct the hate ideologies and subsequent genocidal regime. Nazi ideology was the most developed philosophy of a world based on amoral power. Here and in what follows we draw heavily on the writings of Franz Neumann (1943, 1957); Neumann's brilliant and insightful work is far too little known today.

Today, almost everyone has forgotten the pervasive reach of fascism and anti-Semitism in Europe and America (see Hilberg, 1992). Most people seem to think it was a German madness, and a temporary one at that. Not so. *All* the central and south European countries went fascist. Some did only after German conquest, but all had had huge, powerful fascist movements long before.

The Nazis were financed, backed, and encouraged by much of the German business and industrial sector, including Krupp, Bayer, Farben, and other major firms. The industrial elite thought they could control the Nazis and use them to win popular support and concessions. What happened, of course, was that the Nazis soon took control, leading to increasingly deadly policies that eventually devastated Germany and its economy. This dynamic was already clear by the middle 1930s, when it was brilliantly described by the Czech author Karel Čapek in his novel *War with the Newts* (1937). (Čapek's earlier play, *R. U. R.* [1923], had anticipated this by portraying the takeover of the robots; this play in fact introduced the word "robot," from the Czech for "work." See Čapek, 1990.) Sinclair Lewis, meanwhile, wrote a novel, *It Can't Happen Here* (1935), about a United States in which it did indeed happen; in fact, the United States came perilously close to fascist takeover (see below). We advise modern readers, especially in the United States, to read these works. *War with the Newts* is especially chilling, given what is happening in the United States today.

Italy was, of course, fascist before Hitler, but Italian and Spanish Fascists were less anti-minority. East Europe was not so gentle; most East European countries had huge pro-Hitler movements, and these often exterminated Jews more thoroughly than Germany did. France had a long anti-Semitic tradition, stretching from the Middle Ages to the Dreyfus affair, and a third of the French supported Hitler up to, and even into, World War II. There was no lack of collaborators to staff the Vichy government that Hitler installed. England's fascist Osbert Mosely had a large following, though it wilted quickly as Hitler turned warlike.

Poets loved fascism's forward-looking, strong, Nietzschean character. T. S. Eliot and e.e. cummings were supporters who wrote viciously anti-Jewish poetry. William Butler Yeats climbed briefly aboard, largely because Ireland's fascist movement opposed England, Ireland's old oppressor and enemy. D. H. Lawrence and Carl Jung were fascist sympathizers; Jung briefly joined a fascist movement and Lawrence flirted with one (as is memorably described in his novel *Kangaroo*). Most of these sages fell away as Hitler showed his true colors. Jung's flirtation was particularly brief. But Ezra Pound, Roy Campbell, and a few other poets remained rabidly pro-fascist right through World War II. Pound was confined in a mental hospital for this, having made some statements interpreted as treasonous. There is still debate about whether he was genuinely ill or simply a political prisoner. More than a few scientists also came on board, cooperating with the Nazi ideas on race (Stocking, 1988).

The United States had an enormous pro-Hitler movement. Martin Dies, longstanding congressman from Texas and founder of the House Un-American Activities Committee, was the major political supporter. Charles Lindbergh, the famous "flying ace," was a Hitler supporter until World War II. When the present authors were growing up in the United States, Hitlerian fascism was still a living force. World War II had ended outright support for the Nazis (and thus Martin Dies's career), but Nazi ideology was widespread, glorifying militarism, force, violence, strength, will power, and racism. Bernarr McFadden, who founded the physical education movement in America, became a passionate Hitler supporter in the 1930s, and many physical education specialists became followers. ENA well remembers the fascist sympathies of many "jocks" and physical education teachers in the 1940s and 1950s.

Worthy of special note in all this is the large number of people who heroically sheltered and protected Jews and dissidents through it all (see e.g., Colby and Damon, 1992; Monroe, 2004; Oliner and Oliner, 1988). Oskar Schindler made "Schindler's list" proverbial. This is a phenomenon seen in all well-documented genocides (recall the Applegate family on the Rogue River), though more in some than in others. Humanitarians everywhere risk the worst sorts of torture and death to protect persecuted people who are often perfect strangers. This fact may give a better insight into humanity and the human condition than does the existence of genocide. Worthy of note also is the work of those, such as Simon Wiesenthal (1998; Weinstein, 2005) who have hunted down refugee Nazis since 1945. Countless Nazis and collaborators who carried out genocide escaped to all corners of the world, where many were patiently tracked down and brought to trial, often in a world that seemed more inclined to forget them (see chapter 7).

Fascist democides occurred in Spain in the 1930s and after (under Franco), in Portugal (throughout the mid-twentieth century, under Salazar), and in Argentina in the late 1970s. Chile in the 1970s and 1980s, and one or two other well-off, stable countries, have had smaller campaigns of fascist repression involving mass murder. These have been controlled and systematic rather than meltdown or civil war situations. They appear to owe everything to Hitler's precept and example.

Other fascist nations in Europe largely followed Hitler or took his orders, but Japan had a separate (though allied) autocracy, with its own murders in Korea and China. (As usual, a notably valuable overview is in Kiernan 2007). In particular, Japanese treatment of Chinese ranged from using Chinese as experimental subjects in disease and biological warfare experiments to the Rape of Nanking. The total number of war dead in China from 1937 to 1945 will never be even approximately known, but it was in the tens of millions. We also will never know how many of these deaths were due to direct killing by Japanese, how many to Chinese civil strife, how many to famine, how many to disease. But certainly the Japanese killed millions. This was not genocide—the Japanese had no intention of exterminating the Chinese, and in any case the Chinese were enemies in an ongoing war—but mass murder it most certainly was.

Stalin killed millions of Soviet citizens from the late 1920s into the 1950s, eliminating not only political rivals and imagined rivals but also whole ethnic groups such as the Crimean Tatars. He drove Poles, Germans, and other groups out of Russia with great loss of life, and his repression of the Ukrainians involved such appalling unnecessary slaughter that it must qualify as genocide in spite of not being total (see, as usual, Kiernan, 2007). After the fall of Stalin, other Communist regimes killed large numbers. Usually these were political murders—politicide rather than true genocide. An oft-neglected chapter in modern genocide is the mass murder or displacement of East European Germans by Stalin and other Communist governments in East Europe just after World War II (Langenbacher, 2009). It went far beyond "payback" (bad enough in itself) and became a general campaign to get rid of German minorities that had long been hated and feared by prejudiced elements in many countries. The various campaigns under Stalin, Mao, and other Communist leaders involved motives ranging from desire to take land to sheer ethnic difference ("nationhood"), religion, and political conflicts.

All Communist countries, even Cuba, have records of democide. Most often, the democide took place when the regimes were consolidating their hold after takeover; thus in eastern Europe they usually occurred in the late 1940s (see Rummel, 1994, 1998). Mao Tse-Tung took the lead in sheer numbers, causing the deaths of tens or hundreds of millions of Chinese, especially (but far from solely) in the Great Leap Forward and Great Cultural Revolution campaigns. (See again Kiernan, 2007, but for once he is inadequate, since his mortality figures appear to the present writers to be far too low. ENA's interviews in Hong Kong in 1965–1966, including both refugees and informed Hong Kong residents, suggest figures far higher than Kiernan's or Rummel's estimates. For discussion, and better estimates of the Great Leap Forward toll, see Dikotter 2010.) Most of this was politicide, not ethnic genocide, but Mao's policies toward the Tibetans and a few other minorities have been called genocide and appear to qualify by any reasonable definition; the government does not seem to desire to exterminate the Tibetans, but does appear to be working to destroy Tibetan culture through a mix of massacre, forced re-education, and culturocide. This falls with the United Nations definition of genocide.

One chronic problem associated with genocide is the use of local groups as proxies for great-power conflicts. This often involved making small nations into proxy battlegrounds for major powers. Notably unfortunate in this regard is Afghanistan, where the "Great Game" of the nineteenth century led to the "cold war" of the twentieth and the "jihads" of the twenty-first. The Korean War of the 1950s was another proxy war, a competition between the United States and the leading Communist powers (the USSR and China) with Korea as the cat's-paw. The Vietnam War continued this tradition. Similar proxy wars have been fought in several African countries and in several smaller Latin American ones. Often, these wars spill over into local genocide. North and South Korea and North and South Vietnam all killed large numbers of people in the process of consolidating their regimes. The real combatants may pay heavily in these wars, but the locals pay more; "when the elephants fight, it is the grass which suffers." Most, if not all, of the Third World conflicts summarized below have one of these two backgrounds.

Indonesia's mass murders of 1965–1966 and subsequently have involved ethnicity, religion, "race," politics, class and other economic factors. Like the Armenian genocide in Turkey, the 1965–1966 massacres were anarchic and free-form. Many of them were, however, orchestrated or invoked by Suharto, who took over as dictator. Later, democide, and actual genocide or at least ethnic killings in East Timor and Aceh, were directly planned and methodically carried out by Suharto's Golkar dictatorship. Murder did not stop with Suharto's fall, however, and genocide continues in Irian Jaya, which is largely closed to outsiders in what is widely suspected to be a deliberate attempt to hide the murders. One of us (BA), however, has visited Irian Jaya and thus has direct knowledge of the situation from observation and interviewing.

Indonesia had been savagely repressed under the Dutch colonial regime; when it achieved independence, only some three hundred people remaining in the country had any college education (Kahin, 1970). The legacy of violence, oppressive government, and poor educational and social facilities became self-maintaining, dooming Indonesia to an almost hopeless task. It has fallen farther and farther behind more dynamic

Asian states. The environment has suffered particularly badly. Further meltdowns and mass killings seem more likely there than in almost any other nation.

Cambodia's orgy of murder under the Khmer Rouge (and not only by the Khmer Rouge—a fact not always remembered) is an extremely typical genocide in terms of the risk factors we have identified: It took place during a war, under a new and shaky government trying to consolidate its position, and the government was politically authoritarian to an extreme degree (Maoist-Communist). Accounts suggest also that its extreme intensity had much to do with Khmer culture. Alexander Hinton's superb historical ethnography and Ben Kiernan's histories trace the cultural and historical roots of massacre better than any other accounts we have seen for any genocide anywhere (Hinton, 2002; Hinton [ed.], 2002, 2005; Kiernan, a one-man publishing industry, has written so much that one can cite only his most recent books: 2004, 2007, 2008). It is also the genocide we know best, since Barbara Anderson's thesis research was with Cambodian refugees (Frye, 1989), and both of us have traveled through the nation.

Hinton traces the Khmer Rouge bloodiness to the interaction of high-modern thought (systematic, thorough, rationalized, totalizing), Maoism, and Khmer culture, particularly its stress on honor, "face," revenge, and extreme overreaction to dishonor of any kind (Hinton, 2005). Ironically, Buddhist-Khmer nonviolence and obedience played into it too; according to accounts, victims rarely did much to fight back once seized. In one way, Hinton was in a better position to analyze the situation than are those studying Hitler's Holocaust; the latter tend to think they and their readers "know about" Germany, and thus do not always get deep enough into immediate cultural contexts. Kiernan emphasizes more the primitivist streak in the Khmer Rouge, whose leadership came primarily from outback parts of Cambodia. These leaders wished to clear Cambodia of aliens (westerners, Chams, Vietnamese), educated people, the rich, and indeed almost anyone not a peasant or laborer.

The total population of Cambodia in 1975 was estimated at 8,000,000. By 1980 there were perhaps 6,360,000. Natural increase would have led us to expect the 8,000,000 to become 8,200,000 to 8,300,000—Cambodia's population had been increasing rapidly before the genocide. The total death toll has been estimated at 1,671,000 to 1,871,000 (Kiernan, 2008: 281). Rummel (1998) gives a figure of 2,639,000 for the total dead in Cambodia during the entire Vietnam War period. Any of these figures would make the Cambodian genocide the worst in all history in terms of percentage reduction of total national population: some 25 percent of total population. (Some 33 percent of the population died from genocide, war, and related conditions during the late 1970s.) The Cham ethnic group, especially targeted, lost about 36 percent (Kiernan, 2008; Osman, 2006). Only the Indonesian massacres in East Timor are comparable in percentage figures. Of course the settlement wars in the Americas caused a far greater reduction in the end, but they stretched over centuries, and most of the deaths were due to disease.

Communism collapsed in Yugoslavia in 1989, and Yugoslavia itself did not long survive; it broke up in a new Balkanization in 1991. Serbia seized the initiative to eliminate Muslims, and, increasingly, Catholics too; tens of thousands were massacred. The Communist or ex-Communist military dictator of Serbia, Slobodan Milosevitch, found a large number of willing murderers. He called the process "ethnic cleansing," to avoid being charged with genocide and thus subjected to possible intervention. This term has unfortunately caught on as a euphemism for genocide; it somehow implies something nicer and pleasanter. The reality is the same as in other genocides. The world delayed long (Hirsch, 2002), but eventually intervened, via NATO, and stopped the genocide, but few of the war criminals have since been brought to trial. Serbia remains a rather unrepentant state with a less than reformed government, and the killing could break out again.

Rwanda and Burundi provide another controversial case. They fell apart because of political problems exacerbated by ethnicity. The ethnic conflict owes much to Belgian policies of divide-and-rule during the colonial period (Gourevitch, 1998; Mamdani, 2001; Pottier, 2002; Prunier, 1995, 2007; see also Vansina, 2004, focusing on an even earlier, more peaceful and harmonious age). The Belgians set the Tutsi over the Hutu, using a divide-and-rule strategy and branding the Hutu as inferior or backward. They also created labor discipline of a merciless top-down form, which was later to be pressed into service in mobilizing genocide. Once the Belgians left, Rwanda and Burundi failed to succeed economically. In large part this was due to Belgian colonial policies, including runaway population growth exacerbated by Catholic missionization. A crippled economy could not keep up with rising population. Land was deforested, then eroded, then utterly ruined. The masses of hopeless young people provided ready fodder for ultra-ethnicist zealots. Hutu-Tutsi conflicts arose and worsened over time (Straus, 2006). Tutsi repression of Hutu was close to, if not actually, genocide. When the Hutu—a downtrodden majority—finally took power, they used it to settle scores with the Tutsi.

The world believed "disinformation" on what was happening, or preferred to appear to do so (see Pottier, 2002). The United Nations sent troops, but without arms and without orders; they could only stand idly by. The Hutu hardliners ordered their militias and gangs out. They also mobilized the entire population (Pinker, 2011: 339 claims that the murderers were only the dregs of society, but this is contradicted by all observers). Some seven hundred thousand people were killed in a hundred days, before the Tutsi could rally and slowly take over the country, establishing a regime that endures as of this writing. A majority of Rwandans did not kill. Those who did were influenced by top-down orders and by fear and insecurity (Straus, 2006, esp. pp. 122 ff.; see Hatzfeld, 2005 for personal accounts).

The story has been told in agonizing detail by the commander, Roméo Dallaire (2003). Among other sources, Gourevitch (1998) is highly sympathetic to the final winners in Rwanda. Other accounts (Khan, 2000; Melvern, 2006; Prunier, 1995, 2007; Straus, 2006) are more nuanced and much less pro-winner. The Tutsi, including the Tutsi army invading from Uganda at the end of the genocide, did their share of the killings (Davenport and Stam, 2009), and the whole situation was chaotic; also, since there really are no visible distinctions between most people of the different ethnic groups, many people hid in plain sight by claiming they were of the locally dominant ethnic group, whichever one it might be at the time.

As in so many cases, Rwanda had its hero endangering his life to save others. "Hotel Rwanda," actually the Hotel des Mille Collines, was run by Paul Rusesabagina. He made the hotel a safe zone for hunted officials and ordinary people, and managed by an incredible and harrowing amount of political machination to save them throughout the genocide (Gourevitch, 1998). He deserves to be remembered along with Oskar Schindler and others who saved the hunted in genocidal campaigns.

The violence in Rwanda and Burundi led, in part, to the complex and poorly-documented killings in Congo (D. R., Kinshasa). Tutsi and Hutu militias, and sometimes the Rwandan army itself, have been active there for decades, and so have local gangsters and rebel groups. Killing in D. R. Congo involves formal government to a debatable degree. National government has never functioned well in that prototypic "failed state." It was the scene of mass killings in the Belgian colonial period (including the earlier period when it was not officially a "colony" but was, rather, the personal domain of King Leopold). These, which included local genocides, set the tone for the future political evolution of the Congo. In any case, an already violent situation was vastly exacerbated when the Hutu extremists fled Rwanda and established themselves in eastern Congo. Tutsi followed them, or fled from Burundi. The ethnic conflicts continue in the new zone. Other conflicts between militias in the area are apparently little more than local looting. Another major exacerbating factor is conflict over the rich mineral resources of the area, especially col-tan, the ore of columbium and tantalum; these metals are vital to the electronics industry and are not found in many places worldwide.

In Congo and elsewhere in Africa, child soldiers have been a major part of the action, and present special problems morally and otherwise (an excellent discussion is provided by Rosen, 2007; see also articles in Brainard and Chollet, 2007, and the harrowing memoir of Beah, 2007). Rape is also a routine weapon, as is extermination of whole villages at a time. Claims of fatalities run to over five million people; this is probably a good deal too high (Pinker, 2011: 319), but the need for a hedge indicates not only that it could be that high but, more to the point, that we really have no idea of the toll.

Those who do not like blaming colonial parties for events in ex-colonies would do well to study Belgium's role in Africa, as well as the Dutch role in Indonesia and the British in Myanmar. The legacy of colonialism has been self-maintaining. The decades since independence have not provided adequate time to break free of the institutions and "mentalities" in question.

Sudan killed at least two million and enslaved countless more in the South. After relative peace finally came to that region, a local rebellion in Darfur erupted into fighting in 2003 that led to mass murders of Darfuris by the Sudanese government (sometimes acting through proxies, local Arab gangs known as *janjaweed*; see Totten, 2011a for full review). As in the Rwanda case, colonial policies underlay these problems (Prunier, 2007). Apparently the peace accords with the South were signed partly to give the government a freer hand in Darfur. Sudan's government used vastly superior force to devastate civilian communities, and used the rebellion as an excuse to clear out Darfuris and resettle more congenial "Arab" Sudanese. The overwhelming majority of victims were noncombatants killed by the government and its *janjaweed* proxy forces. By 2009, some four hundred thousand had been killed (Prunier 2007: 155; BBC News Online, April 23, 2008, and August 27, 2009) and three million displaced. It wound down in 2009 and the United Nations declared it ended (as of August 27; BBC News Online for that date; United Nations, 2007), but sporadic action continues. Chad was drawn into the war as refugees attracted pursuers from Sudan. This was further exacerbated by Libyan meddling in the Gaddafi era (Prunier, 2007), and merged into Chad's endless civil strife.

Referring to this as genocide remains a judgment call. It remains "ambiguous," as Prunier points out, because Darfuris fought back and attempted to make the region independent. The utter disproportion of the forces involved and the mass murders of civilians by the Sudan government make it a genocide by most criteria. It was finally declared genocide by the United Nations. However, many still refrain from accusing Sudan's current government of outright genocide (Farley, 2005; Prunier, 2007; Totten, 2011a). Significantly, most of the refrainers represent, or speak from, governments that are major trading partners of Sudan.

One could roughly divide recent genocide and politicide into three vaguely distinct environments: fascist governments and collapsing empires in the early twentieth century; Communist states in the mid-twentieth; and failing African states and other economically and politically challenged entities since then.

The closely related case of out-of-control violence, with mass killing of civilians but without systematic governmental genocide, has also occurred in Haiti, Algeria, and many other places. This sort of near-genocide also affected Liberia and Sierra Leone in the 1990s and early 2000s. Civil war in Liberia turned into general chaos, confounded by drugs. An illicit diamond trade, involving exchange of diamonds for drugs and weapons, fueled the war, especially in Sierra Leone. At least two hundred fifty thousand died in Liberia and fifty thousand in Sierra Leone, but vastly greater numbers suffered mutilation, torture, and rape. Around five hundred thousand fled these countries. Cannibalism, sometimes involving people forced to kill and eat their own relatives, occurred (Stepakoff et al., 2006). The reasons for violence escalating so far out of control remain somewhat obscure. Somewhat less horrific meltdowns are common in the historical record. They do not count as "genocide," because particular ethnic groups are only incidentally targeted and because the government is not systematically and coldly acting, but they provide a valuable sidelight on the issue.

THE PERMANENT NATURE OF GENOCIDE

The effect of genocide on a society is permanent. They are often told to "get over it," but they do not. Not one group subjected to genocide has "gotten over it," no matter how many years have passed. Our Maya friends in Mexico still talk about the Spanish Conquest and Bishop Diego de Landa's psychopathic reign of terror. After 450 years it is still fresh in their minds. Among many smaller indigenous societies victimized by settler wars, the endlessly lingering effects of genocide devastate the survivors and drive them to substance abuse, depression, and hopelessness. These may linger for generations. At best, the lingering memories lead survivors to dedicate their lives to justice, human rights, and the agenda summarized by the phrase "never again" (Kidder, 2009).

Genocide is bad enough; pretending it did not occur merely adds more suffering. The denial of violence may be almost as damaging as the actual violence itself, as we note from the outrage of victims of abuse who are not believed. Turkey still denies the mass killing of Armenians, though it happened a century ago under a totally different government regime (cf. Bloxham, 2005). Germany has its skinhead Nazis again, and they deny that the Holocaust amounted to much; more serious are the Holocaust-deniers and anti-Semitic extremists in other countries, including high officials in Russia and Iran. Japan refuses to apologize, let alone recompense, for its atrocities in World War II (McNeill, 2007), including the atrocities perpetrated against the "comfort" women (Chang and Kim, 2007). One of the authors (BA) has listened to young Cambodian-Americans who deny the Khmer Rouge atrocities, in spite of the Tower of Skulls and other unequivocal memorabilia. The authors have walked those killing fields, witnessed the remains of human bodies at these sites, and seen the scars on the bodies of survivors. Closer to home, we have heard many doubts cast on the genocidal nature of America's Indian "wars." Grim though they may be, Holocaust memorials are necessary to remind us, "never again."

SEVEN

Causes and Some Predictions

REVIEW OF THE CAUSES

In summary, *the basic, deep, constant problem that allows genocide is human social or group hate, due to fear*. While fear and individual hate merely expose the weak side of humanity, group hatred leads to ascribing evil intentions to the targeted group. The targeted group is blamed for the problems of life. The human tendency to seek group solidarity and approval leads to compliance with violence once it has been socially sanctioned. "Othering," if not dehumanization, takes place. However, hate and fear exist in all societies; they slide over into mass killing only when inflamed by politicians or violent individuals for cynical or divisive motives.

Hate and fear are naturally exacerbated by *poverty and insecurity, but above all by decline in economic well-being, social status, and overall security*. A society that is in decline and fears worse is *primed for takeover by autocratic governments, which then very often move toward genocide* as they consolidate rule. Hopelessness, often occurring when there is downward mobility, a downturn in economic security, or a sense of internal or external threat, may result in rigid absoluteness. This becomes a defensive posture, eroding the social value of tolerance. The predatory nature of genocide could be stopped at any of these steps if social stability and hope intervened.

After this, the critical step can be either *fears in the mind of a powerful but insecure authoritarian leadership, or ongoing conflict—typically either strong government support for settlers' strife for land held by a weaker group or sudden setbacks in an ongoing war*.

The usual threat situations that concern such leaders include the following: (1) Consolidation of a new regime that feels threatened by strong opposition or general unpopularity. This was commonest in the cases of

Communist takeover of governments. Rummel reports bloodbaths in virtually every case; they reached extreme levels in Mao's China and Pol Pot's Cambodia as well as the USSR. Other cases, however, include the exact opposite: the fall of Communism, when it was replaced by right-wing dictatorship. This happened in Serbia in the 1990s. Yet other examples of consolidation of totalitarian rule through genocide include Suharto's Indonesia, Iran after 1979, the military rule in Argentina in the 1970s, Pinochet's Chile, Rwanda in 1994, Idi Amin's Uganda, and other cases. Shoring up shaky autocracy through mass killing has occurred in Colombia, El Salvador, Guatemala, Haiti, Sudan, and many other places; some of these involved newly elected "democratic" governments that actually exercised military powers well beyond normal democratic functions. (2) Civil war and unrest, especially when identified with particular ethnic groups. The temptation is to solve the problem by eliminating the ethnic group—or even turning against an ethnic group that was not involved at all but that presents a convenient scapegoat. (3) External war, especially when it is not going well for the autocratic regime.

Of course, all these can occur together, producing a real witch-cauldron. External war, with the imminent threat of losing, certainly affected the Young Turks in Turkey and Hitler in Germany. Indonesia's invasion of East Timor turned to genocide when the Timorese resisted. Suppression of small revolts turned into mass genocide—not always confined to the group in rebellion—in Burma, El Salvador, Guatemala, Nigeria (Biafra), Pakistan (in the attempt to suppress independence for Bangladesh), Philippines (under Marcos), Sudan, and several minor cases. A fourth possibility is that the leader will become genuinely paranoid or psychotic, as seems to have happened with Zhu Yuanzhang and Robert Mugabe, and possibly Mao Zidong.

More with individuals than with governments and more with governmental regimes than with nations, a record of previous genocide is also an ominous risk factor. Nations can fix their act (like Germany), but regimes tend to fall back on genocide when threatened. This is frightening now in places like China and Iran, where regimes that once indulged in mass killing are facing an uncertain and challenging future.

However, a history of genocide, so often emphasized by authors on the subject, seems not highly valuable as a predictor. Some countries, including almost all of Europe, most of South America, and all of east Asia except China, have been so thoroughly inoculated (so to speak) by experiences with genocide that they seem virtually riskless today. One cannot imagine Germany returning to the early 1940s under any remotely likely scenario. Democracies that suffered brief lapses into horror, such as Argentina, Chile, and the Philippines, show every sign that they have learned to guard their freedoms—though, especially in the Philippines, corrupt government officials and simmering local rebellions cast a dark shadow.

Cambodia in the 1970s had all possible risk factors. It was a weak, impoverished country sliding into chaos as the Vietnam War spilled over the border. The Khmer Rouge, whose leadership came from a remote backwater of the country, seized power. They consolidated their rule under increasingly desperate economic, social, and military conditions, in a land saturated with weapons and filled with random violence. With this many risk factors, their creation of one of the worst of all genocides is not surprising.

However, the two worst performers in the twentieth century—Stalin's USSR and Mao's China—were different. All three major risks were present at first, but killing did not stop when the regimes were consolidated and the wars over. As long as Stalin and Mao held power, the killing went on and on. Apparently the same was true of Uganda's Idi Amin and a few other cases. New targets were invented and hatred against them was generated, often with no previous history of hating those particular groups; in fact, as we have noted, Mao targeted the groups previously most respected in Chinese society. With the deaths of these leaders, the killings stopped short—almost totally and almost instantly. We must, then, recognize that some leaders are either genuinely paranoid or very close to it, and that they manufacture threats when no independently detectable ones exist. The vast majority of genocides, however, happen when regimes are genuinely or believably threatened.

Civil wars, also, are apt to appear even in stable, long-established, democratic governments—the United States in 1861 being the most obvious example to American readers, as England's in the seventeenth century is to British ones. They rarely become true meltdowns—orgies of undirected mass murder—except in weak but dictatorial governments. Examples of the latter case range from Porfirio Diaz's failing regime in Mexico to the recent meltdowns in Somalia, D. R. Congo, Liberia, and Sierra Leone. Colombia, however, reminds us that an endless civil war with aspects of meltdown can coexist with an imperfect democracy (Escobar, 2008). Many earlier civil wars and jacqueries in Europe were all too reminiscent of twentieth-century meltdowns. Risk factors for war and civil war are different. War often accompanies a militaristic government and culture; economic decline; aggressive rise of a borderland (marchland) state; and a real sense that profits as well as glory can be obtained (Turchin, 2003). Civil war is closer to genocide in origins, differing mainly in that the persecuted group starts the war by rebelling, or else fights back if attacked. Thus external war gives us little understanding of genocide, though the economic decline is a significant variable. Civil war is more useful in understanding genocide, especially for demonstrating the wider economic contexts that make mass murder likely.

A terminally weak, failing government cannot commit genocide because it cannot hold law and order together at all; under stress, it dissolves, leading to chaos. Chinese dynasties, for example, survived and flourished when strong, in spite of incredible death rates from war and famine. But when they finally gave way, dynasties fell rapidly, leading to long periods of total meltdown, in which millions of people died.

Genocide occupies the in-between case. When a government is sorely challenged but not collapsing, it will often try to unify the majority against a minority. This often happens when it is losing a war, as we have seen above. It may also happen when it has just won a war but is very shakily in control.

There are always opportunists or outright criminals waiting to take advantage of any situation in which they can take or consolidate power through violence. In a civil war, such people attract many ordinary citizens who have become desperate and feel that poverty and loss of honor and justice leave them with little else to lose. In a genocide, a small outbreak by small-scale thugs gives even more thuggish elements in government an excuse to butcher. In a genuine revolution, the thuggish element may take only a marginal follower role.

The victims are most often minority ethnic groups. Next come political opponents ("politicide"). Next come religious groups. Minorities that are both ethnically *and* religiously different from the majority, like the Armenians in Turkey and Jews in Germany, can expect the worst treatment of all.

We have pointed out in several places above that genocide bears a striking resemblance to family violence. The "dehumanization" is somewhere between a hollow sham and a desperate attempt to "other" one's own people. The sadism and torture indicate psychological closeness, not distance. Above all, the clear immediate drive is need to control. The spouse abuser desperately wants control of his or her mate. The child-beater wants "obedience." The leaders and organizers of genocide want the same thing. They often feel their situation—their political leadership, in particular—is spiraling out of control, or, as Mao repeatedly said, that it would do so without mass campaigns.

We have progressed from ultimate causes to immediate ones. A causal chain should run from basic underlying factors to immediate, contingent ones.

The ultimate cause is the human tendency to hate and fear other groups that present a conceivable threat to one's own person or group. This, however, in manageable genocide usually remains rare.

Next in the causal chain comes defining a group by its structural opponent status: it is the most salient "other" group within society, or at least one of the most salient. The more tightly and rigidly it is defined, the more the danger. A group seen as a vague, shifting, voluntary thing, such as a club with a fluctuating membership, is often in less danger than a group allegedly defined by important hereditary features. On the other hand, this is not true in politicide, where holding a purely voluntary political ideology is fatal. The sharpness of definition and the sharpness of perceived threat matters more than heredity. In very many modern genocides, Kiernan's "blood" matters much less than political opinion.

Even a hereditarily defined group should be in less danger if people realize that groups mix and blend. Sharply defining a group, however, often moves toward a pre-genocidal situation in which heredity is believed to create extreme differences that cannot be wiped out by admixture. "One drop of black blood makes a person black" in the United States, even today (if we read "the tiniest shred of African-like appearance"). American definitions of "Indians," Australian definitions of Aboriginals, and German definitions of Jews all fluctuated with the level of genocidal attitudes. What is really and deeply important here, as noted earlier, is that *during genocides, the inevitable and numerous ambiguous cases are usually lumped with the clear ones; all are killed.* Arnold Amaury's famous policy resurfaces in every genocide.

In a typical pre-genocidal situation, and during the genocide itself, ordinary people fall in line, not so much because they do not care or because they are natural followers, but because they have lost hope and been made passive by both bad times and deliberate breaking of the spirit by totalitarian governments. Yeats's lines "The best lack all conviction, while the worst / Are full of passionate intensity" ("The Second Coming," written 1919) apply to people in such cases, as indeed were most people in Europe and America in 1919.They also apply with singular accuracy today, which does not bode well. Indeed, Yeats's dreadful Sphinx-like figure that "slouches toward Bethlehem to be born" is an excellent forecast of fascism and genocide. It is ironic that Yeats flirted with fascism himself in the early 1930s.

Next in the causal chain come opportunistic politicians who exploit this ethnic, religious, or political tension. They exaggerate difference, demonize the stigmatized groups, and whip up rhetoric.

A warning step that means the tilt to genocide is nearly irreversible is the creation of a thuggish band of enforcers: Hitler Youth, the Hutu Interahamwe, Mao's Red Guard, and the like. Sometimes the entire army is subverted (as in Guatemala) or a significant chunk of it becomes a band of fascist devotees (as in Argentina), but usually the opportunistic politicians find it expedient to create their own groups—sworn faithful, and outside the ordinary military and legal structure.

Finally, when war or extreme unrest breaks out, insecure but autocratic elites use such means to try to control the situation. If it spirals out of control regardless, genocide becomes almost inevitable.

In short, *genocide can be confidently predicted.* We cannot predict it 100 percent, but there are certainly places to watch. These would be ones where unrest and instability exist, where there is widespread downward mobility, and where ethnic and religious hatred and scapegoating are widespread and are exploited by politicians. We can expect that, if an extremist government comes to power, it will be very apt to turn totalitarian. It will then move quickly toward mass murder to consolidate its position, especially if there is any major move against it.

PREDICTIONS

Many countries have not so far melted down in spite of major risk factors. Their future depends on the trajectory of stability and civil rights over time. Some examples are Bangladesh, Burkina Faso, Kenya, and Nicaragua; more could be found. These have avoided falling into exploitation of hate speech, have stayed either democratic or at least stable, and are developing slowly. Other countries have not been so responsible.

Let us make some testable predictions. Examples of nations at extreme immediate risk as of this writing include both Congo-Brazzaville and D. R. Congo, Egypt, Indonesia, Myanmar, Niger, Nigeria, and Sudan. These six countries have all the risk factors: mobilized hatreds, economic problems that leave many worse off, ongoing violence, and dictatorial regimes in need of shoring up their power. We originally listed Chad and Syria as well, but events overtook us, showing that our predictions have some value. All have histories of recent ethnic and religious killing, with Indonesia, Nigeria, and Sudan guilty of major genocides. Congo (Brazzaville) is dealing with the oil curse and has a weak government and considerable ongoing violence; conditions for much of the country appear to be worsening.

Egypt is a special case, one in which we can advance a prediction that genocide is highly probable. Civil unrest led to the fall of Mubarak. A shaky democracy has been restored, under military domination. Islamic parties dominated the elections, with extremists gathering over 20 percent of the vote. The chances of a new government remaining democratic and religiously tolerant are slim. The Egyptian economy was impacted by the unrest, and shows little sign of reviving at this time. Violence against the Coptic Christian minority has escalated and shows no sign of easing; it is being exploited by Islamic extremist politicians. At the very least, politicide is probable, and the world should be preparing for perhaps ten million Coptic refugees. In short, every risk factor is present.

Indonesia has a particularly violent history of recent genocides, a low-key settler war in Irian Jaya, a weak government, a huge extremist Islamic movement, and oil. Moreover, in spite of paper growth, most of its people are not doing well, if not actually getting worse off. Indonesia's chances for genocide in the near future are well over 50 percent. Myanmar has a shaky dictatorship in poor control of the ethnic-minority parts of its country, and a dismal economy; the government will quite likely try to reassert control at some point "by any means necessary." Nigeria has a long history of genocide and political murder, and an unstable and volatile situation in its oil districts; it also has religious violence in the Muslim north, with bombings of Christian churches. If it faces some downward mobility, it will probably suffer from some form of civil violence. Sudan needs no elaboration beyond what has been said in the last chapter. In short, all these cases have potential for trouble, but only if one or two of our risk factors become more salient; however, there is a strong risk that this is exactly what will happen.

It seems likely, given the risk factors, that genocide or at least mass civil killings are also a serious risk in the following nations, which we judge to have three risk factors present: Burundi, China, Eritrea, Guatemala, Iran, Iraq, Mali, North Korea, and, of especially high concern, Pakistan, with its nuclear arsenal and its loss of control of remote areas close to Afghanistan. The problems with the countries noted above should be obvious from what has gone before. In addition, Libya and Tunisia are now transitioning to some unclear form of governance, and cannot be assessed, but are obviously of major concern.

China is a slightly longer-term risk, but a terrible one. China evolved from glorifications of the successful in pre-Communist times to hatred of the well-to-do in the 1960s to scorn for rural and "backward" people in the 1990s—a 180-degree turn. Political opportunists, combined with powerful political and financial interests, defined "friend" and "enemy." They used and built upon existing historical hatreds to craft political hatreds. "The enemy" had to be defined to allow a general term for anyone disliked or falling outside of the fold. At present, increasing corruption, and consequent breakdown of civil society, environmental protection, and economic welfare nets, are stressing a society whose economic foundations are built on sand. A major turnover of government personnel, elevating a new and younger leadership, is due as of 2012, and would very possibly unleash a power-consolidation genocide of the sort seen in China in the 1950s and 1960s, and in other Communist lands. A major economic downturn—a certainty, given China's suicidal environmental policies—would almost certainly unleash a wave of hopelessness and a consequent wave of violence.

Colombia provides a special case. It has calmed down its drug violence, paramilitary squad operations, and ethnically targeted murdering (see Escobar, 2008), and is currently doing well economically, and thus has no risk factors operating at present (except for a less than fully democratic government), but this could easily reverse. Meddling by outside influences, including the United States, could restart the civil war there, though at present some stability and economic growth are protective. Iran continues in a near-genocidal state, having eliminated its real or fantasized opponent groups after the Islamic coup of 1979, but still cracking down on dissidents of all sorts, real or imagined. It is not flourishing economically, though some growth occurs and so far is protective. Like Colombia, Sri Lanka seems peaceful and democratic, but until recently it had all four factors present and was indeed genocidal. It could erupt again.

Extremist Islam is on the rise in several countries, many of which had virtually no such movement forty years ago. Pakistan, Bangladesh, and Malaysia are examples. However, of these, Pakistan seems to be the only one that is clearly in immediate danger, with political breakdown leading to the rapid rise of extremism. A regime change, especially a military takeover such as has happened before, would surely trigger major bloodletting. Bangladesh is currently relatively stable, harmonious, and not at risk. Malaysia has been saved by, among other things, a rapidly rising economy and modernizing infrastructure, though a downturn in this ethnically polarized country could be dangerous. Related conditions exist in several other countries. The Arab Spring of 2011 led to reforms that reduced risks in some countries (notably Algeria), but led to Islamic extremist power grabs in others (notably Egypt), with results that are at least destabilizing and at most extremely dangerous. At this writing, civil war seems imminent in Libya, ongoing in Syria, and barely averted in Yemen, and results might include genocide in both countries.

Even Europe is not immune, in spite of lessons that should have been learned. Russia is stressed by criminal gangs and corruption, and, as of this writing, Vladimir Putin shows ever more dictatorial colors. Russia came close to outright religious war in the Caucasus, and a great deal of anti-Islamic hate speech and activity is reported. Russia's economic woes are relieved only by oil—the worst possible thing to have as one's economic salvation; ordinary people's economic situation is parlous. Russiais moving very close to being a four-risk country. Elsewhere in Europe, Belarus is still a Communist dictatorship, though a stable and peaceable one at present. In other countries, anti-Roma sentiment has turned into more and more ominous legislation, especially in Slovakia and Hungary. The constituents of the former Yugoslavia are still somewhat unstable.

Less immediate risks, but not to be forgotten, are the countries that have had genocidal violence lately but now seem stable. Rwanda is probably the most shaky of these. Angola, Equatorial Guinea, Madagascar, Uganda, and Zimbabwe are also major risk candidates. The rest of Africa seems currently stable, but regime change could be troubling at any point. El Salvador, Guatemala, Haiti, Honduras, and Nicaragua are not entirely out of the woods, but show no current risk factors except ongoing economic doldrums with some civil unrest. The rest of Latin America seems secure, though local genocide of small Indigenous groups still could happen in Brazil and neighboring countries.

Turkey could crack down violently on the Kurdish minority, though full-scale genocide would probably require a major change of policy and regime. Cambodia, Laos, Sri Lanka, and Vietnam seem well out of danger. The rest of Asia outside the Arab countries seems stable, but one or another of the inner Asian daughter republics of the USSR could flare up if there is a massive coup or other regime-change violence.

Other violence based on classic "difference" factors has happened recently in India, Ivory Coast, Kenya, Nepal, and elsewhere, but has always stopped well short of genocide; this could change, but shows no sign of it in those states at present. These countries are mostly democratic, are reasonably stable economically, and are not in danger of totalitarian takeover; they have no immediate risk factors.

The international community should show extreme vigilance in the three worst general cases: when a powerful settler group invades a new land, as with Indonesia's current colonization of Irian Jaya; when a powerful but shaky leadership tries to consolidate control of a fractured realm, as in Sudan and Myanmar today, and above all when a new and autocratic regime comes to power, as in Egypt; and when a war seems to be spiraling into defeat or into endless and hopeless violence, as in Afghanistan and Congo (D. R.) today.

Other countries, including Colombia, Indonesia, Sudan, and several Central African and Middle Eastern states, seem so addicted to mass murder as a problem-solving method that they can be expected to continue as long as current government structures persist, but even in these cases we doubt if actual genocide will ensue without at least one or two of the above four conditions coming into play.

POLITICAL FRAMEWORK: IT CAN HAPPEN HERE

On the other hand, genocide in the United States seems quite likely, even probable, at this writing. The rise of extremist right-wingism in America in the 1990s and 2000s dramatically changed conservatism there. The long-established American conservative political tradition featured fiscal discipline, free rein to large corporations, environmental protection, "old-time" genteel Christian religion, boot-strap success, and the acquisition of power veiled in respect and deference. It was not defined by sexuality or reproductive choices. In fact, opposition to abortion was largely confined to the Catholic church, which was generally in low regard among old-time conservatives.

After 1980, for several reasons, American conservatism produced a new blend of thinking. Environmental conservation, respect and deference, and old-time decorous Christianity were abandoned and even vociferously repudiated. Fiscal conservatism was honored in name but not in deed; Republican governments were generally bigger spenders than Democratic ones. Fiscal conservatism turns out to be an ideology of those out of power; it is a defense against the spending priorities of the ruling group. Thus, fiscal responsibility, which was in any case never applied to the military or to subsidies for the rich, was abandoned by whichever party had power. As Republicans became the majority party and increasingly dominated government decisions, conservative Republicans abandoned it, while many Democrats adopted it over the decades. The return of Democrats to dominance in 2008 brought fiscal conservatism back to Republican rhetoric, but the Republicans continued to prioritize tax breaks and subsidies for the wealthy, as well as military spending, over any fiscal concerns.

More important was the transformation of right-wing religion and politics into a virulently sexist, anti-gay, and racist "fundamentalism." Fear-based ideas—hatred of women and minorities and glorification of strength and bigness—became central. American conservatism became defined partly by opposition to gays, abortion, women's rights, and liberals in general (cf. Westen, 2007). Republican campaigners even used the term "faggot" for Democrat politicians (including some thoroughly heterosexual ones) in the 2008 election campaigns (our personal observation).

Meanwhile, funding for American conservatism became dominated by the giant resource-based corporations, for example, oil, tobacco, agribusiness, mining, and forestry. They were overwhelmingly the biggest donors in politics, and their money went largely to conservative causes. By early 2006, fierce conflict had broken out between conservative and liberal factions over spending priorities, for example, immigration restraint, religious expression, reproductive rights, and torture of prisoners.

During the immigration debates after 2006, conservative leadership proposed measures designed to strengthen the political infrastructure for business and extractive industries: migrants would be controlled and kept as a low-paid workforce, easily deported if they attempted to object, let alone unionize. Conservative legislators directed extreme rhetoric at Hispanics. The huge numbers of non-Hispanic illegal immigrants, such as Chinese, Russian, or Canadian, were notably absent from the dialogue. Rhetoric came perilously close to calling for genocide. Attempts are being made to insure that citizens providing assistance to illegal immigrants are in defiance of law. In 2010, Arizona passed legislation that specifically singled out and targeted Hispanic Americans, legal citizens as well as illegal immigrants. A large number of other states followed suit. Throughout the United States, Republican parties that formerly worked hard (with Democrats) to provide public education, conservation, and other services cracked down on immigrants. They also attacked unions, organizations that provide reproductive care to women, independent health providers, and a range of other social service providers. Republicans that took over state governments on a promise of small government rapidly assumed near-dictatorial powers, at least in regard to labor unions, religious groups, and public education. Bills were introduced to forbid teaching about sexuality (or at least homosexuality), global warming, Darwinian evolution, and a host of other concepts, in the public schools.

The contrast with the Republicans of Eisenhower's and Nixon's days is striking. The similarities to extremist movements worldwide are even more so. The resemblances to extremist Islam are particularly close.

Not to be left behind, the left developed an equal share of untruths, conspiracy theories, and extremist ideas, but the American left was vanishingly small and essentially powerless.

The Tea Party on the right and Occupy movements on the left remained incoherent. The incoherence of the latter probably dooms it to early extinction, but the Tea Party's extreme fringe movements fuse with the illegal militias, surviving hate-based organizations, and extreme conspiracy movements. These present real and present danger. If an extremist Republican becomes president, the urge to crack down and use such militias to enforce a hate-based order will be virtually impossible to resist. Declaring a state of emergency, suspending the Constitution, and launching a mass murder campaign against political opponents, gays, and other groups can be fairly confidently predicted.

We are deeply concerned about the future of the United States. The United States has recently seen the meteoric rise of hate politics reminiscent of the politics of Germany in the early 1930s. This rise has been ongoing since the 1990s, but has become truly terrifying with the economic downturn of 2008. On the right, specialized professional hatemongers (the most visible being commentators on Fox News) have advocated major political crackdowns, and have been successful enough to give us the Patriot Act nationally and a discriminatory immigration control bill in Arizona, with imitations arising in other states. The left has been quieter of late, but has certainly had its moments, including a great deal of hate material circulating on the web during the George W. Bush administration. The level of political polarization, and above all the lack of reason and moderation, is frightening.

Anyone thinking that genocide is based on some simple root ideology like purity, agrarianism, or nationalism would do well to look at group hate in the United States, as reflected tens of thousands of times daily on talk radio and in the anonymous comments on articles in online news sources. As in Hitler's Germany and Mao's China, almost any group is attacked for one or another imagined sin. People who describe themselves as "real Americans" hate Blacks because the latter are supposedly dirty, lazy, and stupid; Hispanics because they are all on welfare yet somehow are taking all the "white people's" jobs, and also because Hispanics "breed like rabbits"; intellectuals because intellectuals are smart, act superior, question authority; Native Americans because they were "savages" and keep expecting respect for their "savage" cultures; gays for various pseudo-religious reasons; Jews because Jews are smart, successful, and devious; Muslims because 9/11 "proves" that Muslims are terrorists who want to destroy the United States; mainstream Christians for being (in the words of Jerry Falwell) "children of the Devil," and tolerant of sexual latitude; and liberals because liberals disagree with group-hatred politics. It is clear that the only ideology here is hate for anyone weaker or for any rival group. Naked group hate based on naked fear, and the need of dictators to consolidate their power, are the real "ideologies" behind these movements.

The United States situation is particularly frightening because many giant corporate interests have partnered with hate groups and hate radio, using the platform to spread disinformation about global warming (Hoggan, 2009; Oreskes and Conway, 2010) and many other important environmental and health issues. The partnership of hate interests and giant corporate ones is exactly what Hitler arranged in Germany in the 1930s, and the United States appears to be uncomfortably close to a political takeover of the same nature.

EIGHT

Sowing Good Seeds

Sustaining the Soil of Community

THE RISE OF PEACE IN THE LAST THREE HUNDRED YEARS

In thoughtful contrast to the gloom that pervades most literature on violence today, Steven Pinker, in *The Better Angels of Our Nature* (2011), shows that violence of all types has decreased over the last three hundred years or more. This applies especially to war, but also to murder, feuds, and even violence toward animals. Pinker also shows that wars got fewer, smaller, and more tractable to intervention in recent decades. Before that, wars arose in a quite random fashion; neither poverty nor cycles nor regime types predicted war. Also, a few wars and genocides did most of the killing; most wars and genocides are small. Pinker resorts to exhaustive statistical analyses and databases, most of them very recent or even under development, allowing him to see patterns previously unsuspected. His work is impeccable on these points, in spite of some negative reviews. (Reviewers can get far from rational when their favorite cynicism is gored; Robert Epstein, in *Scientific American Mind* [Janurary–February 2012, p. 68], distrusts Pinker because chimpanzees fight and kill. Besides the obvious points that chimps are not humans and that Pinker fully acknowledges chimp violence, there is also the point that we are as closely related to the peaceful and loving bonobos as to the savage chimps. So are we bonobos or chimps? We are neither, and Epstein's point is irrelevant.)

Pinker also points out that bloody-minded ideology, political stances, and even literature—notably children's literature—have changed a great deal (see, e.g., pp. 292ff). We well remember the Grimm's fairy tales, Greek myths, and retold medieval epics of our childhood—too much for our grandchildren, and this after only a few decades. Truly, the public mind has changed, and not only in the west.

Moreover, the decrease in violence is only part of a wider increase in public alleviation of suffering. Public health, medical care, famine relief, and other such matters have grown exponentially, and resulted in saving as many lives as genocide ever took. A highly relevant sidelight is that Pinker notes the rise in inoculations for major diseases from 5 percent of children to 75 percent of children, worldwide, between 1974 and today. A point he does not mention is that this was largely the result of the bulldog tenacity of *one* man, James Grant, head of UNICEF from 1980 until his death in 1995 (UNICEF, 2004). That one man saved perhaps as many lives as Hitler took, yet everyone knows Hitler's name and almost no one knows James Grant's. If that situation were reversed, perhaps people would see more benefit in doing good and less in committing genocide.

Genocide has declined too, but only over the last forty years; before that, genocide spiked, in the incredible orgies of murder under Hitler, Stalin, Mao, and their ilk. (He sees Mao's China as already at a lower level, but that is at least partly because he underestimates the level of killing there.) However, especially since the 1990s, the decline is real, and—as Pinker points out (pp. 314–16)—has much to do with the rise of genuine international intervention, first in Bosnia and then in several African countries.

The general secular decline is more interesting. Pinker attributes it in part to Norbert Elias's "civilizing mission" (Elias, 2000, orig. 1939). This is a dubious enterprise. Elias held that Europe had gone on a long civilizing mission, to make the uncouth medieval souls, who spit on the floor and urinated in public, into proper courtiers. Pinker believes that a part of this was banishing violence, including torture and cruelty to animals. However, Elias was writing at a time when medieval history was poorly known and grossly distorted by bias (noted above); he also believed Freudian nonsense about the dark, brutish inner soul of humanity. He apparently believed that everyone, everywhere was basically Id until the European civilizing mission. In fact, we now know that all cultures have their own politeness codes, often very involved and rigid. The medieval period was a time of quite elaborate etiquette, at least in urban areas. The civilizing trends noted by Elias had more to do with educating barbarians and rustics than with changing the whole culture. Moreover, they were often Arab norms imported via Spain and Italy into high-class surroundings, where they contrasted with earlier upper-class behavior that was different but not necessarily bestial.

This said, Elias had a point: European behavior got less uncouth from the high middle ages onward. What is not so believable is Pinker's application of it to violence and torture. For one thing, we know that torture, witch-burning, and horrific behavior toward heretics and religious dissidents increased dramatically from 1200 through the 1400s and even

1500s. The early medieval period had been much more civil, and even the Dark Ages were a great deal less dark than the Renaissance, if fiendish torture applied by state and religious authorities is the measure. For another, the rest of the world was civilized from much earlier times, without it having done much to alleviate war and torture. Elias is speaking strictly of Europe, and Pinker is generally Eurocentric in his book (though he tries to escape that trap). Thus both of them miss the point that the Chinese have been famous for their ritual, politeness, and excessive detail in etiquette codes since time immemorial, but 3,000 years of this did not diminish war or violence one iota. Confucius, who idealized such extreme civility, thought it went back to the origins of civilized life. Yet the killing merely got worse over time. China's most horrifically violent eras were (so far as we know—admittedly on the basis of very bad statistics) the interdynastic wars, especially the fall of Song and rise of the Mongol Yuan; the fall of Yuan in turn and the rise of Ming; the inevitable later fall of Ming and rise of Qing; and above all—most bloody and prolonged of all—the fall of Qing, troubled "Republic" phase, and rise and consolidation of the incredibly murderous Communist state. (The fabled violence of the Qin Dynasty, 221–207 BCE, is clearly exaggerated in the standard histories; the later violent episodes, including those under Mao, tend to be understated.)

It gets worse: the Mongols themselves are poster children for what a civilizing mission can do. Before Genghis Khan, they were relatively peaceable and fair as "barbarians" went. They were minding their flocks in relative content (with only a few raids a year) until Genghis Khan set out to conquer the world. He and his successors learned from their more civilized neighbors the arts of life and the arts of war. As they grew more and more civilized by the standards of the time, they grew more and more bloody. Contrary to the myth that the Mongols were somehow an apocalyptic new step in war, they were merely doing what everyone did in the civilized world of the 1200s. They rank as the greatest killers in premodern history partly because they themselves vastly exaggerated their bloodiness, to scare others into submitting without a fight (Weatherford, 2004). Also, they killed more because they won more. If we had records that assessed killings per one hundred thousand people (like Pinker's statistics for modern times), we would probably see the Mongols as quite average. In any case, their rapid and dramatically successful attempts to change themselves from uncouth sheepherders to refined kings and courtiers certainly did not make them peaceful. The same could be said of countless other semiperipheral conquerors: the Babylonians and Assyrians, the Arabs and Persians, the Greeks and Romans, the Aztecs and Incas. And of course centuries of civilizing missions did not stop the Germans and Russians from the genocides we have recorded above. For one thing, Elias's civility played best among the nobility, who remained the most militant and bloody-handed class.

Yet Pinker is most certainly right that violence declined, and that the Enlightenment of the eighteenth century was the major break—the major turning point. He speaks of a Humanitarian Revolution that began then and continues, fed by rising literacy and world awareness. It was in the eighteenth century that torture started to fall from grace (as in the United States Constitution) and that people proposed—for the first time in all human history—that slavery was bad and should be abolished. As Pinker points out, much of the reason was the escalating and increasingly meaningless bloodshed in the wars of religion, which basically started with the Cathar genocide and peaked in the sixteenth and seventeenth centuries with the decimation of the Huguenots and other minorities. It finally became obvious to everyone that depopulating whole districts over a Latin word or a particular way of baptizing the young was not in anyone's interest.

However, there is more to this. The classic view has been that the Enlightenment was to some extent a self-defensive move by merchants, urbanites, intellectuals, crafts workers, small farmers, and other rising "bourgeois" classes, who were squeezed between increasingly autocratic governments (Perry Anderson, 1974) and increasingly powerful landlords and magnates. They were trying, with increasing desperation, to save themselves from being forced down into the lower classes. Their first real victory was an ironic refutation of Hobbes on his home turf: Hobbes got his wish, the Civil War ended with an unprecedented and total autocracy (owing much to Hobbes's teachings), and the public got fed up with it very rapidly. John Locke theorized, and the Dutch carried out (with widespread English support), a "Glorious Revolution" in 1688 that would restore broad-based rights, especially to small property-owners and tradespeople. This was really the opening shot of a world revolution that is not yet complete; it led directly to other, increasingly radical revolutions (including America's in 1776) that steadily broadened the number of people involved. In particular, the working classes got the message and quickly organized (Thompson, 1963). (The above brief analysis is traditional in the literature, but is shunned by Pinker, presumably because it smacks of Marxism; however, it was also the near-universal consensus analysis of capitalist historians in our student days, and we accept it as such.)

The aristocrats and autocrats had been the ones who stirred up, led, and profited by violence; the bourgeois and working classes had been the ones who paid the price. In times of rising economies, when these classes were doing better, hope and confidence inspired them to take on the powerful. There is *no* case of human rights reforms being won without a struggle. In almost all cases it required revolution, or at least mass demonstrations. There is also no case of a completely happy, harmonious finish to the story. A large percentage of Americans and Europeans still vote along strictly racial and religious lines. A large percentage of them still dream of war, genocide, and exclusion. And of course most of the world has yet to get the rights that Europeans and Americans largely enjoy.

Pinker draws heavily on Immanuel Kant, both as example and as innovator. Kant argued in many publications that a more open society would be a fairer, less bloody one. Pinker picks out, and discusses at length, "the Kantian triangle of democracy, open economies, and engagement with the international community" (Pinker, 2011: 310). He is able to show that across time, across space, across continents, and across ethnic and religious lines, these are indeed the predictors of peace—including freedom from genocide. They are broadly self-explanatory, and we have discussed them above. Recall that an open economy is *not* one that is merely open to the ravages of giant international firms from which it cannot protect itself; it is one that is open to free, fair, widespread trade. And engagement with the international community does not mean giving one's sovereignty up to the World Bank and World Trade Organization; it means actual engagement in meaningful ways with as many other countries as possible, including openness to international peacekeeping by diplomacy or by on-the-ground peacekeepers. Pinker discusses a number of ways to use carrots and sticks to persuade even the lowest dictators to listen to international reason. The threat of intervention and the compliment of being invited to the international negotiation table are often enough—so long as they are combined. Some aid may be promised, giving us a form of the approach known in Spanish as *plata o plomo*, "silver or lead."

Pinker holds forth much optimism, but admits that the future cannot be predicted. One reason is individual variation even within modern democracies. Voting figures (notably the vote for one-issue racial extremists like Strom Thurmond in 1948 and George Wallace in 1968 in the United States and Jacque Le Pen in many elections in France) show that 10 to 20 percent of people in the most "enlightened" countries will always vote for such candidates. It is reasonable to suppose that individuals like Wallace and Le Pen would happily carry out genocides. Ethnic violence, hate speech, and inflammatory media stories both maintain the levels of hate and show that extremist hate continues to dominate a sector of the public that hovers around 10 to 20 percent. If such candidates appeal to a broader base by promising to cope with an economic downturn or to "restore law and order," they can win democratic elections with a majority or plurality of votes, as did Hitler, Efrain Rios Montt, and Ferdinand Marcos (among others). This is a very real danger in the United States today. Pinker's broad-brush characterizations of people in general and of public ideologies tend to blind him to the importance of such individual variations and contingent histories.

Perhaps the most interesting change flagged by Pinker is the steady expansion in the size of the group(s) we consider "ours." The hunting-gathering band of fifty to one hundred fifty expanded slowly over prehistory. With the rise of the state, group size leaped to a few tens of thousands. States grew and formed alliances, empires rose, and the size of the average human community rose to a million, then to many millions. Religions tracked this; then in the Axial Age, roughly from 600 to 300 BC, they suddenly made a conceptual leap to all humanity. After that time, any self-respecting religion applied to all persons, and often attempted to convert them. With this came a few rights, but the next real development was separation of human rights from religious participation, largely after 1700. Finally, in the twentieth century, people for the first time took "animal rights" seriously. This process of extending rights, ending with the animals or even with all life-forms, has been traced by many animal rights advocates (see esp. Singer, 2000). It seems unlikely that animals will get many rights any time soon, but the human species is now one family, and all but the most benighted individuals and regimes recognize that at least some human rights are here to stay. (Oddly, and ironically, most of the opposition comes from self-appointed spokespersons for world religions, but that is another story.) Pinker notes that more and more rights, consistent with ideals of personal safety and social fairness, are coming on stream, at varying rates of speed, throughout the world. Pinker traces some of this to the rapid spread of media of all sorts, bringing innovations in morality to the world in quicker and quicker time (Pinker, 2011: 476ff).

Pinker hopes that the civilizing mission will go on, and violence will continue to decline. There are many reasons to think this is too rosy a prediction.

First, the recent worldwide economic downturn brought out the expected civil problems, though no genocides so far. It is probable that they will occur if the slide continues. The slide was started by the irresponsible behavior of several banks and governments, which incurred or acquired excessive amounts of bad debt. However, behind this lies a worldwide crisis in population and resources. Growing population reduces wages by producing ever more competition for limited spots; those who claim that more people mean more jobs have to explain away the obvious fact that unemployment is sky-high and not falling in precisely those countries which have rapidly increasing populations, from Egypt to South Africa, and for that matter in the United States (with due allowance for rather lower increase rate); conversely, countries with stable populations or low increase rates—most of Europe and east Asia—are doing relatively well at present. As basic resources such as fresh water, farmland, and forests become scarcer, nation-states and international agencies will have more and more trouble keeping order and preventing fear. It is well to remember that the Enlightenment was a product of the steadily rising middle class, especially the urban components of it. They were tired of being oppressed by the rich and were in a position to do something about it; they were also self-aware and self-conscious enough to figure out what to do, and to organize accordingly. Only continued rise of middle-class fractions of the body politic can guarantee a continued rise of Enlightenment policies. In a world where resources are running out and the gap between the rich and the rest is getting rapidly wider, such continued rise is unlikely.

Second, violence is currently low, but could easily escalate everywhere if the current economic and military power of the United States and the European Union continues to decline. The world is kept in relative order now by the countries that have internalized the Enlightenment. Most of the rest of the world has not, and chafes under the yoke of peace and prosperity.

Third, hate speech, hate ideologies, and hate politics are more common than ever. We have noted that the United States is in a terrifying crisis of public polarization and hatred. It is not alone. Europe and east Asia are more civil, but extremism is common elsewhere. Campaign rhetoric and religious rhetoric in particular seem to be following trends dramatically opposite to Pinker's hopes. It is thought-provoking, at the least, to see that no one predicted the dangerous combination of rising extremist religion worldwide coupled with steady and rapid decline of other forms of religion. The mainstream denominations, which broadly teach love and help, have been in precipitous decline for decades in the west; similarly, extreme religion is rising at the expense of the traditional, more liberal interpretations (Maliki, Hanafi, Shafi'i) of Islamic rules; radical Hinduism is espoused by the BJP political party in India and is leading to communal violence there; apparently the same thing is happening with Buddhism, judging from our admittedly unsystematic observations in southeast Asia.

Fourth, regime changes are inevitable, and seem imminent in many countries. The attendant risks are not well recognized or addressed by the international community. China's aging leadership is being replaced by a new young group. Egypt, Libya, Tunisia, and other countries of the Arab Spring are in transition. Aging leadership from Sudan to Zimbabwe guarantees changes in the not too distant future. And so it goes, worldwide.

How, then, can we keep the anti-violence part of the civilizing mission going, and make it ever stronger?

HUMAN RIGHTS

Possibly the first and most basic need is to recognize human and civil rights—the rights of all people to life, property, some degree of dignity, and above all *equal treatment under the law*. A recent disturbing trend in certain western intellectual circles is a full-scale, outright attack on the whole concept of human rights because they are "western," and imposing them on other peoples is "colonialist" (see, e.g., Mutua, 2002; Shell-Duncan, 2008). This literature echoes the line of genociders from Milosevich and Karadzic to Saddam Hussein and Pol Pot, as well as more general defenses of human rights abuses by dictators from Singapore to China. Of course the west—more accurately, Britain and France—developed the modern concept of human rights, but the concept builds on religious teachings from all the world's religions, as well as on Chinese, Islamic, and traditional European political philosophy and practice. Few premodern societies advocated or practiced genocide. In fact, as we have seen, true genocide is a fairly modern western idea, and if people like Mutua really want to protect their societies from western political concepts, they should be opposing genocide.

Even if Mutua were right, genocide generally appears a bad thing from the point of view of the victims, and imposition of colonialist western values might appear preferable to being exterminated in a "culturally appropriate" way. Of course, all decent humans, victims or nonvictims, protest against genocide and other human rights violations. Rogue governments like those of Sudan and Myanmar, to say nothing of China, devote great effort to holding down protests by indigenous human rights advocates. China has a robust human rights tradition millennia old, and the claims that the current type of repression and persecution is somehow "traditional" are flat lies (Leys, 1985). We are back to the classic question of who gets to define the "culture" and its proper attitudes. Milosevich and Karadzic do indeed represent all too many Serbs, but do they represent all Serbs, or all Serbian culture? If not, why do other positions get no hearing? Nonwestern opponents of human rights such as Mutua deny their own cultures' real heritages (see Goodale, 2006, and commentary therein; Nagengast, 1994).

There is also the wider question of whether the world can afford to indulge those cultures that resort to genocide as a regular, "culturally appropriate" thing. Is the modern global community—desperately short of food, fuel, and tolerance—big enough to accommodate, comfortably, the current behavior of Sudan or Myanmar? Can nations really afford to tolerate this behavior because, though it is a pure western invention, it has allegedly become a norm in certain nonwestern cultures? Obviously not.

The same logic applies that led to requiring motorcycle helmets in California: the individual is free to choose his or her fate, but if taxpayers are stuck with the bill—as they were in many, many motorcycle accident cases—they have a right to insist on minimally sane behavior. The motorcycle zanies did not have the right to impose on taxpayers the costs of their failure to wear safety equipment or buy insurance. The same applies worldwide. The rest of us all pay terrible prices for genocide. We have to deal with refugees, supply humanitarian aid, and deal with the international crises and wars. Far worse: we have to face the extremely high risks of genocide in our own nations. Once it is acceptable behavior, it is inevitably acceptable everywhere, from America to Japan. The recent past of Chile, Argentina, and Serbia shows that highly developed, educated, reasonably prosperous countries can commit genocide with little warning or reason. Recent political events in the United States and elsewhere are clearly pre-genocidal. Zero tolerance for genocide, worldwide, is a price for national survival in every country.

In short, human rights in one or another form are widespread among civilizations, but genocide is essentially a western idea—exactly the reverse of the situation claimed by Mutua. This being the case, we can safely begin with grounding human rights in some level of tolerance, and then protecting them through civil institutions.

FIRST CONCERN: DEALING WITH HATRED AND THE POLITICAL EXPLOITATION OF IT

Clearly, the first and most necessary line to hold against genocide is making sure that hatred is limited as much as possible. There is only so much hope in that direction, since people seem unable to keep from hating other groups. This should be minimized if possible, but more important in the short run is *immediately launching total attacks against public manipulation of social hatreds for political or selfish ends*. The ways that Hitler manipulated public opinion were copied or paralleled in almost all subsequent genocides. Particularly notable public campaigns occurred in Mao's China and Pol Pot's Cambodia, as well as in Rwanda under the Interahamwe. More recently, the rhetoric is extreme in Egypt, Iran, and some of their neighbors, and increasingly serious in China, where all manner of dissidents are now seriously attacked for being agents of westernization and other sinful things.

Free democratic nations, unfortunately, have not avoided this. The degree to which American media have gotten away with attacks on gays, Hispanics, and other minorities is absolutely terrifying. No society can stand this sort of public erosion of morality for any length of time; not only a bloodbath but a meltdown of the whole country is certain to occur unless this situation is dealt with.

The beginning is simply getting the word out—spreading news and educating people about genocide and human rights violations. This has been done by a succession of courageous and single-minded individuals like Simon Wiesenthal (see above) but including many others (Dawes, 2007). There is even an 812-page anthology of poetry of witnessing: *Against Forgetting* (Forche, 1993). However, it needs to be much more widely stressed. Schools should teach more than they do about Hitler and

Stalin and what actually got the populations of their countries to go along with their killing.

Revisionist history has had an extremely unsavory role in denying the horror of genocide. Germany has been very sensitive to this issue. Recently British Bishop Richard Williamson was convicted in a German court for incitement and publicly denying the reality of the Holocaust, a criminal offense in Germany ("World Briefings: Bishop Guilty of Holocaust Denial," Los Angeles Times, April 17, 2010, A–11). The Australian massacres of Aborigines have been denied in a flagrantly misleading revisionist literature (Wildschuttle, 2002; see scholarly disproofs in Dawson, 2004; Elder, 2003; Kiernan, 2008; Manne, 2003). In short, almost everywhere, in time, the horror of genocide spawns a denial literature by those looking to again create targeted hatred. The horror must be faced and the lies inherent in denial and revisionist history must be confronted. The United States has a long way to go in teaching what really happened to its own Indigenous population; even sober college textbooks tend to blame "introduced diseases" and say almost nothing about violence.

Hatred, however, is not the only problem. The link of genocide with domestic violence and schoolyard bullying has not been missed; Hamburg (2010: 170) quite correctly identifies constant, vigilant action to prevent bullying as a key to stopping genocide. We add that every move against domestic violence, especially against viewing it as normal or even desirable, is a move against mass violence. Thus, constant vigilance against these small-scale manifestations of cowardly violence is necessary. The actual gangs of thugs mentioned in the previous chapter can grow from bullying and woman-suppressing packs.

Educating the public in human rights and the international need for peace and justice has a long way to go, in the United States as elsewhere; Herbert Hirsch has thoughtfully written on this issue in his book *Anti-Genocide* (2002).

Hate speech and dishonest historical revisionism need to be exposed to the light of day. Banning it merely drives it underground and encourages it by discouraging refutation. Hate crimes, on the other hand, must be firmly and rigorously suppressed and the perpetrators brought to justice immediately. This is particularly true not only at local and national levels, but also at the international level, where abuses frequently go unchallenged. Rational discourse does not privilege extremism. Taking a high rhetorical position that exaggerates the differences between political sides, essentializes these, and then demonizes one's opponents is a deadly mix. Damping down the vicious spiral into genocide begins with cooling the rhetoric and ceasing to define groups as absolutes.

All this involves a major concern for inclusion and participation. Dealing with the ultimate causes of hatred is necessary too. A major need in today's world is *to stop defining groups as absolute, essential entities. Reality gives us vague, shifting, ill-defined, and blending categories. The more people lose sight of this truth, the more danger of genocide and structural violence.*

One angle into human thought is provided by what works in psychotherapy (Roth and Fonagy, 2005). Notoriously, any sympathetic ear, or even a sugar-and-water placebo pill, can help with personal problems. Cognitive-behavioral therapy works well. So does family therapy. Roth and Fonagy (2005) do not rate it highly, but experience suggests that it deserves a much higher rating (see, e.g., E. Anderson, 1992). Reason, however defined, is valuable but inadequate. It is a valuable aid, not a basis.

Generalizing from individual psychotherapy to mass psychology is difficult but not impossible. Starkly, the problem with the world is hate, especially group hate. Hate is based on fear, especially of real attack or of downward mobility in the world. At individual and social levels, we simply have to face this and deal with it, by psychological methods as well as others. One goal for the future is identifying the sort of leader or potential leader who might become genocidal, and warn voters accordingly.

All this requires individual liberty and responsibility, but it must be coupled with an ideology of caring for others. Competitive individualism tends to bring us right back to mass conflict, since individuals who compete almost always form coalitions that eventually tend to become warring factions (a point stressed at great length by America's Founding Fathers; see esp. Hamilton et al., 1961).

The necessary cure, then, would start by banning gratuitous harm, but would be much more seriously targeted at fixing one-down defensiveness in general and group hatreds in particular. It would be focused, then, on three things: conflict resolution; promoting appreciation and tolerance rather than hate; and, most centrally of all, giving people mature ways to cope with cruelty, misfortune, putdowns, and general oppression.

An important realization is that the fears that produce hate and defensive violence in many people produce passivity in others. Fear leads to a fight-flight-freeze response. If the "fight" option is picked, scapegoating and group hatred are easy to arouse. But if the "flight" and "freeze" options are picked, people seem calm and docile—until genocide begins. Then, through a combination of passive giving up and released tension, they may suddenly become killers. Our research, including interviews of Cambodian refugees, suggests that this is the reason for the oft-mentioned paradox of ordinary people following orders to kill. They were conformist, docile, and passive, due to fear and stress; they thus followed orders, and often suddenly galvanized into out-of-control killers on a mass scale. This is reported for, and by, "good Germans," Cambodian peasants, Rwandan Hutus and Tutsis, and (perhaps most extensively)

Chinese sucked into the Red Guard and Cultural Revolution hysteria of the 1960s.

Thus, we feel that *one absolutely critical need in world education is to teach people to cope proactively with trouble and to be independent thinkers*. Unless people have been trained to analyze situations and solve their problems, they will be easily led astray. Unfortunately, world education today seems bound in the opposite direction. Mindless memorizing of facts for mindless standardized tests is now the accepted definition of education in the United States and most other countries. We have more or less returned to the old days when education consisted of memorizing sacred books "in a tongue not understood of the people" (as the Church of England's Book of Common Prayer puts it), where even minimal comprehension, let alone independent thought, is viewed as a threat rather than a benefit. Even preschool students are forced to sit and memorize rather than play, create, and follow their interests (Tullis, 2011). This remains a serious and dangerous problem. It is possible that education for passivity is even more dangerous than hate speech, since the latter naturally calls forth opposition and debate (if free speech is allowed!). Passive learning by memorization is the method of choice for those who want to regiment citizens rather than enlighten them. As such, it has become the darling of dictators, who want followers, not thinkers. (On this and related matters, see our posting "Saving American Education in the Twenty-First Century," on our website, www.krazykioti.com.)

In fact, there is serious need to teach children and adults not only proactive and rational coping, but also pragmatic and realistic hope. Both utopian dreams (Kiernan, 2007) and hopeless despair are serious risk factors for genocide. Serious coping, among other things, involves raising children by making them deal with progressively harder problems, while always providing support. They must deal on their own but they must know that parents and other adults "have their backs." This sort of combination of independence and mutual support is one of the best inoculations against all manner of violent and irrational responses to life's problems. We suspect that this kind of training alone would render genocide very rare.

Teaching outright racist untruths is less common than it used to be, but still far from rare. Teaching religious bigotry is much commoner, being endemic in some parts of the world and not unknown even in liberal democracies. Some countries, including Iran, teach that the Holocaust never happened. Obviously, some kind of control on school curricula is essential. Nations need to get a firm grip on their educational establishments, and insure that at least minimal accuracy is enforced in the educative process. Freedom of speech is necessary, but total anarchy in academic curricula is a quite different question.

Teaching specifically for tolerance is a serious need, but is not well worked out in sources we have been able to find. However, an excellent summary of some needs is provided by Claude Steele (2010: 216), a leading expert on stereotyping and prejudice. He gives a list of needs for the modern socially and ethnically diverse classroom, to reassure minority students of all kinds and to reduce prejudice in general:

- critical feedback as intellectual rigor, sedulously avoiding anything that could sound like personal rejection;
- have more people from the minority in question; there is reassurance in numbers;
- foster intergroup conversation and keep the class from the usual tendency to break up into ethnically defined groups;
- get students to affirm their core values, in writing and in speaking (this one is incredibly effective); and
- reframe problems as situational rather than personal or wired into the system.

It turns out that in multicultural situations *both* involvement in one's culture of origin *and* involvement in mainstream culture are valuable (Smokowski et al., 2009). Confidence in one's own traditions is important for learning others' traditions well. It seems highly valuable to get everyone involved in this. However, exposure to the sort of "multiculturalism" that essentializes cultures and makes them seem highly separate and incommensurable can and often does shore up prejudice. The middle ground does not seem difficult to find: teach respect for other cultures, and also teach the degree to which cultures fuse, blend, and interpenetrate.

The great religious teachers have always argued something similar: love or compassion for all, following peaceful ways, justice and fairness. Yet they typically become excuses for more hate. Christianity, with its explicit and unequivocal charge to love all and to turn the other cheek when struck on one cheek, has as bloody and hateful a record as do the religions that teach vengeance on enemies. Clearly, religion must be the beginning of the solution to world evil. Equally clearly, it cannot be the end.

We need a renewed respect for the human spirit and its accomplishments. A paternalistic, belittling sort of "care" is no help. Life is about love, but love in the sense of active, caring, warm interest—not blind devotion or dependence. Richard Crisp and Rhiannon Turner (2009) have found that even imagining pleasant, mutually beneficial intergroup contact significantly reduces bias and prejudice. Their research built on the long-known and most unfortunate fact that imagining *bad* intergroup contact is one of the worst problems. Obviously, most genocide requires such evil imagining. No group is remotely close to being as bad as genociders portray it. Imagining the "others" as human, with all the normal human virtues and salt-of-the-earth pleasant traits, appears to be startlingly effective as a counter.

Most of the literature on preventing genocide does not touch on education, or if it does it confines its concern to genocide itself. We feel that the first and most important line against genocide is a comprehensive education that teaches children and adults to cope rationally with problems rather than coping through scapegoating and hate.

It should be obvious, but is not obvious to most politicians, that hate speech by political and media figures should be immediately confronted with honesty, dignity, and directness. Nothing except trouble comes from sinking to the level of the hate merchants who make money or gain political capital through sowing hatred, but every citizen—especially those with political power—should immediately stand up against such speech and provide measured but incisive refutation. Currently, religious bigotry—especially gender hatred bearing the false name of "religion," such as the current attacks on gays—is privileged speech; it seems that no one dares to oppose it. The one clear exception is worse than nothing: the countering of radical Islam by even more radical hate speech and even legislation. This is trivial in the United States, but a major and serious problem in Europe, where even heads of liberal states (notably Sarkozy in France) have resorted to what can only be called bullying.

There is a sliding scale from the endless tirades from the lowest levels of society—annoying but not serious—up to this sort of highest-level troublemaking. The more the volume, and the higher-placed the speaker, the worse the risk.

Finally, to return to the little-known James Grant, and to Oskar Schindler, Paul Rusesabagina, and many other heroes, known and unknown. We owe it to our children and their children to teach more about the people who have helped the world, who have done something about human suffering—and less about the generals and warmongers, the murders and genociders. Heinrich Heine said almost two hundred years ago, "The tree of humanity forgets the labour of the silent gardeners who sheltered it from the cold, watered it in time of drought, shielded it against wild animals; but it preserves faithfully the names mercilessly cut into its bark" (Gross, 1983: 323). The time is long, long overdue to change this. If we can make one point in this book, let that be the one. It is surprisingly absent from the literature on these concerns.

SECOND CONCERN: PREVENTING ECONOMIC AND CIVIL DOWNTURNS

Economic downturns create a fertile field for genocide. Few have focused on this, though several writers are aware of it (see Pinker, 2011). As we have seen, being on the losing side in World War I and then facing the Great Depression were highly correlated with fascism and genocide in the 1930s and 1940s. Stalin's and Mao's failures at economic development and economic hard times in many smaller countries preceded genocides. The terrifying explosion of anti-immigrant, anti-gay, and anti-liberal sentiment in the United States following 2008 raises the real possibility of genocide there.

The downturn need not be national. If a large group, *especially a dominant majority*, is downwardly mobile, the danger is as real as if the whole country were downbound. This presents a measurement problem: given the poor quality of statistics on such matters, how do we know? National growth, income, and development figures are averages, and they often conceal the fact that a tiny minority is getting better and better off while the vast majority are getting worse off. We know that this has been the situation in the United States for the past several years, but we do not have very reliable figures for, say, China, or Indonesia, or Egypt. China, for instance, does not count the environmental and health costs of its "growth," and most independent authorities agree that if they did their growth rate would be close to zero, rather than the reported high figure (Fu, 2008; Qiu, 2011a, 2011b). The poor bear most of the costs, and are clearly downwardly mobile by reasonable standards, whatever official statistics may say (cf. Abe and Nickum, 2009). *Thus not only economic development, but some degree of fairness therein, is necessary*. In fact, from the point of view of minimizing violence of all kinds, the fairness is more important than the development—though we are most certainly not calling for choosing one or the other; both are needed.

Steven Pinker concisely summarizes clear indications: "The decline of genocide over the last third of a century, then, may be traced to the upswing of some of the same factors that drove down interstate and civil wars: stable government, democracy, openness to trade, and humanistic ruling philosophies that elevate the interests of individuals over struggles among groups" (Pinker, 2011: 342). This line is hard to beat; it should be inscribed over very many doors of governments and—*above all*—of supragovernmental organizations from the United Nations to the World Bank.

The price of eliminating genocide certainly includes some reform of the world economic pattern as it exists in the early twenty-first century. The meltdown of 2008, beginning in the United States and propagating worldwide, led to several regime changes, many of them distinctly worrisome and others not yet clearly resolved. We cannot afford this sort of world economic disaster. In the near future, population will reach nine or ten billion and resources will progressively diminish. Forests and wild-caught fish will be gone from most of the world by 2050, and fresh water is already overallocated. The resulting squeeze will not cause genocide in itself, but if it causes massive economic downturns, the hopelessness and despair caused in many people by those downturns will be taken out on scapegoats by a significant fraction of the world's political actors.

While it is difficult indeed to solve all of the world's economic problems, eliminating major downturns of the sort seen in 2008 is not so hard. It simply involves some sort of control on rampant speculation; on taking on inordinate amounts of debt in speculative ventures or for governmental programs; and on rampant destruction and waste of natural resources with no real investment or development to show for it. There is nothing wrong with debt per se if it is incurred for investment, especially when the investment can produce high returns, as in education, scientific research, environmental conservation, and public health. The problems that led to 2008 were quite different: real estate speculation in which the same piece of property—without any change—was bid up to astronomical prices; government spending on subsidies and tax breaks to people already rich, including the idle rich; government spending on duplicated, inefficient, or unwatched activities and enterprises; outright corruption; and the like. Most governments have or had laws to prevent this, but in the United States the laws protecting consumers and businesses against fraudulent and shady speculation were repealed in the gilded 1990s, making a previously impossible collapse into a certainty.

The other problem so large that it cannot be ignored, even in a book not intended to be an economic text, is the corrupting and distorting effects of giant extractive corporations on the world's governments—particularly, but not only, in small impoverished countries. The oil industry is the worst offender (Juhasz, 2008), with mining and agribusiness far behind but still quite visible. Another major player is international construction, because of the distorting, corrupting, and usually economically ruinous effects of megaprojects such as big dams (Anderson, 2010; Scudder, 2005). Even the most conservative and pro-business commentators have been unable to miss the "resource curse" and the correlation between oil extraction and civil war or genocide (see Anderson, 2010; Bunker and Ciccantell, 2005; Bjerga, 2011; Clarke, 2009; Collier, 2007, 2010; Humphreys et al., 2007; Juhasz, 2008; Pinker, 2011; Stiglitz, 2003; many sources cited in those works). The correlation is partly direct, through the corruption and violence that often accompany resource extraction, and partly indirect, through the effects of environmental devastation, economic distortion (e.g., injection of huge amounts of cash into the economy), and increasing the gap between rich and poor. We believe the worst problem is that uncontrolled resource extraction may make a tiny elite better off, but it makes a large percentage of the affected people worse off, and the effects of declining welfare on hope and hate come fully into play.

As usual, the problem is largely one of dictatorships. Extractive concerns almost always support, and sometimes install, dictatorships. Democracies can be corrupted—as the United States certainly has been, with its multi-billion-dollar subsidies to big oil and big agribusiness—but clearly oil has had much less negative effect on Norway and Scotland than it has had on Equatorial Guinea and Sudan.

For the record, we are not advocating either extensive government regulation or extensive deregulation. We are agnostic as to how free the world economy should be. We do not know how to fix the world economy. What we can say is that the survival of capitalism and world trade, the survival of the world's poor and minorities, and possibly the survival of the human species, depends on regulating the most flagrant abuses. There seems no need to bring glowing prosperity to all. All that is needed is to prevent downturns that seem so out of control that they produce widespread hopelessness, despair, and scapegoating. Even the Great Recession following 2008 did not cause a noticeable uptick in genocides. It did, however, certainly contribute to the rebellions of the Arab Spring, the resurgence of right-wing and racist extremism in the United States and Europe, the resurgence of violence in Sudan and Congo, and many other troubling local manifestations. The end is not yet, and only vigilance, warnings, and above all the restoration of hope will prevent future killings.

In short, we are making a point apparently new in the genocide literature: controlling rampant speculation, corruption, waste, resource abuse, and uncontrolled resource extraction *is an absolutely critical part of controlling genocide*, as well as being desirable for many other reasons.

THIRD CONCERN: VIGILANCE DURING WARS AND CIVIL UNREST IN AUTOCRATICALLY GOVERNED NATIONS

When a dictatorship is facing a civil war, or is losing in an international war, or even winning but with difficulty in any war, *genocide is an extremely likely outcome*. Dictatorial governments seem unable to avoid it under those cases. The world should expect genocide, should warn the government in question, and should be fully prepared to intervene.

Experience teaches that there is almost no hope of dealing with such cases except by *force majeure* or the threat of it. The case of Bosnia and Serbia in the 1990s was a solid test: jawboning, diplomacy, moral suasion, and the like had no effect, but NATO troops stopped the genocide in short order, and there has even been some bringing to trial of perpetrators.

This being the case, the world community should be on standby when any regime in times of unrest abrogates normal democratic procedures, for instance by declaring a "state of emergency." Such measures are the biggest of red flags for genocide.

The only problem is deciding what counts as violent unrest. Clearly, an ongoing war is more dangerous than random violence, and ethnic and religious fighting is more dangerous than ordinary crime. We are not concerned about Russia's high murder rate so much as about its near-genocidal approach to the problems of the caucasus. Further research, however, is necessary to show exactly what levels of violence, and what kinds of violence, are the most risk-related.

FOURTH, DEALING WITH AUTOCRATIC LEADERS, IN ORDINARY TIMES

The most direct, immediate, and constant correlate of genocide is a newly-empowered autocratic regime. In autocratic regimes, the first dictator is generally the worst, and the first years of his reign are often the worst in his tenure—though if he has to deal with a serious war, it usually produces worse killing than simple seizing of power. There seems to be little to be said about this, beyond the obvious: the world has to be on standby at such times.

For autocracy in general, there is again a measurement problem. When does democracy slide over into authoritarianism? This question is especially serious when democratically elected leaders drift toward dictatorship, as Ferdinand Marcos did in the Philippines in the 1970s. Moreover, if Steven Pinker (2011) is right, failing or pseudo-democracies are more dangerous than secure totalitarian regimes, at least for civil war if not for genocide. These matters require further attention.

More hope attaches to controlling dictators and autocratic governments in general. This concern naturally falls under several heads. Most of them—the routine diplomatic questions—have been thoroughly explored by Gareth Evans and others in sources cited below, but some require elaboration here. First is holding the guilty accountable.

There is an old folktale of Alexander the Great and a pirate. The pirate is caught, and hailed before Alexander. The latter asks, "What have you got to say for yourself?" The pirate answers, "I have to say that if I had a thousand ships, and you had one, I would be 'the great' and you would be the pirate." At least in one version of the folktale, Alexander let him go. Another folktale relates that a dictator—accounts differ on whether it was Hitler, Stalin, or someone else—claimed that a man who kills one person is a murderer, but one who kills a million is a hero. The point, in both stories, is that criminals on an enormous scale generally get away with it; only small fries suffer from the law.

Political unity and action to stop genocide was advocated by Lemkin, and again by pioneer genocide scholar Leo Kuper (1985). Many prevention books have focused on dealing with hatred (e.g., Rittner et al., 2002). Several international bodies, notably the United Nations, actively investigate and combat genocide (see Hamburg, 2003, 2010; Heidenrich, 2001; Hirsch, 2002). Unfortunately they have so far been less than effective. As noted above, many countries deliberately block both use of the term "genocide" and doing anything to combat it, obviously on the theory that they may wish to carry it out themselves. Internationally, there has been so little sympathy for combating genocide that attempts to stop it in Rwanda, Sudan, and elsewhere have been actively blocked. Sudan, especially, has been protected and defended in the United Nations and elsewhere by nations that covet its natural resources. Gareth Evans (2008) provides a long and depressing history of ignored genocides and murders over the centuries, as well as a few more hopeful interventions. He concludes: "The cynicism of the great powers about major human rights violations in their own and each other's backyards was understandable enough in purely realist terms. . . . But the trouble with these reactions, like most things taken too far, is that they had a terrible downside" (Evans, 2008: 25) in that genocides not only continued but got worse in the 1990s. Evans (a former foreign minister of Australia) has been active in world peacekeeping.

Leaders of genocide usually get away with it. Hitler resorted to genocide when he was beginning to lose his war, and died soon after his victims, but few other genociders come to such a bad end. Pol Pot escaped, as did Idi Amin, who took refuge in Saudi Arabia. Stalin, Mao, and many others retained their leadership positions until their deaths. Often the self-interest of nations prevents much action against genocide (Smith, 2004).The oil industry is particularly notorious, but agricultural, mining, and other interests are often involved.

Leaders who survive and face trial are notoriously unrepentant and proud. Milosevitch of Serbia, Pinochet of Chile, Rios Montt of Guatemala, Saddam Hussein of Iraq, and the Hutu leaders of Rwanda maintained their righteousness to the last. Augusto Pinochet's last major act, before he died (peacefully, of old age) in 2006, was to write a public letter maintaining everything he did was right and best for Chile (Gallardo, 2006). Yet, his leadership of the Chilean genocide occurred without even the excuse of rebellion or serious threat of any kind. His fascist leadership co-opted Chile's social institutions in ways devastating not only to dissenters' lives but also to women's reproductive health, the rights of indigenous people, and justice for the poor. Though less fatal than most, it was one of history's most flagrant, inexcusable, and chilling exercises of terror by government.

From 1966 to 1998, Suharto presided over genocides in Java, Sumatera, East Timor, and Irian Jaya, involving the deaths of at least a million noncombatants—probably two or three times that many. He began an environmental onslaught that continues today and has turned Indonesia from one of the world's richest nations in natural resources to one of the poorest. Suharto died peacefully in bed in 2008, unrepentant and rich; neither he nor his henchmen suffered any repercussions. Of his life, Brad Adams, head of Human Rights Asia, said, "One of the enduring legacies of Suharto's regime has been the culture of impunity" (Adams as cited in

Deutsch, 2008). Milosevich, Karadzic, and Saddam protested, at their trials, that they were the hapless victims of harsh justice. Their own victims were not there to point out the irony. A murderer who kills one person usually spends life in a maximum-security prison; those who kill millions generally remain free. As Shakespeare said, "The evil that men do lives after them."

Oil-producing nations, in particular, commit genocide with impunity. Oil importers, especially China (which desperately needs oil to get its people out of poverty), will protect the worst behaviors. Sudan gets away with genocide in Darfur; Nigeria got away with it in Biafra and continues to massacre indigenous occupants of its oil lands. Equatorial Guinea and Congo-Brazzaville get away with mass shooting of opposition figures, and Angola got away for decades with rampant killing campaigns because the world needs their oil (Juhasz, 2008; Marquand, 2007; Prunier, 2007). The "resource curse" applies also to mining, notably diamonds, the curse of Sierra Leone and Angola among other nations. Genocidal regimes supported by mineral wealth are almost guaranteed impunity. Etcheson (2005) speaks of a "culture of impunity" there and in Africa (this is the phrase echoed by Deutsch, above), and Kiernan (2004, 2008) has also detailed the denial and refusal to bring killers anywhere near justice.

Accountability of those who have bullied a compliant population into genocide is an essential step to reclaiming soil poisoned by genocide, no matter what the cost. Indeed, it seems beyond debate that the failure to punish perpetrators has been a huge factor in causing the explosion of genocides since 1990. This means not only punishment of the leaders; it means full action, *including requirement of economic reparations*, against the firms that backed the genocidal governments. This was done, or at least attempted, after both World Wars, but it has generally been neglected in recent decades. At the least, a combination of publicity, consumer boycotts, and threatened action can be effective, as we have seen in several cases. De Beers, for instance, refused to buy "blood diamonds" in Africa.

Possible hope for the future comes from the arrest in 2008, after thirteen years of impunity, of the Serbian genocider Radovan Karadzic. General Ratko Mladic, his henchman who actually directed the murders on the ground, remains at large. The arrest followed a shift in Serbia away from nationalist isolation and toward union with Europe. The European Union denied membership to Serbia until these men were captured. Economic pressure worked where morality and force had failed. It remains likely that Karadzic will die peacefully before he is actually tried and convicted. One recalls the success of Hitler's many minions in Yugoslavia at avoiding arrest. One actually escaped to the United States and directed the construction firm that used to do all the construction work at ENA's university. He was eventually captured and tried, but he was in his nineties by that time, and died before he could pay any significant debt to society.

Further hope comes from final sentencing of some of the Rwanda genociders. The chair of the Hutu genocidal political party (the National Revolutionary Movement for Development), Matthieu Ngirumpatse, and his deputy Edouard Karemera, were sentenced to life imprisonment by the International Criminal Tribunal for Rwanda in December of 2011, while the then chief of staff of the defense ministry, Theonest Bagosora, was sentenced to thirty-five years in prison ("Rwanda Genocide: Ngirumpatse and Karemera Given Life," BBC News Online, December 21, 2011). Unlike all too many genocide sentences, these will actually be enforced; the villains are in captivity.

Finally, in an incredible flood of good news, the BBC News (on air) announced on January 10, 2012, that Paul Kagame had been cleared of complicity in the murder of Rwanda's president (by shooting down his airplane) and that the killing was actually done by Hutu extremists, as independent observers had generally held; and also that the generals who took over Turkey in a military coup in 1980 had finally been charged and convicted for it. There is hope.

Clearly, the international community must get beyond its extreme aversion to calling out, let alone intervening in, nations that practice genocide. International structures, treaties, and agreements are all in place; they are not honored. Many ways of dealing with international law and order have been proposed (Heidenrich, 2001; Hirsch, 2002), and these need to be implemented.

ACCOUNTABLE GOVERNANCE

Rudolph Rummel, author of *Death by Government* (1994) and *Statistics of Democide* (1998), suggests that the solution to accountable governance is to come very close to eliminating government—not a very practical idea. He has, however, shown that genocide is rare in democracies, that it usually occurs in top-down authoritarian regimes, and it is *nonexistent* when individuals have civil rights that are actually respected by the government. As Charles Tilly states, "Democratic regimes, on the average, harbor less collective violence than undemocratic regimes. Broadening of political participation, extension and equalization of political rights, regularization of nonviolent means for making claims, and increasing readiness of third parties to intervene against violent resolution of disputes over claims all dampen the processes that generate violent contention" (Tilly, 2003: 44).

Even structural violence has the same epidemiology. Recall Sen's findings, quoted above, that famines do not occur in true democracies (Sen, 2009: 342). Famines are usually labeled "acts of God," but Sen showed they were really acts of government. Floods may be due to rain, but flood damage is usually due to government or private irresponsibility. The same is true of most "natural" disasters (see, e.g., Steinberg, 2006).

Mercifully, evil societies rarely last long. Some self-destruct, like Hitler's Germany and Pol Pot's Cambodia. Others change after a ruler dies (Mao's China, Stalin's USSR) or after the people rebel or take control back (Ethiopia after the Dergue, Haiti after the Duvaliers). Sometimes neighboring countries are finally pushed to intervene (Bosnia, Idi Amin's Uganda). However, some countries manage to be incredibly badly run for decades or centuries (Guatemala, Haiti) and some manage to be truly evil for decades with no sign of falling so far (Iran, Burma).

On the other hand, relatively good societies are very rare but can also last for long periods: Scandinavia, the Low Countries, New Zealand. These nations have stayed out of war, have very low crime and poverty rates, and have powerful ideologies of the common good.

Many democratic nations have experienced periods of fascistic despotism in their histories, often drenched in blood, that were followed by successful restoration of freedom and peace. In fact, most European nations have managed this after periods of fascism or communism in the twentieth century. Argentina, Brazil, Chile, Peru, Philippines, and several other countries outside Europe have also managed this feat. Uruguay threw off a brief fascist rule, emerging into democracy. Korea evolved into peaceful democracy under military-dictator tutelage in the 1960s. Particularly interesting is the case of Sri Lanka, involved in a bloody civil war with little quarter asked or given almost throughout its career as a nation, and facing a declining economy—yet it remained democratic, and even its somewhat imperfect and war-torn democracy was enough to prevent a "final solution" to the Tamil problem. Peace eventually prevailed. It was a near thing at times. Statements by local strongmen left absolutely no doubt that things could have very easily gone differently. As it was, the bloodshed was horrific and involved countless local massacres, but the Tamils survived. Colombia, Indonesia, and Pakistan currently present "cliff-hanger" situations that are rather similar. Violence and brutal massacre are common in all, civil rights are weakly enforced at best. In the future, these nations could go up toward more democracy, and therefore peace, or down into totalitarianism and mass murder.

Countries where the government is not only voted in or out, but is *actually accountable legally*, are the safest. What matters is the *degree* of democracy—more exactly, the protection of civil rights. Majority rule is not a protection. The only protection is civil rights, enforceable through recourse by the injured. There is a strong contrast, too often ignored in the United States, between "majority rules" democracy and "minority rights" democracy (see Rawls, 1971; Sen, 2009). The latter, of course, has majority rule also—it just ensures that the majority cannot vote to exterminate or oppress the minorities. Governance without accountability of civil rights can devolve into limitation on freedom of speech, religion, and political activity. Even repressing all hate speech is counterproductive; all it does is validate that the speakers of hate are credible. However, freedom of speech, in functional minority-rights democracies, does not extend to false witness, denial of civil rights, or hate crimes.

All this implies that simply having the right to vote is really not enough. The more ways a nation has of enforcing accountability on the government, the safer are its people. A national ombudsman, full civil and human rights protection, full protection for whistle-blowers, and bureaucratic channels to air grievances are all necessary. The ancient Chinese (and some other Asian regimes) placed a drum at the capital gate, and charged anyone with a serious complaint about the government to beat that drum and make his case. This evolved into a unique imperial Chinese institution, the censorate; its job was not to censor literature but to censor government acts, even the emperor's, that were harming the people. This institution operated for millennia with astonishing success; it was often weak and corrupt, but often far from so; countless censors endured banishment or death for their forthright denunciations of abuses—truly "fearless speech" in Michel Foucault's terms (Foucault, 2001). Han Yu in the eighth century, for instance, was banished to the remote south for stinging criticisms of the emperor (see e.g., Lewis, 2009). The world could use institutions like that, as well as the elective representation that the Chinese sadly lacked (and still lack).There is a worldwide crisis of accountability in governments today, and that is one of the major reasons that genocide is allowed to go on.

Ethnic tolerance, valuing of diversity, and confronting targeted hate are all necessary but not sufficient. They will survive only in a social environment that promotes ecological sustainability, economic stability, a sense of hope about the future, and full civil rights. Rummel is basically right: genocide tracks authoritarianism, exclusion, and targeted hatred. For the long term, accountable democratic governance remains the only hope of preventing genocide (Rummel, 1998).

Democracy is no guarantee of safety if full civil rights are not extended to all (cf. Brown, 2003; Tilly, 2003: 44). Multicultural democracies can get bloody. They are safe only for citizens and for those with civil rights; noncitizen or disenfranchised minorities have not fared well. Recall the situations of Native Americans before 1924, Australian Aborigines before 1973, and black Americans prior to the civil rights movement. Significant massacres of these groups stopped short when citizenship or civil rights were granted. Moreover, democracies sometimes elect people who take dictatorial powers and the commit genocide. Hitler is the obvious example—he was duly and freely elected chancellor, though with a small plurality rather than a majority. Ferdinand Marcos initially was democratically elected in the Philippines. Efrain Rios Montt won free (if not fair) elections in Guatemala, and his henchmen were elected by reasonably free and fair elections in the 2000s. Significantly, in the later case, they could not restart the genocides they carried out in the 1980s; world attention and Guatemalan civil society had both matured.

Conversely, even undemocratic regimes may escape genocide if they have stability and accountability, for example, Tanzania, Tunisia, and Singapore. Zambia was relatively well-run by Kenneth Kaunda and Cote d'Ivoire by Felix Houphouet-Boigny. Cote d'Ivoire fell apart as soon as Houphouet-Boigny died, but the result was civil war—with intervention by neighboring states helping to prevent it from getting totally out of hand—rather than targeted hatred and genocide toward any specific groups. Other protective factors include ecological viability, economic stability, and a sense of hope in the society. But, always, the vital key is civil rights for all citizens.

Democracy protects, and we return to the point that democracy correlates with trade and commerce, economic security, open opportunities and perceived hope, while totalitarianism correlates with militarism and with a stagnant economy based on primary production, as well as with downward mobility. Militarism, in turn, feeds on a genuine need to defend the country against outsiders. It thus is common in vulnerable countries with rich resources such as Iraq, and even commoner in highly unstable, hard-to-conquer areas like mountain ranges. Still, contingent history is far more important, and winds up being a major predictor of mass murder.

Measures that should be undertaken anyway—moves to increase commerce, grow the economy, and get away from primary production—are desirable also as preventatives of genocide. Worldwide, at all times, teaching tolerance and valuing diversity are the mainstay, but they will never be enough. International vigilance must never fail, above all in clear risk situation.

For the time being, international involvement is working fairly well. World violence in general continues to decline (Pinker, 2011). Diplomacy, backed up by international peacekeeping missions (heavily armed), have reduced conflicts by 40 percent in comparison with the blood-drenched 1990s (Evans, 2005, 2008). Still, there were twenty-five major local wars ongoing as of 2004 (Evans, 2005), with full-scale genocide ongoing in Sudan. Yet the momentum continued, and by 2010 even Sudan was more peaceful. The world was remarkably free from war and mass murder. The many governmental and bureaucratic ways of preventing, minimizing, or dealing with genocide have been superbly reviewed in very important books by John Heidenrich (*How to Prevent Genocide*, 2001) and Donald Hamburg (*Preventing Genocide*, 2010), and we can do no better than recommend these works. They should be on every politician's desk (see also Hirsch, 2002; Mills and Brunner, 2002; Totten, 2008b provides a very comprehensive bibliographic volume). Meanwhile, however, we have to rescue the victims (Levenstein, 1983), and that is usually done grudgingly or not at all; the world has millions of refugees from genocides living in misery and squalor in camps (the authors have visited many of these and found the conditions appalling).

Fortunately, genocidal wars have decreased. International war is rare now, and civil wars—always the most deadly pretext for genocide—have diminished. There were eleven long-running civil wars ending in the 2002 to 2005 period (Ferguson, 2005). Some continue, stuck at a rather low level without actual genocide occurring, as in Afghanistan. International intervention accounts for this, with the United States sometimes playing a key role (notably in ex-Yugoslavia in the 1990s as well as in Afghanistan). The United Nations has taken a stronger stand since late 2005. Economic growth and ecological protection are both important in diminishing risk. Benjamin Friedman's conclusions, amplified by our cases herein, prove that *a top priority for anyone caring to prevent genocide is to figure out how to use resources sustainably and efficiently, so as to permit growth and prevent decline.*

Still, for the long term, genuine democracy remains the only hope. Not only does democracy render democide very difficult; democracy also is the best preventive for economic and ecological problems, which so clearly influence democide and war. Directly important is the absolute necessity of *international* legal measures to bring rogue governments and government officials to account. Clearest and most imperative is for the international community to be extremely vigilant, and prepared to act, if an autocratic regime is in a shaky position: newly established, strongly challenged, or facing possible defeat in war.

Gareth Evans, mentioned above, concludes that we must move to the "right to intervene" and then beyond it to a "responsibility to protect." This was defined by the International Commission on Intervention and State Sovereignty, of which Evans was co-chair, in 2001. It is just what it says: nations have a responsibility to protect groups of innocent people that are being massacred. Inevitably, it has been attacked as a bit of western imperialism by certain dictatorial regimes and individuals (Evans, 2008: 55ff). He notes that it goes beyond humanitarian actions but does not require military force; he also disassociates himself, and it, from the Iraq War, which was seen by some as an all too revealing bit of "intervention," clearly motivated by a desire to steal oil rather than to stop genocide (Evans, 2008: 69–71). Evans sees more hope in diplomacy. He identifies warning signs: previous atrocities and conflicts, weak governance and accountability, and receptivity to international influence (Evans, 2008: 74–75; on p. 83 he notes, and dismisses, several general predictive models of conflict). (It will be seen that this is quite a different list from ours. In particular, we find that new governments are the most dangerous, rather than those with a long track record.) In practice, he observes that hatred whipped up by governing elites is particularly important as warning.

He provides a chart of needed actions (Evans, 2008: 87).The international community should intervene to "promote good governance," provide diplomacy and aid, "support education for tolerance," and provide carrots and sticks economically. All nations need to provide human rights, rule of law, legal recourse, confidence, and civilian government. Failing all this, increasing military deployment and show of force will be necessary if human rights are being massively threatened.

All this is more easily said than done; unless that involves watching for the warning signs—the cynical manipulation of hate, the economic problems, the shaky leader—we will intervene too late.

If a crisis occurs, diplomacy, sanctions, and massive international effort is needed; also, on a more direct and local level, progressive measures, such as safe havens, no-fly zones, and threats of force. Evans even forthrightly recommends jamming the regime's public media (Evans, 2008: 107). The next stage is international peacekeepers. Peacekeepers very often fail, being inadequately armed and empowered (as in the case of Rwanda), but they have defanged crises in several African nations more recently (Evans discusses the case of Kenya: Evans, 2008:106). At worst, fighting is necessary. Finally, Evans very usefully—and uniquely—gives a great deal of detail on rebuilding: the international community must take responsibility for reconstructing a functional government that guarantees rights and justice (see esp. p. 150). One recalls that the United States successfully did this in Germany and Japan after 1945, but on the other hand has had very shaky success (at best) in Iraq recently, and barely tried in Indochina. Rebuilding is not an easy task, and requires a kind of hope and will that the United States evidently had in 1945 and did not subsequently have to such a degree. As Heidenrich thoroughly covers legal matters, Evans thoroughly covers direct aspects of governance and foreign policy.

VANISHING THE TIGER

The call to action for this book is to encourage every citizen to intervene when targeted hatred is manifested. While every genocide is unique, commonalities outweigh the differences. Only by looking at genocide as whole, identifying the predictive variable, can we frame strategies to prevent or halt such enterprises (again, for legal and political details, see Heidenrich, 2001; see also Straus, 2006: 224ff., which reaches the same conclusions as ours above, though we wrote before being aware of his book).

Group and mass hatred may not predict actual genocide events, but it is so serious in the world today, so dangerous, and so universally correlated with genocide, that addressing it must remain a basic concern. This means retooling world education to teach tolerance and the value of individuals. Spotlighting particular ethnic groups may backfire (as in Serbia); it essentializes them, generally stereotypes them, and unwittingly defines them as structural opponents. On the other hand, in writing history curricula, valuing and including the contribution of leaders from any and all groups is essential in educating our children.

This involves recognizing that group hate is far stronger, more insidious, more widespread, and more socially accepted than individual hate. It is a different and much more deadly phenomenon. We cannot totally stop group hate; it is too deeply rooted in humanity, unfortunately. But we can still go a long way to preventing genocide, by constantly raising the truths about the wrongness of racism, the social costs of intolerance, the values of cultural diversity, and other relevant eternal verities. *We need not end all group hate; we merely need to inoculate people against the blandishments of the leaders and firms that mobilize group hate to take over countries or get political and economic advantages.* We also need not worry much about the sleazy excuses ("purity," "agrarianism," "renewal," "antiquity," and so on) that are provided for group hate. See through them and go for the hatred itself.

It is the cynical use of group hate that actually does the direct damage. Dealing with this is difficult, however. Yugoslavia tried hard and sincerely to create a nation and minimize group hate, but failed; the nation broke up and its daughter states dissolved in hate, one into outright genocide. So eternal vigilance is the price of even minimal tolerance, as well as of liberty. Since fear and hate are strong emotions, typically the strongest political emotions (Westen, 2007), they triumph unless the counter-pressure is constant, strong, and sincere.

Then, when leaders do arise who manipulate group hate for their own purposes, *we need to call them on it, immediately.* The extreme tolerance shown by the international community to religious hate is especially sinister, but any and all group hate is dangerous. Opposing it is ideally left to citizens of the country involved, but that is never enough. First, those who exploit hate silence their opponents, often by politicide. Second, the international community simply has to keep itself in order and on watch. The current situation, in which "inaction" is cultivated by genocidal and would-be genocidal powers, is intolerable; it will bring the current world order down eventually. In the United States, among other countries, the most flagrant hate-merchandising by people whipping up bias and prejudice to sell political positions or economic nostrums has gone almost without protest or remark, putting the United States in a pre-genocidal situation. Particularly dangerous situations (to repeat) are ones in which an autocratic government is consolidating power or is challenged by war or revolt. Extreme and militaristic ideologies are contributing factors.

Finally, when killings do begin, the international community must move immediately, with open publicity and investigation followed by genuinely condign economic sanctions, then armed response if sanctions and speeches fail.

We have proposed that solidarity and complicity are strong factors in acquiescing to hate strategies and abdicating the political power that lead to genocide. These same factors are strong coping strategies in the prevention of genocide and the promotion of a peaceful society. We all need to feel secure and that begins by managing fear. As Franklin Delano Roosevelt stated, "The only thing we have to fear is fear itself." President Roosevelt not only understood the role of fear in social breakdown but also the importance of a warm, emotional, and supportive approach to handling fear. His "fireside" radio chats sustained America facing the Great Depression and World War II. In order to pull the nation together, we needed rational reasons combined with emotional warmth (cf. Damasio, 1994).

John Rawls, in *A Theory of Justice* (1971), memorably advocated considering what you would do if you were "behind a veil" that kept you from seeing who you are, and thus would have to decide matters on the assumption that you could be a Black in the South, a Palestinian in Israel, a poor farmer in India. This he hoped would make people decide cautiously and morally. Unfortunately, he was writing for "reasonable" people (see Amartya Sen, 2009: 43). People are not reasonable. The person behind the veil could be a masochist, a terrorist, a psychopath. Even among ordinary people, many decide happily to suffer and die if they can take even one or two members of a hated group with them (Atran, 2010). In the world today, there are thousands of suicide bombers and no identified saints. If humanity is to survive the twenty-first century, we have to create a moral climate that turns that ratio around. Appealing to reason will not do it. Appealing to fear that oneself will be next is some use, but not enough. We need to teach concern for humanity, and indeed for all life. This has failed before, and produced genocides; we now can spot the warning signs that a religion of mercy is sliding insidiously toward becoming a religion of hate, and do something about that slide. However, this requires vigilance and "fearless speech."

If people are secure, they will strive to make their lives better. They are less likely to feel the need to hate. If they are scared enough, they resort to a hierarchy of coping strategies moving from defensiveness to targeted aggression to genocide. The bully leader builds upon this fear and articulates the source of fear in targeted hatred; the inclusive leader asks for a wide base of inclusion and participation and speaks to hope.

Human beings are all one family. We are all in this together. This is especially clear now, with resources so desperately short, creating an imperative need to plan on a worldwide basis. Either we recognize that we are all in this together or we will destroy ourselves—all of humanity—in more and more desperate fights over dwindling resources.

Hope is all important. Humans are capable of great love, sacrifice, and creativity, but the mobilization of these qualities requires an inclusive leader. Such a leader articulates the critical role of individual participation in society and the righteousness of civil rights, sowing the seeds of content and hope. The inclusive leader attacks evil, but in the mode of the traditional Hindu representation of the goddess Durga saving the universe by killing a buffalo-demon. Durga is always shown in art as looking out with love and care at the universe she is saving—never looking down with ferocity at the demon she is killing. The inclusive leader embodies action, based not upon fear but upon participation, civil rights, and justice.

The only way for humanity to survive the future is through firm commitment to human rights and to "Never again." Far from telling others to "get over it," we must tell ourselves *not* to get over it. Our challenge is to teach our children to resist overzealous solidarity, to recognize dehumanizing behavior, to confront the injustice of targeted hatred, the deadly seeds that poison the soil, strangling all of us. May we learn from the experiences of genocide and be audacious in hope that our children and their children can live together in peace.

Appendix I

Statistics of Genocide, with Risk Factors

When possible, to maintain comparability, the totals below are from Rummel, *Statistics of Democide* (1998: 351–55). His cutoff date is 1987. He gives a range from low to middle to high estimates. His middle figures are used here unless otherwise specified. They are often clearly underestimates, but usually more reasonable than his highest figures. Notes are ours.

We evaluate each country for our four risk factors. "Hatred" means political mobilization of hatred, *not* simple hatred itself. "Economics" refers to poverty, but with special attention to downturns and wartime disruption, since it is downward changes rather than simple want that are associated with genocide. "New regime" means a new government that is shaky but seizing autocratic power, or, in some cases, we note that the regime is not new but has encountered a sudden challenge that makes the leaders feel threatened. "War" refers to either external or civil war, or both. We believe these four things are the actual causes of genocide, and that most or all of them must be present for genocide to occur. The material below is our evidence. Sources are Rummel's works and general histories cited in text, above.

We do not include the many small-scale political killings that Rummel lists but that do not constitute genocide under our definition. For example, several small, imperfectly described cases from the World War I era, and a few from modern Africa, are not summarized below (see Rummel's book); the figures are vague, and the situations are poorly described in literature available. Many of them seem more like mere civil unrest than genocide. Conversely, we have added a number of cases, mostly those occurring since Rummel's book.

Since 1987, figures are from works cited in main text (for the specific area, and cited also below where controversial).

The great "classic" genocides remain those of Turkey in 1915–1921; Germany and German Europe in World War II; the USSR under Lenin and Stalin; some USSR satellites in the late 1940s; China under Mao; Indonesia in 1965–1966; Cambodia under Pol Pot; Guatemala in the 1980s; Nigeria in the Biafra War; Brazil in several cases where small Indigenous groups were exterminated. The major true genocides since 1987 have been the cases in Burundi, D. R. Congo (ambiguous), Indonesia,

Rwanda, Serbia, Sudan, and possibly China (depending on interpretation of stories from Tibet and Xinjiang).Otherwise, in the list below, we are generally dealing with political murders—what Rummel called "democide" and Tilly called "politicide." However horrific they may be (as they certainly were in Argentina, Chile, Myanmar, and many other places), they do not appear to represent attempts to exterminate entire ethnic or religious groups. They were, however, attempts to exterminate entire segments of the political spectrum—not just targeted killings of opponents. Families of dissidents, groups that might be dissident, individuals who show sympathy with dissidents, and random people suspected for no real reason, all are fair game. Thus they deserve a major place in this book.

Also, ethnic violence with massive killing, very near the genocide level, has occurred in dozens of countries—far too many to list. Much is civil war rather than genocide (Colombia, Liberia, Sierra Leone, etc.), or is "ordinary" political murder (Myanmar, Turkmenistan, etc.). The risk factors for genocide generally predict these cases, and the need to prevent such violence remains with us.

AFGHANISTAN, 1978–1987, 228,000

> Since then, war has led to hundreds of thousands of further deaths, but breaking out the figures is impossible. War is ongoing at this writing, and has been almost continually since 1978.
> Hatred: Wahhabite Islamic extremism mobilized by Taliban and Al-Qaeda; fear of terrorism mobilized by the United States
> Economics: extreme, and, for many, worsening for decades
> New regime: Taliban in 1990s, Karzai's regime afterward
> War: Long conflict with USSR evolved into civil wars

ALBANIA 1944–1987, 100,000

> Largely in WWII and its aftermath and in consolidating the Communist regime. Killing largely ended when Enver Hoxha's regime was secure, and did not significantly pick up when it fell.
> Hatred: Various ethnic rivalries
> Economics: Extreme poverty, wartime devastation
> New regime: Communist
> War: WWII and major civil conflicts after it

ALGERIA 1962–1987, 50,000, MANY SINCE

> Hatred: French/Algerian morphing into moderate/Islamist

Economics: Poverty and disruption by civil war
New regime: military government after the French
War: Independence followed by increasing civil unrest; largely ended in very recent years

ANGOLA 1975–1987, 125,000, MANY SINCE

Hatred: Independence movement dissolving into wars between militias with political (and sometimes ethnic) differences
Economics: Extreme poverty, plus dominance by mineral-extractive interests, always a danger
New regime: Newly independent warlords, in conflict for decades after independence
War: War of liberation morphing into civil war. Killing largely ended with peace and consolidation of the regime in the 1990s

ARGENTINA 1976–1983, 20,000

Virtually all other sources say 30,000. Particularly bloody and unprovoked. Thirteen thousand admitted by the government. Killings ended sharply and suddenly with fall of military dictatorship. Killings largely political, but Jews specially targeted, and at least some outright advocacy of exterminating them; Hitler's *Mein Kampf* was (and had long been) required reading in the military academies.
Hatred: Military hatred of Jews, intellectuals, and political liberals
Economics: Troubles and economic downturns in the 1970s
New regime: Right-wing colonels seized power in a coup and tried unsuccessfully to consolidate their hold
War: Civil unrest; singularly ill-advised aggressive war against England for the Falkland Islands, leading to rapid and humiliating defeat, and the fall of the colonels, which ended the killing

AUSTRALIA, NINETEENTH–EARLY TWENTIETH CENTURY

Unknown number of Aboriginals; absolute numbers small, but the total number of Aboriginals in Australia in the first place was only a few hundred thousand, and many groups numbered a few hundred at most. Thus genocides could be, and were, very "small" yet very total.
Hatred: Organized campaigns and racist extremism against Aboriginals
Economics: Settler war; prosperous, democratic country, unlike more typical genocides

New regime: No
War: Minor civil strife with Aboriginals used as (very thin) excuses for massacre, and subsequently for culturocide through kidnapping children

BANGLADESH 1972–1987, 25,000

This is since the war of independence (the toll of which is counted under Pakistan). Largely consolidating of rule after that war. Consolidation involved genocidal killing and expulsion of minorities suspected of having opposed independence. Many of these were called "Biharis," though far from all came from Bihar. ENA observed "Bihari" refugee camps in India in 1978; conditions were appalling, with starvation common. Indigenous "tribal" people in the mountainous parts of Bangladesh were also targeted for many massacres (Arens, 2011).
Hatred: Bangali hatred of (West) Pakistan oppression and of those who sympathized with it, lumped as "Biharis"
Economics: Poverty, and sense of more and more neglect by (West) Pakistan, which allegedly exploited Bangladesh and kept it down
New regime: Newly independent, essentially oligarchic
War: War of independence from Pakistan, leading to killing and expulsion; ended with consolidation of new regime

BRAZIL/AMAZON 1900–1987, 465,000

An appalling, but thoroughly sober, reasonable, and well-documented, figure for a very underrated genocide: the continuing Brazilian genocide campaign against its Native American citizens. Killing continues today, though no longer with government support. The total also includes many killings of political opponents, opponents of big ranching interests, and the like. Neighboring countries, especially Colombia, have done their share as well.
Hatred: Majority hatred of Native Americans; taken advantage of to settle scores also with environmentalists, small farmers, and so on.
Economics: Poverty and insecurity, but this is a typical settler war situation, with economic downturn not an issue most of the time (though exacerbating conflict during depressed periods)
New regime: Irrelevant until relatively liberal democracy reached Brazil in the 1980s–1990s, ending most of the killing
War: Ongoing small-scale local conflicts with Indigenous groups

BULGARIA 1944–1987, 222,000

Largely early on, in WWII and its aftermath and subsequent consolidation of Communism.
Risk factors as for Albania.

BURMA (MYANMAR) 1944–1987, 53,000

The vast majority under the present regime; killings continue, and the total now would be far above 100,000, but even estimates are difficult to find.
Hatred: Burmese/minority conflicts
Economics: Impoverished country, but we believe (from observation, interviewing and experience) more important was the neglect by the British, leading to resentment and unrest
New regime: Military dictatorship
War: Ongoing conflicts with larger minority groups, some of which are de facto independent as of this writing

BURUNDI 1965–1973, 140,000; ADDITIONAL DEATHS IN RWANDA

Rummel underplays this ongoing killing; the figure is from Pinker, 2011: 340. Tutsis systematically killed Hutus during this period, setting the stage for greater genocides in the 1990s.

CAMBODIA 1958–1987, 2,639,000

The vast majority—1,671,000 to 1,871,000, probably closer to the higher figure (Kiernan, 2008: 271) of these—were killed in the Khmer Rouge period, 1975–1979, but it is well to recall that another 700,000 or more died before and after this. Includes many war dead killed in actual battles, but the *vast* majority of deaths in both categories were outright democide.
Rummel's higher estimate of 3,888,000 may well be the true figure for total deaths, but it includes the war dead.
Hatred: Cambodians were notably tolerant before the 1970s. However, even before the Khmer Rouge, problems were noted with minorities, especially immigrant Vietnamese, and with resentment of westernized elites. The Vietnam War exacerbated hatred of Vietnamese and of foreigners. The Khmer Rouge whipped up hatred of these and of Chams and other minorities, and of all educated individuals.

Economics: Wartime devastation following colonial stagnation; neglected colony
New regime: The ruthless Khmer Rouge, including a core of peasants from outback areas
War: Increasing spillover of the Vietnam War was the direct precipitating event for the Khmer Rouge takeover and the subsequent genocide.

CENTRAL AFRICAN REPUBLIC/EMPIRE, 1970S, THOUSANDS

Not even approximate figures exist, and precious little information of any kind available. Rummel's estimate of two thousand is a guess, certainly far too low. Most died during Bokassa's rule of terror.
Hatred: Local tribal tensions, but largely consolidation of dictatorship under J. Bokassa
Economics: Neglected colony, probably actually declining economically
New regime: Bokassa's dictatorship
War: Not serious; military coup

CHAD 1962–1987, 10,000

War spilled over from Sudan in the 2000s, causing several thousand further deaths.
Hatred: Local tribal and minority tensions
Economics: Chronic poverty and want exacerbated by global warming, which has almost dried up Lake Chad
New regime: Revolving-door coups; complex history of militarism
War: Post-independence troubles after 1962; renewed troubles with spillover of Darfur conflicts

CHILE 1973–1987, 10,000

Politicide or democide but not true genocide, since there was no attempt to wipe out whole groups, except for Pinochet's personal opponents. However, it was so extreme, bloody, systematic, and a notorious "murder by government" that it presents a specially important case.
Here Rummel's higher estimate, thirty thousand, is closer to the truth, as disclosed since Pinochet's fall shortly after Rummel's cutoff date.
This is an extremely atypical genocide, showing that all that is really necessary to launch democide is a new fascist regime.

Hatred: None relevant
Economics: Nothing significant; prosperous country with healthy growth
New regime: Pinochet's fascist dictatorship; Pinochet consolidated it by bloodshed
War: No

CHINA 1923–1987, 58,916,000

Low figure; most of the deaths from 1958 to 1961 were due to famine caused by the Great Leap Forward, and thus are ambiguously attributed to genocide or simple hunger. True figures are, in any case, impossible even to estimate. Rummel estimates around ten million for various political campaigns in the warlord years of the 1920s–1940s, and Pinker estimates nine hundred thousand killed in various warlord campaigns 1916–1928 (Pinker, 2011: 316). These, however, were arguably civil war deaths, not genocide. Truly genocidal tolls reached at least one hundred million between 1957 and 1966. ENA's interviews in Hong Kong in 1965–1966, if they are even remotely representative (and we believe they are), show that most estimates of the deaths in the Great Leap Forward and Great Cultural Revolution are too low. Killings largely political, not ethnic, but repression in Tibet killed thousands and was coupled with extreme cultural repression, leading to widespread and credible charges of genocide. There were many other smaller ethnic episodes involving Mongols, Hui, and other minorities. Religion was repressed in particular, with countless thousands or millions of Daoists, Buddhists, Christians, Muslims, and others killed simply for being religious practitioners or even for merely practicing religion in a country committed to "atheism."
Many, probably most, of the above deaths were from starvation and random killing. Systematic government murder accounted for a large but unknown percentage of the total.
Killings continue as of this writing, but at a low level, though probably enough to be numerically significant as politicide if the actual total were known.
Hatred: Previously, serious tensions between Tibetans and Chinese, Uighurs and Chinese, Muslims and non-Muslims. Under Mao, these all were exacerbated, and hatred of almost every imaginable category of society—ethnic, religious, class, occupational, educational, political—was tried out as excuses for local bloodshed. This history seems unique in the sheer number of groups targeted and the lack of any visible rationale for targeting them.

Economic: China's economy was devastated by rebellions and militarism in the nineteenth century, again by the fall of the Chinese Empire in 1911 and by natural disasters, again by the Depression, Japanese invasion and World War II, again by the civil war between Communists and others, and again by the excesses of Communism under Mao—a unique record of misfortune.

New regime: Consolidation of Maoist Communism; with the death of Mao and the final consolidation of the regime, killings greatly diminished

War: As above

COLOMBIA 1948–1987, 152,000

Political killings as well as extermination of Native Americans. Worse since 1987, with drugs more and more involved; figure now at least doubled.

Hatred: Largely political, but ethnicity involved, with major repression of Afro-Colombians (Escobar 2008) and Native American groups

Economic: Major problems from drug economy

New regime: Series of "democratically elected" regimes in a very compromised "democracy" with major military and paramilitary involvement in elections

War: Continual civil war since 1948

CUBA (CASTRO) 1959–1987, 73,000; HIGH ESTIMATE OF 141,000

Largely early on, consolidating. The toll of the Castro revolution is often forgotten or ignored.

Hatred: Class; some ethnic but not apparently serious

Economic: Major doldrums for poor under previous Bautista dictatorship (itself murderous enough, a part of the problem)

New regime: Communist

War: Some conflict during the takeover, but not a major war

CZECHOSLOVAKIA 1945–1948, 197,000

General bloodbath, more civil war than democide.

CZECHOSLOVAKIA (COMMUNISTS, 1948–1967), 65,000

Again, largely in early years; regime consolidation.
As for Albania, but far less problems and therefore less killing

EQUATORIAL GUINEA 1958–1979, 50,000

Further killings in 2009–2010; no totals to date; apparently a few thousand.
Hatred: Anticolonial; local groups
Economics: Classic oil state, increasingly run by giant multinational oil corporations through local kleptocracy
New regime: Worst problems follow coups
War: Anticolonial wars early; oil-related strife, sometimes involving corporations behind the scenes (see Anderson, 2010)

ETHIOPIA 1974–1987, 727,000

In this case, Rummel's high figure of 1,287,000 is much more credible. Much of this was famine death but counts as deliberate killing because food aid was deliberately withheld. (For this and later deaths, see also Kissi, 2006.)
Est. 150,000 intellectuals, opponents, and miscellaneous positions killed directly by order of Mengistu Haile Mariam alone (Yahoo News online, January 10, 2007). Mostly politicide but much ethnic targeting
Hatred: Extremist political regime; religious and ethnic prejudices and strife
Economics: Economic downturn (near collapse) and famine during Dergue regime
New regime: Dergue
War: Continual civil unrest and local rebellion but no real war

FRANCE, VICHY 1940–1944, 70,000

Part of the German fascist genocide

GERMANY 1933–1945, 20,946,000

Obviously counting many war deaths; the classic figure of "six million" still stands, for the outright genocide. The figure of 20,946,000 is far too high for the genocide and far too low for the war deaths.
Oddly, Rummel does not mention the consolidation of Communist power in East Germany, but it was not done bloodlessly.
Hatred: Not just Jews; also other minorities, political dissidents, homosexuals, handicapped persons, many other groups
Economics: Major problems after Germany's defeat in WWI; worse in the Great Depression

New regime: Hitler consolidating dictatorship
War: WWII

GUATEMALA 1954–1987, 136,000

Rummel's high figure of 174,000 is more accurate; both include the very few killings by the rebels; the vast majority of killings were by the government. Most estimates are higher, around 200,000.
Hatred: Certain Maya Indigenous groups targeted, but general massacre of dissidents or suspected ones, villages claimed to be harboring guerillas; also labor organizers, teachers, aid workers, intellectuals, anyone suspected of helping the poor.
Economics: Chronic poverty and insecurity, exacerbated pre-genocide by repressive regimes with erratic policies
New regime: Efrain Rios Montt seized de facto dictatorial policies with classic fascist ideology
War: Local guerrilla movement used as excuse, but it was tiny and soon crushed

HUNGARY 1945–1987, 67,000

Probably a very low figure. Again, most killings were in the earlier years, during the rundown of WWII and then the consolidation of the Communist regime. There was also genocide by Hitler's forces and Hungarian sympathizers of Hungary's Jews, Roma, and other minorities, between 1939 and 1945.
Hatred: Many collaborated with Hitler in WWII genocides. This was reversed after the war, with persecution of Germans and right-wingers. Communists coming to power then eliminated opponents.
Economics: War and postwar were devastating.
New regime: Fascist, then unsettled, then Communist—all with agendas of democide
War: WWII and violent, unsettled aftermath

INDONESIA 1965–1987, 579,000

Unquestionably far too low. Rummel's high figure of 1,016,000 is closer to other estimates, but many other estimates go up to 1,500,000 or even 2,000,000. The vast majority of these killings were in the 1965–1966 chaos, but killings continued at a high rate. Many or most of the deaths were due to local and random violence, but the Indonesian military bears most of the blame (directly or indirectly), and Suharto, the rising dictator, was the single most responsible individual. His consolidation of power during this period was a classic case of the new-dictatorship type of democide.

Since 1964–1966, tens of thousands more in various local wars. The attempted conquest of East Timor (1979–1999) led to 120,000–170,000 (Kiernan, 2008: 281–82) or perhaps even 183,000 (Deutsch, 2008) deaths; some of these were in actual conflict, since the Timorians resisted fiercely and in the end successfully, but most were cold-blooded murder. This was some 20 to 25 percent of the East Timorese population. Over 100,000 New Guinea tribal people were killed in Irian Jaya (Deutsch, 2008), and this was almost pure genocide; there was some local tribal resistance, but it was basically spears against bombs and machine guns. Continual conflict in Aceh was actual war, not genocide—the Acehnese rebelled, and fought tenaciously—but they got little mercy and many massacres. Killings continued through the Suharto dictatorship and have not totally ceased with the return of democracy (see Sidel, 2006). On the other hand, outright genocide has ceased.

Hatred: In spite of alleged tolerance and easygoing nature, Indonesia has proved to be one of the most genocidal countries, if not the most. The major problems were under the long-lasting Suharto dictatorship, which targeted, at various times, Chinese, Communists, Javanese peasants, labor organizers, Timorese, New Guinea Indigenous peoples, and many smaller groups.

Economics: Chronic poverty; major economic collapse in early 1960s opened the way for chaos, taken advantage of by Suharto's Golkar movement. After that, corruption, oil politics, agrarian problems and other ills kept the country economically weak and unstable.

War: Major civil war in 1965–1966; attempted conquest of East Timor; successful conquest of former Dutch New Guinea, involving bloody repression of local people to allow settling of Javanese and others from more western islands.

IRAN (SHAH REGIME) 1954–1979, 16,000; IRAN (ISLAMIC STATE) 1979–1987, 55,000

Both figures probably too low. Total for Islamic state now certainly higher. An uncertain but huge number died in the repression of the freedom movement of 2009.

Hatred: Shah repressed political enemies (but no more than that). Islamic state since 1979 has eliminated dissidents and suspected dissidents, repressed local autonomy movements, and, above all, targeted religious minorities, Islamic liberals and moderates, women in general, and various forms of "immorality."

Economics: Oil and other industries make Iran a prosperous, growing state, far from the usual case of genocidal states.
New regime: Worst problems, predictably, came when the Shah and later the Ayatollahs took power.
War: No

IRAQ 1963–1987, 189,000; HIGH FIGURE 407,000

Repression under Saddam Hussein, including extreme, genocidal repression of Shi'a Muslims and of Kurds.
Figures were far higher by the time the United States invaded in 2003. Since then, killings are literally beyond counting; enormous debates have erupted over the number of deaths and the percentage that were outright genocide as opposed to battle deaths. At least several hundred thousand died in wars and repressions after 1987. Estimates at the final, official end of the Iraq War, in December of 2011, ran over 105,000 civilians and many thousand Iraq troops, as well as some 4,484 American soldiers (Zucchino, 2011).
Hatred: Main problems political, but Sunni-Shi'a fighting may have killed many more people.
Economics: Oil carries the state, but the wars led to chaos and disruption, affecting most people.
New regime: Saddam Hussein consolidated power at first, and later whenever threatened, by indiscriminate mass killing. Then unsettled conditions prevailed after his fall.
War: First Gulf War in 1992; Iraq War 2003–2011

JAPAN IN CHINA 1937–1945, 5,964,000; HIGH FIGURE 10,595,000

Real figure certainly much higher. To this should be added a large number in Korea and in Japan itself, and many in Taiwan. Rummel does not give estimates, but the toll in Korea was appallingly high.
Not a true genocide by this book's definition, but close enough to be included here, because the Japanese massacred millions of noncombatants in zones they controlled and held as their own territory.
Hatred: Japanese vs. Chinese, Koreans, and others
Economics: Great Depression, then WWII disruption
New regime: Fascist militarists basically controlled Japan from early 1930s through 1945
War: Sino-Japanese conflicts, evolving into WWII

KOREA, NORTH 1948–1987, 1,663,000

Many more by now.
Hatred: Political repression of opponents and imagined opponents
Economics: Poverty after the Korean War, but then worsening situation with isolated, repressive form of Communism.
New regime: Communist—the problems were worst at the initial takeover and during the Korean War, but have remained at a level unusually high for a quite stable regime.
War: Korean War clearly triggered the major atrocities.

KOREA, SOUTH, 1946–1948, 1950–1953, 150,000+

Hatred: Anti-Japanese; political factions; later anti-Communism
Economics: Incredible devastation after WWII; possibly the poorest country in the world at that time.
New regime: Fascist military dictatorship developing and consolidating (it rapidly evolved away from fascism and rather soon restored democracy
War: WWII and unsettled aftermath followed by Korean War

LAOS 1960–1987, 94,000

Spillover of Vietnam War; see Vietnam.

MEXICO 1910–1920, 1,417,000

Rummel's high figure 3,290,000, probably too high. Rummel's mid-range one is close to the usual estimates. About one-tenth of the Mexican population died violently. This was a civil war rather than a true democide. Countless massacres occurred, but they were local and in the heat of battle, not coldly calculated, centralized policy. Risk factors irrelevant except to point out that neither economic downturns nor a new regime in actual control were involved, making this a good case of the risk factors not being present and genocide duly failing to occur. It might well have otherwise, since local genocides of Indigenous groups had been attempted.

MOZAMBIQUE 1964–1987, 201,000

War of liberation rather than true genocide. However, by the end of the period a leftist regime was consolidating position with some killing. Killing continued after 1987 but has now ceased. This was a

many-sided civil war with indiscriminate killing; governments killed (politicide) when they could. The complexities have been teased out by Carolyn Nordstrom (1997, 2004).
Hatred: Largely of political opponents and sympathizers with the former colonial power.
Economics: One of the poorest countries, and extremely affected by war of liberation, which devastated the economy.
New regime: Leftist power
War: Anticolonial and then civil war between political factions

NIGERIA 1967–1970, 377,000

This was the Biafra "War," a hopeless rebellion by the Biafra area that turned into a genocidal massacre and looting of Biafrans. Other estimates run close to a million. Nigeria has had a murderous regime before and since, the total slain being beyond even rough estimate.
Ongoing conflicts in the Delta, due to injustices related to oil extraction, have led to thousands of political killings. They are not systematic genocide, and thus are outside our purview, but they need mention here.
Hatred: Largely ethnic, but political and oil-company factors involved
Economics: Conflicts over oil wealth in an otherwise totally impoverished country
New regime: Succession of military coups and rigged elections guarantee fairly frequent turnover of military dictators
War: Biafra War, a one-sided conflict that ended up being a wholesale massacre of Biafrans

PAKISTAN 1958–1987, 1,503,000

High figure 3,003,000; includes 150,000 to 500,000 Bengalis killed in the independence war of Bangladesh, 1971. The huge range of the figures is typical of genocides everywhere. A considerable amount of random killing persists.
Hatred: Religious, then ethnic (Bangalis)
Economics: Gradual decline of formerly prosperous regions
New regime: Succession of military dictators during this period
War: Bangladesh war of independence turned genocidal early on

PHILIPPINES, MARCOS 1972–1986, 15,000

Small figure, but significant, because of the revealing nature of Marcos's short, bloody reign in a country that has otherwise been peaceful and democratic.
Hatred: Simple political repression
Economics: Major and long-lasting economic decline preceded the Marcos takeover
New regime: Ferdinand Marcos seized dictatorial powers in 1972; the killings were a classic, straightforward case of political repression by a new dictator consolidating power.
War: No

POLAND 1941–1944, 1,585,000

Nazi murders of Polish Jews, partisans and dissidents (as opposed to war dead)

POLAND, 1948–1987, 22,000

Consolidation of Communist rule.
Risk factors as for Germany and Hungary.

ROMANIA 1948–1987, 435,000

One of the bloodier Communist consolidations and subsequent repression, under Ceaucescu.
Oddly, Rummel does not count the Nazi murders, possibly lumping occupied Romania with Germany. But killings under the Nazis were extreme; ethnic violence in the post-WWII unsettled period was also extreme.
Risk factors as for Germany, Poland, and Hungary.

SOUTH AFRICA 1934–1987, 6,000

Too low, but the total figure of direct killings would still be a low one; the real damage was done by "structural violence"—denying the majority black population the food and medical care routinely received by the whites.
Hatred: White vs. black and colored; Afrikanders vs. British.
Economics: Great Depression; WWII dislocation.
New regime: Extremist Boer power seizure in post-WWII period
War: No

SPAIN 1939–1975 (FRANCO PERIOD), 275,000

Enormous bloodshed 1936–1939 counts as civil war, not genocide, but the line is close. A huge percentage of it was sheer repression.
Hatred: largely political.
Economics: Great Depression and WWII dislocation.
New regime: Worst excesses under Franco's early consolidation of power
War: Spanish Civil War and, soon after, WWII

SRI LANKA 1952–1987, 5,000

Since 1987, the war of independence by the Tamils in northern Sri Lanka escalated and was finally crushed in 2009, with huge loss of life; this was a true war, with the Tamils giving as good as they got whenever they could, but the Sri Lankan majority government used it as an excuse to kill so many noncombatants, for purely ethnic reasons or simply because they were political dissidents, that it has to be ranked as genocidal. After 1987, at least several thousands more died by cold-blooded governmental murder. The totals for murder by government, however, cannot be broken out from the totals for military casualties. This case is interesting in that it proves that genocide can go on for decades under genuinely democratically elected governments, if conditions are bad enough. In this case, Sri Lanka's steadily declining economy and its ongoing war created pressures intolerable even for democratic regimes.
Hatred: Tamil/Sinhalese (religious and ethnic hate)
Economics: Steady deterioration in Sri Lanka's economy; a classic case of downturn correlating with genocide.
New regime: Not relevant, and a *very* unusual case in that ongoing genocide took place in a genuine democracy for decades. The steady economic decline was presumably critical here.
War: Ongoing until 2009

SUDAN 1956–1972, "AROUND 500,000" (PINKER, 2011: 340)

Further discussion below, since much more happened after 1987.

TURKEY 1909–1918, 1,883,000; HIGH FIGURE 3,204,000

To this may be added 95,000 Armenians killed in or near "independent" Armenia during this period and on to 1921. Another 878,000 or more fell in the next two years, in Atatürk's rule, but these deaths seem to be associated with actual warfare.

There was also a good deal of killing of Greeks and Kurds, with massacres of Greeks after 1922 (but again there was a real war: Greece invaded Turkey) and with massacres of Kurds in later decades.

Hatred: Turk/Armenian (and later other groups)
Economics: WWI devastation of the economy
New regime: The "Young Turks" were responsible during the worst years.
War: WWI, later Greek invasion (much later, Kurdish civil unrest)

UGANDA 1971–1979 (I.E., UNDER IDI AMIN), 301,000

Rummel's high figure of 501,000 probably closer to truth. Pinker (2011: 340) gives a low estimate of 150,000, but this seems unlikely. Another 255,000 died in conflicts after Idi Amin's fall; killings have continued. Recently, rebel groups have murdered thousands more in terror campaigns.

Hatred: Ethnic, political, religious—a general send-up
Economics: Poor country, made poorer by Idi Amin
New regime: Seizure and consolidation of power by Idi Amin as military dictator
War: General civil war

USSR 1917–1987, 61,911,000

Rummel's high figure is 126,891,000; includes deaths outside of USSR, that is, mostly killing of POW's by Nazis in WWII; internal figure 54,769,000 (high 114,757,000). This would make the USSR—which, of course, fell two years after Rummel's cutoff date—the bloodiest regime in history, though only because of Rummel's absurdly low estimates for Mao's China. However, note that Rummel's estimate conflates internal purges (actual genocide), Nazi killings of war prisoners, and many war deaths. The number actually killed in genocides under Stalin has been estimated at minimally 20,000,000, probably up to 50 percent higher (Chalk and Jonassohn, 1990: 320).

In the Ukraine in the 1930s, mass murder and deliberate starvation killed six to seven million (*World Almanac*, 2012, p. 745); this was partly associated with "civil war," but as in many other cases it was such a one-sided war by the 1930s that it counts as genocide.

Hatred: Almost every imaginable group of people, defined by any means imaginable, was targeted at one time or another. Attention focused on political dissidents and on Central Asian and Caucasus minorities that Russians had traditionally hated and despised, but

even the small, nonthreatening, and culturally close Lithuanians were decimated (on top of Nazi decimation in WWII, leading to a million of the three million Lithuanians being killed or displaced; Budryté, 2004).
Economics: Failure of Communism after extreme-left policies began in 1928; Great Depression, wars, failure to recover after WWII
New regime: Only in early years
War: Civil war, then later WWII

VIETNAM, 1945–PRESENT

Very many political killings, but so confused with war casualties and the like that it is impossible to establish clear figures. Rummel estimates about four million, but this includes the war deaths, which is not reasonable, and at present there is no way of breaking out the actual political murders from the war dead.
Hatred: Political repression; some ethnic tensions
Economics: Downturns associated with wars
New regime: Communist consolidation
War: War of liberation from France; then the Vietnam War

YUGOSLAVIA 1944–1987, 1,072,000

Since Rummel, the Serbian genocides have claimed tens of thousands more.
Risk factors as for other East European countries.

ZAIRE/D. R. CONGO 1960–1987, 31,000

Vastly more since.
Hatred: Largely ethnic, but much repression of political enemies.
Economics: Complete chaos and meltdown
New regime: Succession of military dictators constantly trying, not very successfully, to impose control: Patrice Lumumba to Laurent Kabila
War: Continuous civil unrest. War since 1990 has killed literally millions, but no one knows how many.

SUBSEQUENT GENOCIDES

Subsequent genocides, plus notes on some covered above; when possible, figures are from Pinker, 2011, esp. p. 240; Pinker has "trawled the databases" and come up with very good consensus figures.

Appendix I

Both the databases and Pinker are well worth following for consistency and general reliability.

ALGERIA, 1990S, POSSIBLY 150,000

Meltdown rather than genocide, but much systematic genocidal massacre by government, military, and Islamic groups locally in control. The Islamists massacred schoolgirls (education for girls being banned by their form of Islam—in rather flagrant defiance of the Quran and Muhammad).
Hatred: Military vs. Islamists
Economics: Not a major factor, but chaotic and damaged by fighting
New regime: Military dictatorship trying to stave off Islamic extremist takeover
War: Ongoing civil war, winding down without true resolution; many reforms since; situation apparently defanged but could erupt again

ANGOLA, 1975–2002

Civil war rather than genocide, but several local mass murders by government would qualify as genocide; total deaths literally countless; "hundreds of thousands" (BBC Country Profile online), possibly even more
Hatred: Political and ethnic rivalries
Economics: Worst possible case of a former colony, liberated in spite of civil conflicts, dominated by oil and diamond extraction, preyed on by rival oil corporations, and characterized by extreme poverty and inequality.
New regime: Jockeying for control through 1980s and into 1990s
War: Civil war for years.

BURUNDI, 1990S, PERHAPS 200,000; GENOCIDE

Hatred: Tutsi vs. Hutu; colonial problems left by Belgian divide-and-rule strategy
Economics: Poverty, land exhaustion
New regime: Military, usually Tutsi control
War: Rwanda's conflicts spilled over rapidly and remain poorly resolved; fighting has spilled into Zaire.

CHAD, 2000–2010, PRIMARILY 2004–2005; LARGELY SPILLOVER FROM SUDAN

Hatred: Various ethnic groups, complicated by political jockeying for power
Economics: Poverty and giant oil corporations have had their usual deadly interface (see Juhasz, 2008).
New regime: Military coups
War: Sudan conflicts over Darfur spilled over into an already unstable situation.

CONGO (ZAIRE), 1990S ONWARD

No one has any realistic idea how many, but an estimated four million by 2008, and things have escalated since. Much of this is ethnically targeted, including continuation outside Rwanda and Burundi (now peaceful) of the conflict between Tutsi and Hutu militias.
See above under Zaire.

EL SALVADOR, 1979–1980S, AT LEAST 75,000

Politicide; "civil war," but again almost all the killing was done in cold-blooded non-combat situations by government forces.
Hatred: Extremist right-wing government repressing the "left," meaning anyone left of the extreme right wing.
Economics: One of the poorest Western Hemisphere countries, and getting poorer with war and rampant crime
New regime: The worst killing occurred when the right-wing dictatorship seized power.
War: Left-wing guerrilla action triggered repression. Murder of American Maryknoll nuns went without any action by the American government, reassuring the dictatorship. Later, Salvadoran drug gangs in the United States opened branches in the homeland, which inevitably formed links to repressive politicians, and now have great power.

GUATEMALA 1980S–EARLY 1990S, >200,000

Genocide (Maya groups like the Ixil targeted for total extermination) and some politicide
Hatred: Latino/Maya, right/left, and a wave of general murders (see main text)

Economics: One of poorest Western Hemisphere countries; economy devastated by civil conflicts in 1980s
New regime: Worst under consolidation of rule by Efrain Rios Montt, who was democratically elected but seized dictatorial powers
War: Small-scale leftist guerrilla insurrection used as excuse for mass genocide

HAITI, 1960S–1990S, THOUSANDS

Hatred: Diffuse; general breakdown
Economics: Poorest country in Western Hemisphere, perhaps in world (since it lacks the subsistence resources of those poorer in dollar income).Economy in shambles after dictatorship and then storms and earthquakes.
New regime: Serious already under "Papa Doc" Duvalier; worsening with consolidation of rule by his successor "Baby Doc" Duvalier; fall of the latter and restoration of (imperfect) democracy did not stop endemic violence.
War: None, but constant conflict

IRAQ, 2000S, HUNDREDS OF THOUSANDS

(An example of the difficulty of getting statistics on these matters is that even the relatively "transparent" and well-reported Iraq War has produced wildly conflicting accounts of Iraqi death tolls.) While this was largely in the course of a war for quite other reasons, it degenerated into mass murder along religious lines, with clearly genocidal attempts to eliminate whole religious minorities. Saddam Hussein was particularly murderous toward the Kurds; up to 100,000 Kurds were killed in a genocidal campaign (Paddock, 2003).
Hatred: General, but actual mass murders tend to be along religious lines, especially Sunni/Shi'a
Economics: War caused massive collapse of economy
New regime: Saddam Hussein consolidated power by mass murder; his fall due to American invasion in the Iraq War unleashed more killing until control was reasserted slowly
War: As above

IVORY COAST, EARLY 2000S

Few thousand in small civil war between political factions. Not a genocide.

Hatred: Mix of political and ethnic rivalries
Economics: Not a major problem; one of better-off African states
New regime: Death of F. Houphouet-Boigny released civil strife among successors
War: Civil strife as above

KYRGYZSTAN, 2010

Major ethnic violence, neither genocide nor civil war but hundreds of thousands of Uzbeks expelled with many ethnic murders.
Hatred: Kyrgyz and others expelled Uzbeks
Economy: Collapse of national economy after USSR dissolved
New regime: Newly independent regime consolidating dictatorial rule
War: No

LEBANON, 1980S–1990S, TENS TO HUNDREDS OF THOUSANDS

Political and religious conflicts. Probably better called "civil war" rather than "genocide," but enormous numbers of massacres for purely religious and political reasons.
Hatred: Christian vs. Sunni vs. Shi'a vs. Druze; worst violence from Shi'a, supported by Syria
Economics: Not a factor; highly prosperous, successful country before the war
New regime: Governments democratically elected (with the usual complaints about unfair elections), but militias aggressively support candidates
War: Said militias and their political parties battled for control. Eventual top militia is Hizbollah, thanks to Syrian support. A fascist group supporting the Christian side still exists but seems to have lost power.

LIBERIA, LATE 1990S, TENS TO HUNDREDS OF THOUSANDS

Meltdown, but much killing ethnically targeted. See Hoffman (2011).
Hatred: Ethnic and political
Economics: Poverty, but not a case of decline
New regime: Coups and countercoups
War: Basically a civil war between political factions, not genocide

NEPAL, 1990S–2000S, FEW THOUSAND

Local meltdown and government repression.
Hatred: Political—largely a Maoist insurgency vs. everyone else
Economics: Poor country failing to progress
New regime: No, a kingdom with a powerful monarch; unrest eventually terminated his power and created democracy, which largely ended the killing.
War: As above

NICARAGUA, 1980S, FEW THOUSANDS

Politicide
Hatred: Left/right
Economics: Another poor and economically unstable country (unusual by Western Hemisphere standards)
New regime: Fall of Somoza dictatorship, brief democratic triumph by leftists; rapid shifts since but largely democratic and peaceful.
War: Killings during the conflict that eventually led to the fall of Somoza, the limiting of the left, and the eventual triumph of something like democracy (a very rare partial-success story in this grim roll).

PARAGUAY, MOST OF TWENTIETH CENTURY

Murders and repression, especially under the dictator Alfredo Stroessner; not many deaths but significant in such a tiny country. Stroessner fell in 1989, ending most of the killing. Indigenous groups were often targeted and some substantially wiped out (Hitchcock et al., 2011). Anthropologists may be complicit, having worked with some of these groups during the period in question, denied killings, and—to the detriment of anthropological theory—used findings in a general way as if the findings applied to all humanity, without noting the special conditions of the case.
Hatred: Right-wing dictator, fascist with old Nazi ties, vs. political dissidents and Indigenous peoples.
Economics: Poverty and failure to progress; some decline after Stroessner's fall
New regime: At first yes, when Stroessner took power, but he continued the killings throughout his long career. Stroessner's eventual fall led to actual peace and democracy (if not perfect).
War: No

PERU, 1980S AND SINCE, 69,000 (WORLD ALMANAC, 2012, P. 823)

Largely under "neoliberal" regimes, ended by ouster of Fujimori (who was convicted of murders in 2007) and return of democracy; political, but indigenous peoples heavily targeted; whole indigenous communities exterminated in local genocides on the excuse that they were suspected of harboring Shining Path rebels
Hatred: Left/right and Hispanic/Quechua
Economics: Increasing inequality; progress of many sectors while Quechua and similar groups fell farther and farther behind
New regime: Democracy, but Fujimori seized dictatorial powers, though he was ousted without significant bloodshed
War: Genuine guerrilla war by Shining Path, merciless Maoist rebels; government repression even more merciless

RUSSIA/CHECHENYA, 1990S, TENS OF THOUSANDS

Civil war, but including genocidal massacres by Russians of whole noncombatant Chechen communities
Hatred: Russian/Chechen, partly a religious issue (Christian/Muslim)
Economics: Major economic decline after collapse of USSR
New regime: New regimes in both places after USSR
War: War of liberation by Chechenya

RWANDA, 1990S, ALMOST OR QUITE 1,000,000 (700,000 IN 100 DAYS MINIMUM 1994)

Genocide
Hatred: Tutsi/Hutu
Economics: Extreme poverty, inequality, land abuse; probably worsening before the conflict, certainly during and after
New regime: Seizure of power by Hutu militants unleashed genocide
War: Not significant before, but increased as Tutsi refuged in neighboring countries and reinvaded (eventually successfully)

SERBIA, BOSNIA (EX-YUGOSLAVIA), 1992–1995, 200,000 TO 225,000 (*WORLD ALMANAC*, 2012, P. 745)

Also many in Croatia as part of the same breakdown; purely genocidal (in spite of the euphemism "ethnic cleansing")
Hatred: Serbian Orthodox Christians vs. Catholic Croatians and Muslim Bosnians, Montenegrins, Albanians
Economics: Decline and deterioration after collapse of Yugoslavia

New regime: Slobodan Milosevitch, Communist, took over Serbia and instituted dictatorship—more fascist than Communist
War: No

SIERRA LEONE, LATE 1980S TO EARLY 1990S, ESPECIALLY LATE 1990, 50,000 (LOW ESTIMATE)

Meltdown, much ethnic targeting (see Hoffman, 2011). This is another of those rather rare cases in which some scientific evaluation of statistics is found; thus, though this case is not a true genocide, the statistics are worth reporting. The civil war displaced a quarter of the population; approximately 140,000 civilians were beaten or injured, 95,000 arbitrarily detained, thousands (uncounted) amputated, at least 25,000 raped, 10,000 used as sex slaves, uncounted thousands dead. Charles Taylor and his Liberian militia seem to have been the worst problem; the Sierra Leone army and Civil Defense Force did only about 3 percent and 4 percent of it. Note that even *Science* magazine gave up all hope of even estimating the number killed.
Hatred: Political and ethnic
Economics: Poverty, instability; decline during bloodshed
New regime: Revolving-door coups
War: Constant civil war

SOMALIA, 1980S AND SINCE, TENS TO HUNDREDS OF THOUSANDS

Meltdown rather than true genocide.
Hatred: Largely extremist vs. moderate Islam
Economics: Extreme poverty collapsing into total destitution and mass starvation
New regime: None emerging; control of capital by moderates, of most of the rest of the country by Islamist extremists; northern Somalia has declared independence and is a stable (if poor) polity under the name "Puntland"
War: Constant for decades.

SUDAN, 1970S–2004, SOUTHERN TRIBESMEN, 1,000,000–2,000,000; DARFUR, 2003–2008, 373,000, PLUS 2,000,000 DISPLACED

A rare scientific investigation of the figures estimated at least 170,000, almost certainly over 200,000, very possibly 250,000 or more, as of

2006; the wide differences in even the best possible estimate is typical.
Hatred: Dominant extremist Islamist faction of the Arab ethnic group, vs. both Christian and animist southerners and Islamic minorities, notably but not only the Darfuri.
Economics: Worst-case scenario of giant oil corporations meddling in a poor country (see Juhasz, 2008)
New regime: No; stable for decades
War: Civil war eventually led to independence of south; Darfur and other conflicts continue in what remains of the Sudan.

TADZHIKSTAN, 1990S, FEW THOUSANDS?

Ethnic alignments in a general meltdown of civic order
Hatred: Tadzhiks vs. Turkic groups, but apparently more a matter of power elites vs. all challengers.
Economics: Deterioration after collapse of USSR
New regime: New regime after collapse of USSR
War: No

TURKEY, 1980S–1990S

Kurdish nationalists and villages thought to harbor them, thousands killed, including several massacres that were clearly genocide
Hatred: Turks vs. Kurds
Economics: Not an issue overall, but Kurds impoverished and subjected to discrimination—for example, big dams on their land which displace Kurds without compensation while benefiting Turkish landowners and urbanites (our research)
New regime: No; ongoing under successive democratically elected governments
War: Civil conflict, low-level

There have been minor episodes—none truly genocidal, but all with some ethnic overtones—in Congo (Brazzaville), Dahomey, India, Kenya, Mauritania, Niger, Pakistan, Russia (outside Chechnya),Georgia, Azerbaijan, Armenia, South Africa, Turkmenistan, Uzbekistan, Yemen, and so on. Note that most of these have more diversified economy and lack the deadly link of tyranny and giant primary-production interests. The two exceptions have strong centralized governments left over from the Soviet period.By contrast, countries with major ecological, political, and economic problems that have *not* had mass murders.

NEW WORLD:

Bolivia (revolving-door coups prevent the political stability necessary for systematic mass murder)
Ecuador (relatively prosperous and democratic till recently; now a prime candidate for testing the predictive power of this theory)
Honduras (somewhat successful land reform)
Mexico (meltdown with massive deaths in 1910-1921 seems to have inoculated the country against further mass murder. Democracy. Some undemocratic impoverished areas *have* had very local meltdowns)

AFRICA:

Botswana (stable democracy—one of very few in Africa)
Burkina Faso (local troubles, no meltdown; an amazing survivor story)Egypt (semblance of democracy, but this is in extreme danger after Mubarak. The country has economically declined sharply because of the fall of Mubarak. Democratic elections returned an Islamic majority, keen to consolidate power, clearly at expense of Christians and others. A totalitarian regime followed by genocide or meltdown is a frighteningly likely future)
Eritrea (at first too busy fighting Ethiopia to melt down; since then, escalating violence and human rights abuses; prime candidate for future genocide)
Ghana (prime candidate, test for theory)
Kenya (prime candidate—initially saved by good government and economic growth, but has lost these and is drifting into bloody chaos. Democracy and international intervention has saved it so far. See Evans 2008.)
Madagascar (diversified economy; French aid. Nearly came to civil war in late 1990s under fascist-type dictatorship and after 2008 because of coup. Very high risk at this time; genocide probably prevented only by the fact that the central government is too weak to do it)
Malawi (probably too closely tied to South Africa to be very unstable)
Mali (an amazing survivor story; most risk factors present, yet peace had prevailed until breakdown in 2012. Intensive foreign aid has helped)
Morocco (highly "legitimate" monarch; more prosperous economy; safety valve of mass migration to Europe; reforms fairly successful)
Senegal/Senegambia (relatively good, stable government)
South Africa (amazing self-salvation by democratization; significant also is the fact that the international community actually cared and

helped in this case, showing what might have been in the rest of Africa)

Tanzania (highly "legitimate" government, at least till recently; now losing this, and thus increasingly a risk area)

Togo(Considerable killing; the country is too small for its rates of killing to show up as democide)

Tunisia (successful modernization under strong leaders, followed by genuine democratic revolution—arguably the greatest success story in Africa. However, ironically, democracy brought Islamist government to power, and the future is clouded)

Zambia (strong, effective government)

Zimbabwe (democide reduced by political sharing of power under pressure from the international community, especially neighboring states)

ASIA:

Bhutan (highly "legitimate" monarch)Laos (too busy with genuine wars for meltdown; now, ironically, a more serious risk, with failing development under a Communist government)

Malaysia (killings in the anti-Communist war of the 1950s and the civil unrest of the 1960s almost qualify. There was a near-genocide when Mahathir bin Muhamad seized power in 1972, but he had an amazing change of heart and became progressively more liberal, open, and tolerant, in very striking contrast to the usual progression of strongmen; this assessment based on personal research by ENA, in Malaysia in 1970–1971 and by interviewing since)

South Korea (strong, respected governing structure, and consequently a strong economy, but the extreme forbearance of the military regime of the 1950s is worth attention. This is one case where a dictatorial regime actually gave up power, and a country successfully democratized and found peace and prosperity. Clearly a model to follow)

Syria (powerful but unpopular government; stresses from mass refugee situation; in 2010 we wrote that this is a prime candidate for near future; as we now write in mid-2012, the country has declined into civil war with mass killings by the government)

Singapore (prosperous, with strong civil society)

Thailand (highly legitimate monarchy; otherwise, constant military adventuring, repression of minorities, and economic problems consequent to these make it a risk if royal power fades or the economy turns sour)

OTHER

Island countries and other micro-states do not normally have meltdowns, except for extreme cases like Haiti. Fiji has come close. Continuing "tribal" wars and violent crime in Papua-New Guinea indicate a shaky future.

Appendix II

Genocide Compared

This is a somewhat arbitrary choice, since, for example, civil war in Cote d'Ivoire and political killings in Gabon, Ecuador, and various other nations might be included.

Below, we compare democracies with dictatorships; then, industrialized countries with poorer agrarian countries.

DEMOCRACIES: GENOCIDE/POLITICIDE COMMITTED BY ELECTED GOVERNMENTS

Colombia
El Salvador
Guatemala
Haiti
Peru
Serbia
Sri Lanka

All other cases of genocide and politicide were committed in totalitarian regimes. Some of these had been democratically elected but had declared dictatorships long before genocide; Hitler's Germany is the most obvious and clear example. All the above short list could easily be moved into that camp. Guatemala and Serbia in particular had lost all claim to being working democracies by the time the murders got well under way. Sri Lanka remains a unique example of a country that went through several democratic changes of government while continuing a policy of mass murder that, if not outright genocide, was certainly very close.

Significant (as noted in text) is the fact that many genocides took place in countries that were not only autocratic but were ruled by one person, with genocides stopping short when he was deposed. Hitler's Germany is not a clear case, but Stalin's USSR and Mao's China are clear cases: dictatorship continued when Stalin and Mao died, but mass murders instantly stopped. In some other cases, such as Pinochet's Chile and Marcos' Philippines, the overthrow of a single dictator ended killings.

It is clear that Rummel was basically, though not quite entirely, correct: "Power kills, and absolute power kills absolutely" (Rummel, 1998).

INDUSTRIALIZED OR INDUSTRIALIZING NATIONS

Argentina
Bulgaria
Chile
Czechoslovakia
France
Germany (including capture and killing of Jews in occupied countries—Netherlands, Belgium, Finland, Greece, etc.—where the German regime, not those nations, was in control and carried out the genocide)
Hungary
Iran
Italy
Japan
Poland
Portugal
Rumania
Serbia
Spain
Turkey
Uruguay (brief and minor)
USSR (including subsequent killings in daughter republics)
Yugoslavia

The earlier cases involved major killing campaigns during WWII. There was substantial postwar politicide in Spain and USSR, and some in Portugal.

Consolidation of Communist regimes after WWII were involved in Bulgaria, Czechoslovakia, Hungary, Poland, Rumania, and Yugoslavia. Political killing continued in Rumania throughout the Ceaucescu dictatorship.

The cases of Argentina, Chile, and Serbia do not fit any pattern except consolidation of regime. Threats were trivial. Yet in Argentina and Serbia the killings got worse and worse until the regimes fell.

In three cases—USSR, Spain, and Chile—political mass killings kept on over a long period rather than being confined to periods of unrest or consolidation.

IMPOVERISHED AGRARIAN COUNTRIES

(at time of genocide; several, such as Mexico, China and the Koreas, have industrialized since)

Afghanistan

Appendix II

Albania
Algeria
Angola
Bangladesh
Brazil
Burundi
Cambodia
Central African Republic
Chad
China
Colombia
Congo (D. R.)
Cuba
El Salvador
Equatorial Guinea
Ethiopia
Guatemala
Guinea
Haiti
Honduras
Indonesia
Iraq
Korea, N.
Korea, S.
Laos
Liberia
Mexico
Myanmar
Nicaragua
Nigeria
Pakistan
Paraguay
Peru
Philippines
Rwanda
Sierra Leone
Sudan
Uganda
Venezuela (brief and minor)
Vietnam

Every case, with two exceptions, involved regime consolidation, or external war going badly, or civil unrest, though sometimes the civil unrest was so trivial as to be a mere excuse. Many involved two and some involved all three. The main exception is China, which indulged in a historically unique orgy of mass murder throughout Mao Zigong's entire period of rule; the killings largely stopped at his death. The other, far less salient, is Paraguay, where Alfredo Stroessner's fascist regime indulged in political and ethnic killings throughout its long tenure.

References

Abe, Ken-Ichi, and James E. Nickum (eds.). 2009. *Good Earths: Regional and Historical Insights into China's Environment*. Kyoto: Kyoto University Press; Melbourne: Trans Pacific Press.
Adler, R. N., C. E. Loyle, J. Globerman, and E. B. Larson. 2008. "Transforming Men into Killers: Attitudes Leading to Hands-on Violence during the 1994 Rwandan Genocide." *Global Public Health* 3: 291–307.
Akçam, Taner. 2012. *The Young Turks' Crime Against Humanity: The Armenian Genocide and Ethnic Cleansing in the Ottoman Empire*. Princeton: Princeton University Press.
Alexander, Marcus, and Fotini Christia. 2011. "Context Modularity of Human Altruism." *Science* 334: 1392–94.
Alinsky, Saul. 1971. *Rules for Radicals*. New York: Random House.
Allport, Gordon. 1954. *The Nature of Prejucide*. Reading, MA: Addison-Wesley.
———. 1995. "Diversity and the Family Forum." In *Make Us One: Celebrating Spiritual Unity in the Midst of Cultural Diversity*, ws. D. Baker. Boise, ID: Pacific Press Publishing Association.
Anderson, Barbara. 2005. *Reproductive Health: Women and Men's Shared Responsibility*. Sudbury, MA: Jones & Bartlett.
Anderson, Benedict. 1991. *Imagined Communities*. 2nd ed. London: Verso.
Anderson, E. N. 1992. "A Healing Place: Ethnographic Notes on a Treatment Center." *Alcoholism Treatment Quarterly* 9, 3/4: 1–21.
———. 1996. *Ecologies of the Heart*. New York: Oxford University Press.
———. 2010. *The Pursuit of Ecotopia*. Santa Barbara, CA: Praeger.
Anderson, Perry. 1974. *Lineages of the Absolutist State*. London: NLB.
Appadurai, Arjun. 2006. *Fear of Small Numbers: An Essay on the Geography of Anger*. Durham, NC: Duke University Press.
Arendt, Hannah. 1964. *Eichmann in Jerusalem: A Report on The Banality of Evil*. London: Penguin.
Arens, Jenneke. 2011. "Genocide in the Chittagong Hill Tracts, Bangladesh." In *Genocide of Indigenous Peoples, Genocide: A Critical Bibliographic Review* 8, Samuel Totten and Robert K. Hitchcock, eds. New Brunswick: Transaction Publishers. Pp. 117–42.
Arrow, Holly. 2007. "The Sharp End of Altruism." *Science* 318: 581–82.
Atran, Scott. 2003. "Genesis of Suicide Terrorism." *Science* 299: 1534–39.
———. 2010. *Talking to the Enemy: Faith, Brotherhood, and the (Un)Making of Terrorists*. New York: HarperCollins.
Atran, Scott, and Jessica Stern. 2005. "Small Groups Find Fatal Purpose Through the Web." *Nature* 437: 620.
Balakian, Grigoris. 2009. *Armenian Golgotha*. New York: Knopf.
Balakian, Peter. 2003. *The Burning Tigris: The Armenian Genocide and America's Response*. New York: HarperCollins.
———. 2009. *Black Dog of Fate: A Memoir*. New York: Basic Books.
Bandura, Albert. 1982. "Self-Efficacy Mechanism in Human Agency." *American Psychologist* 37: 122–47.
———. 1986. *Social Foundations of Thought and Action: A Social Cognitive Theory*. Englewood Cliffs, NJ: Prentice-Hall.
Barnaby, Wendy. 2009. "Do Nations Go to War over Water?" *Nature* 458: 282–83.
Baron-Cohen, Simon. 2011. *Zero Degrees of Empathy: New Theory of Human Cruelty*. London: Allen Lane.

Bartlett, Steven James. 2005. *The Pathology of Man: A Study of Human Evil*. Springfield, IL: Charles C. Thomas.
Bartov, Omer, and Phyllis Mack (eds.). 2001. *In God's Name: Genocide and Religion in the Twentieth Century*. New York: Berghahn.
Baumeister, Roy. 1997. *Evil: Inside Human Violence and Cruelty*. San Francisco: W. H. Freeman.
———. 2005. *The Cultural Animal: Human Nature, Meaning, and Social Life*. New York: Oxford University Press.
———. 2006. "Violent Pride: Do People Turn Violent Because of Self-Hate, or Self-Love?" *Scientific American Mind*, August–September, 54–59.
BBC News. 2008. "Africa 'Being Drained of Doctors.'" BBC News Online, January 10, 2008.
Beah, Ishmael. 2007. *A Long Way Gone: Memoirs of a Boy Soldier*. New York: Sarah Crichton Books.
Beck, Aaron T. 1999. *Prisoners of Hate*. New York: HarperCollins.
Beck, Aaron, John Rush, Brian Shaw, and Gary Emery. 1987. *Cognitive Therapy of Depression*. New York: Guilford Press.
Beck, Ulrich. 1992. *The Risk Society: Towards a New Modernity*. Translated by Mark Ritter. Newbury Park, CA: Sage.
Beckham, Stephen Dow. 1996. *Requiem for a People*. Original edition, 1971. Corvallis, OR: Oregon State University Press.
Bengali, Sashank. 2007. "Wars Have Cost Africa an Estimated $284 Billion Since 1990." Yahoo News Online from McClatchy News Service, October 11.
Bernhard, Helen, Urs Fischbacher, and Ernst Fehr. 2006. "Parochial Altruism in Humans." *Nature* 442: 912–15.
Bernheimer, Richard. 1952. *Wild Men in the Middle Ages*. Cambridge: Harvard University Press.
Bjerga, Alan. 2011. *Endless Appetites: How the Commodities Casino Creates Hunger and Unrest*. Hoboken, NJ: John Wiley.
Bloxham, Donald. 2005. *The Great Game of Genocide: Imperialism, Nationalism, and the Destruction of the Ottoman Armenians*. Oxford: Oxford University Press.
Boehm, Christopher. 1999. *Equality in the Forest*. Cambridge: Harvard University Press.
Borger, Julian. "Deterioration in Darfur." *Guardian*, October 1.
Bourdieu, P. 1991. *The Political Ontology of Martin Heidegger*. Translated by Peter Collier. Stanford: Stanford University Press.
Bowles, Samuel. 2006. "Group Competition, Reproductive Leveling, and the Evolution of Human Altruism." *Science* 314: 1569–72.
———. 2008. "Conflict:Altruism's Midwife." *Nature* 456: 326–27.
———. 2009. "Did Warfare among Ancestral Hunter-Gatherers Affect the Evolution of Human Social Behaviors?" *Science* 324: 1293–98.
Bowles, Samuel, and Herbert Gintis. 2011. *A Cooperative Species: Human Reciprocity and Its Evolution*. Princeton: Princeton University Press.
Boyd, Robert. 1999. *The Coming of the Spirit of Pestilence: Introduced Infectious Diseases and Population Decline Among Northwest Coast Indians, 1774–1874*. Seattle:University of Washington Press.
———. 2006. "The Puzzle of Human Sociality." *Science* 314: 1555–56.
Boyd, Robert, and Peter Richerson. 2005. *The Origin and Evolution of Cultures*. New York: Oxford University Press.
Brainard, Lael, and Derek Chollet (eds.). 2007. *Too Poor for Peace? Global Poverty, Conflict, and Security in the 21st Century*. Washington, DC: Brookings Institution Press.
Brown, Dee. 1971. *Bury My Heart at Wounded Knee: An Indian History of the American West*. New York: Holt, Rinehart and Winston.
Brown, Donald O. 2003. "Plural Societies' Prospects for Violence/Peace." Paper, American Anthropological Association, annual meeting, Chicago.
Browning, Christopher. 1995. *The Path to Genocide: Essays on Launching the Final Solution*. Cambridge: Cambridge University Press.

References

Buckley, Thomas. 2002. *Standing Ground: Yurok Indian Spirituality, 1850–1990*. Berkeley: University of California Press.
Budryté, Dovilé. 2004. "'We Call It Genocide': Soviet Deportations and Repression in the Memory of Lithuanians." In *The Genocidal Temptation: Auschwitz, Hiroshima, Rwanda, and Beyond*, ed. Robert S. Frey. Dallas: University Press of America.
Buell, Paul D. 2008. "Central Eurasia: Genocide as a Way of Life?" Manuscript.
Bunker, Stephen, and Paul Ciccantell. 2005. *Globalization and the Race for Resources*. Baltimore: Johns Hopkins University Press.
Burger, Jerry M. 2009. "Replicating Milgram: Would People Still Obey Today?" *American Psychologist* 64: 1–11.
Butler, Declan. 2007. "Darfur's Climate Roots Challenged." *Nature* 447: 1038.
Cameron, C. Daryl, and B. Keith Payne. 2011. "Escaping Affect: How Motivated Emotion Regulation Creates Insensitivity to Mass Suffering." *Journal of Personality and Social Psychology* 100: 1–16.
Čapek, Karel. 1923. *R.U.R., Rossum's Universal Robots: A Fantastic Melodrama*. Translated by Paul Selver. Garden City: Doubleday.
———. 1937. *War with the Newts*. New York: Bantam.
———. 1990. *A Karel Čapek Reader*. New York: Catbird Press.
Chalk, Frank, and Kurt Jonassohn. 1990. *The History and Sociology of Genocide: Analyses and Case Studies*. New Haven: Yale University Press.
Chang, Edward, and Min Young Kim. 2007. "Transportation of Korean Sex Slave Laborers During World War II via Kanfu Ferries." *East Asia* 24: 69–85.
Charny, Israel. 1994. *The Widening Circle of Genocide*. New Brunswick, NJ: Transaction Publishers.
Charny, Israel, and Adam Berger. 1991. *Genocide: A Critical Bibliographic Review*. New York: Facts on File.
Cheney, Dorothy, and Robert M. Seyfarth. 2007. *Baboon Metaphysics*. Chicago: University of Chicago Press.
Chirot, Daniel, and Martin E. P. Seligman. 2001. *Ethnopolitical Warfare: Causes, Consequences, and Possible Solutions*. Washington, DC: American Psychological Association.
Chirot, Daniel, and Clark McCauley. 2006. *Why Not Kill Them All? The Logic and Prevention of Mass Political Murder*. Princeton: Princeton University Press.
Choi, Jung-Kyoo, and Samuel Bowles. 2007. "The Coevolution of Parochial Altruism and War." *Science* 318: 636–40.
Clarke, Duncan. 2009. *Crude Continent: The Struggle for Africa's Oil*. New York: Profile Books.
Cockburn, Andrew, with photographs by Jodi Cobb. 2003. "21st Century Slaves." *National Geographic*, September. Pp. 2–25.
Colarusso, John. 2002. *Nart Sagas of the Caucasus*. Princeton: Princeton University Press.
Colby, Ann, and William Damon. 1992. *Some Do Care: Contemporary Lives of Moral Commitment*. New York: Free Press.
Collier, Paul. 2003. *Breaking the Conflict Trap: Civil War and Development Policy*. New York: World Bank.
———. 2007. *The Bottom Billion*. New York: Oxford University Press.
———. 2010. *The Plundered Planet: Why We Must—and How We Can—Manage Nature for Global Prosperity*. Oxford: Oxford University Press.
Collier, Paul, and Ian Bannon (eds.). 2003. *Natural Resources and Violent Conflict: Options and Actions*. New York: World Bank.
Collier, Paul, and Nicholas Sambanis (eds.). 2005. *Understanding Civil War: Evidence and Analysis*. Vol. 1 Africa. New York: World Bank.
Collins, Randall. 2008. *Violence: A Micro-Sociological Theory*. Princeton: Princeton University Press.
Conrad, Joseph. 1995. "Heart of Darkness." In *Youth/Heart of Darkness/The End of the Tether*. (Originally published 1899.) London: Penguin Books, Ltd. Pp. 45–148.

Cozzens, Peter. 2002. *Eyewitnesses to the Indian Wars, 1865–1890*. Vol. 2: *The Wars for the Pacific Northwest*. Mechanicsburg, PA: Stackpole Books.

Crisp, Richard J., and Rhiannon N. Turner. 2009. "Can Imagined Interactions Produce Positive Perceptions? Reducing Prejudice through Simulated Social Contact." *American Psychologist* 64: 231–40.

Croll, Elisabeth. 2000. *Endangered Daughters*. London: Routledge.

Curry, Oliver. 2006. "Review of *The Altruism Equation* by Lee Aslan Dugatkin." *Nature* 444: 683.

Dallaire, Roméo. 2003. *Shake Hands with the Devil*. Toronto: Random House Canada.

Damasio, Antonio. 1994. *Descartes' Error: Emotion, Reason, and the Human Brain*. New York: G. P. Putnam's Sons.

Davenport, Christian, and Allan Stam. 2009. "What Really Happened in Rwanda?" *Miller-McCune*, November–December, pp. 60–69.

Davis, David Brion. 1966. *The Problem of Slavery in Western Culture*. Ithaca: Cornell University Press. 2 vols.

———. 1971. "New Sidelights on Early Antislavery Radicalism." *William and Mary Quarterly* 28: 585–94.

Dawes, James. 2007. *That the World May Know: Bearing Witness to Atrocity*. Cambridge: Harvard University Press.

Dawkins, Richard. 2006. *The God Delusion*. Boston: Houghton Mifflin.

Dawson, John. 2004. *Washout: On the Academic Response to the Fabrication of Aboriginal History*. Sydney: Macleay.

De Dreu, Carsten K. W., Lindred L. Greer, Michel J. J. Handgraaf, Shaul Shalvi, Gerben A. Van Kleef, Matthijs Baas, Femke S. Ten Velden, Eric Van Dijk, and Sander W. W. Feith. 2010. "The Neuropeptide Oxytocin Regulates Parochial Altruism in Intergroup Conflict among Humans." *Science* 328: 1408–11.

De Ruiter, Jan, Gavin Weeston, and Stephen M. Lyon. 2011. "Dunbar's Number: Group Size and Brain Physiology in Humans Reexamined." *American Anthropologist* 113: 557–68.

De Waal, Frans. 1996. *Good Natured: The Origins of Right and Wrong in Humans and Other Animals*. Cambridge: Harvard University Press..

De Waal, Frans. 2005. *Our Inner Ape*. New York: Riverhead Books (Penguin Group).

Demick, Barbara. 2011. "Son Inherits Troubled Nation." *Los Angeles Times*, December 20, pp. A1, A7.

Dentan, Robert K. 1968. *The Semai, a Nonviolent People of Malaysia*. New York: Holt, Rinehart and Winston.

———. 2008. *Overwhelming Terror: Love, Fear, Peace, and Violence among Semai of Malaysia*. Lanham, MD: Rowman & Littlefield.

Deutsch, Anthony. 2008. "Survivors Detail Suharto-Era Massacres." Associated Press, retrieved from Yahoo! News website, January 27.

Diamond, Jared. 2005. *Collapse: How Societies Choose to Fail or Succeed*. New York: Viking.

Dibkowski, Michael N., and Isidor Wellimann. 1998. *The Coming Age of Scarcity: Preventing Mass Death in the Twenty-First Century*. Syracuse: Syracuse University Press.

Dichter, Thomas W. 2003. *Despite Good Intentions: Why Development Assistance to the Third World Has Failed*. Amherst: University of Massachusetts Press.

Dikötter, Frank. 2010. *Mao's Great Famine: The History of China's Most Devastating Catastrophe, 1958–1962*. New York: Walker and Co.

Dillon, Richard F. 1973. *Burnt-out Fires*. Englewood Cliffs, NJ: Prentice-Hall.

Dobyns, Henry. 1983. *Their Number Became Thinned: Native Population Dynamics in Eastern North America*. Knoxville: University of Tennessee Press.

Douglas, Mary, and Aaron Wildavsky. 1982. *Risk and Culture: An Essay on the Selection of Technical and Environmental Dangers*. Berkeley: University of California Press.

Dovidio, John, Peter S. Glick, and Laurie Rudman. 2005. *On the Nature of Prejudice: Fifty Years after Allport*. Maldon, MA: Blackwell.

Doyle, Rodger. 2006. "Modern Slavery." *Scientific American*, January, p. 30.

Dunbar, Robin I. M. 1993. "Coevolution of Neocortical Size, Group Size and Language in Humans." *Behavioral and Brain Sciences* 16: 681–735.
———. 2004. *Grooming, Gossip, and the Evolution of Language*. New York: Gardner Books.
Easterly, William. 2006. *The White Man's Burden: Why the West's Efforts to Aid the Rest Have Done So Much Ill and So Little Good*. New York: Penguin Press.
Ehrenreich, Robert M., and Tim Cole. 2005. "The Perpetrator-Bystander-Victim Constellation: Rethinking Genocidal Relationships." *Human Organization* 64: 213–24.
Eidelson, Roy J., and Judy I. Eidelson. 2003. "Dangerous Ideas: Five Beliefs That Propel Groups Toward Conflict." *American Psychologist* 58: 182–92.
Elder, Bruce. 2003. *Blood on the Wattle: Massacres and Maltreatment of Aboriginal Australians Since 1788*. 3rd ed. Sydney: New Holland.
Ellerman, David. 2005. *Helping People Help Themselves: From the World Bank to an Alternative Philosophy of Development Assistance*. Ann Arbor: University of Michigan Press.
Einstein, Albert. In Albert Einstein Quotes retrieved from www.famousquotes/andauthors.com/authors/albert_einstein_quotes.html, August 14, 2010.
Elias, Norbert. 2000. *The Civilizing Process: Sociogenetic and Psychogenetic Investigations*. Revised edition (German orig. 1939). Cambridge: Cambridge University Press.
Epley, Nicholas, Adam Waytz, and John T. Cacioppo. 2007. "On Seeing Human: A Three-factor Model of Anthropomorphism." *Psychological Review* 114: 864–86.
Escobar, Arturo. 2008. *Territories of Difference: Place, Movements, Life, Redes*. Durham: Duke University Press.
Etcheson, Craig. 2005. *After the Killing Fields: Lessons from the Cambodian Genocide*. Westport, CT: Praeger.
Evans, Gareth. 2005. "The Dogs That Never Barked." *Los Angeles Times*, November 22, p. B11.
———. 2008. *The Responsibility to Protect*. Washington, DC: Brookings Institution.
Farley, Maggie. 2005. "U. N. Report Says Darfur Violence Is Not Genocide." *Los Angeles Times*, January 29, A3.
Farmer, Paul. 2004. *Pathologies of Power: Health, Human Rights, and the New War on the Poor*. Berkeley: University of California Press.
Faroqhi, Suraiya. 2006. *The Cambridge History of Turkey*. Cambridge: Cambridge University Press.
Fehr, Ernst, Helen Bernhard, and Bettina Rockenbach. 2008. "Egalitarianism in Young Children." *Nature* 454: 1079–83.
Feldman, Allen. 1991. *Formations of Violence: The Narrative of the Body and Political Terror in Northern Ireland*. Chicago: University of Chicago Press.
Ferguson, W. Brian. 2003. "The Birth of War." *Natural History*, July–August, 28–35.
Ferguson, Niall. 2005. "Giving Peace a Chance." *Los Angeles Times*, September 19, p. B11.
———. 2006. "The Crash of Civilizations." *Los Angeles Times*, February 27, p. B6.
———. 2007. "The Reality of Civil War." *Time*, February 5, p. 60.
Firth, Raymond. 1961. *History and Traditions of Tikopia*. Wellington, NZ: Polynesian Society.
Fleisher, K. 2004. *The Bear River Massacre and the Making of History*. Albany, NY: SUNY Press.
Flinn, Mark V. 2009. "Why Words Can Hurt Us: Social Relationships, Stress, and Health." In *Evolutionary Medicine and Health: New Perspectives*, eds. Wenda Trevia-than, Eric O. Smith, and James J. McKenna. New York: Oxford University Press. Pp. 242–58.
Forche, Carolyn. 1993. *Against Forgetting: Twentieth Century Poetry of Witness*. New York: W. W. Norton.
Foucault, Michel. 2001. *Fearless Speech*. Edited by Joseph Pearson. Los Angeles: Semiotext(e).

Franks, David D. 2006. "The Neuroscience of Emotions." In *Handbook of the Sociology of Emotions*, eds. Jan E. Stets and Jonathan Turner. New York: Springer. Pp. 38–62.
Friedman, Benjamin. 2005. *The Moral Consequences of Economic Growth*. New York: Knopf.
Fromkin, David. 2009. *A Peace to End All Peace: The Fall of the Ottoman Empire and the Creation of the Modern Middle East*. 2nd edition. New York: Holt.
Frye, Barbara (Barbara A. Anderson). 1989. *Process of Health Care Decision Making among Khmer Immigrants*. PhD dissertation, School of Public Health, Loma Linda University.
Fu, Bojie. 2008. "Blue Skies for China." *Science* 321: 611.
Gallardo, Eduardo. 2006. "In Letter, Pinochet Says Rights Abuses Inevitable." *Seattle Times* (from Associated Press), Monday, December 25, p. A16.
Geen, Russell G., and Edward Donnerstein. 1998. *Human Aggression: Theories, Research, and Implications for Social Policy*. San Diego: Academic Press.
Gellately, Robert, and Ben Kiernan. 2003. *The Specter of Genocide: Mass Murder in Historical Perspective*. Cambridge: Cambridge University Press.
Gibbard, Allan. 1992. *Wise Choices, Apt Feelings: A Theory of Normative Judgment*. New York: Clarendon Press.
Gibbon, Edward. 1995 [1776–1788]. *The Decline and Fall of the Roman Empire*. New York: Penguin.
Gillette, Maris Boyd. 2000. *Between Mecca and Beijing: Modernization and Consumption among Urban Chinese Muslims*. Stanford: Stanford University Press.
———. 2008. "Violence, the State, and a Chinese Muslim Ritual Remembrance." *Journal of Asian Studies* 67: 1011–37.
Gladwell, Malcolm. 2002. *The Tipping Point: How Little Things Can Make a Big Difference*. Boston: Back Bay Books.
Glasser, William. 1981. *Stations of the Mind: New Directions for Reality Therapy*. New York: Harper & Row.
———. 1985. *Control Theory: A New Explanation of How We Control Our Lives*. New York: HarperCollins.
Goldhagen, Daniel. 1996. *Hitler's Willing Executioners: Ordinary Germans and the Holocaust*. New York: Random House.
Goodale, Mark. 2006. "Toward a Critical Anthropology of Human Rights." *Current Anthropology* 47: 485–511.
Gourevitch, Philip. 1998. *We Wish to Inform You That Tomorrow We Will Be Killed Together with Our Families*. New York: Farrar, Straus & Giroux.
Gross, John. 1983. *The Oxford Book of Aphorisms*. Oxford: Oxford University Press.
Guilaine, Jean, and Jean Zammit. 2001. *The Origins of War: Violence in Prehistory*. Oxford: Blackwell.
Gusterson, Hugh. 2007. "Anthropology and Militarism." *Annual Review of Anthropology* 36: 155–76.
Gwynne, S. C. 2010. *Empire of the Summer Moon*. New York: Scribner.
Hagan, John, and Alberto Palloni. 2006. "Death in Darfur." *Science* 313: 1578.
Haidt, Jonathan. 2007. "The New Synthesis in Moral Psychology." *Science* 36: 998–1002.
Hall, Thomas, and Peter Turchin. 2007. "Lessons from Population Ecology for World-Systems Analyses of Long-Distance Synchrony." In *The World System and the Earth System: Global Socioenvironmental Change and Sustainability Since the Neolithic*, eds. Alf Hornborg and Carole Crumley. Walnut Creek, CA: Left Coast Press. Pp. 174–90.
Hamburg, David. 2003. *No More Killing Fields: Preventing Deadly Conflict*. Lanham, MD: Rowman & Littlefield.
———. 2010. *Preventing Genocide: Practical Steps toward Early Detection and Effective Action*. New York: Paradigm.
Hamilton, Alexander, James Madison, and John Jay. 1961. *The Federalist Papers*. Garden City, NY: Doubleday Anchor.
Hancock, Graham. 1991. *Lords of Poverty*. London: MacMillan.

Harff, Barbara. 2005. "Assessing Risks of Genocide and Politicide." In *Peace and Conflict 2005: A Global Survey of Armed Conflicts, Self-Determination Movements, and Democracy*, eds. M. G. Marshall and T. R. Gurr. College Park, MD: Center for International Development and Conflict Management, University of Maryland.

———. 2008. "Development and Inmplementation of Genocide Early Warning Systems: Conceptual and Practical Issues." In *The Prevention and Intervention of Genocide*, ed. Samuel Totten. New Brunswick, NJ: Transaction Publishers. Pp. 63–82.

Harper, Janice. 2002. *Endangered Species*. Durham, NC: Carolina Academic Press.

Harvey, Graham. 2006. *Animism: Respecting the Living World*. New York: Columbia University Press.

Hatzfeld, Jean. 2005. *Machete Season: The Killers in Rwanda Speak*. Translated from French by Linda Coverdale. New York: Farrar, Straus and Giroux.

Heather, Peter. 2006. *The Fall of the Roman Empire: A New History of Rome and the Barbarians*. London: Oxford University Press.

Heidegger, Martin. 1962. *Being and Time*. Translated from German by John Macquarrie and Edward Robinson. New York: Harper and Row.

Heidenrich, John G. 2001. *How to Prevent Genocide: A Guide for Policymakers, Scholars, and the Concerned Citizen*. Westport, CT: Praeger.

Heizer, Robert, and Theodora Kroeber (eds.).1979. *Ishi, the Last Yahi: A Documentary History*. Berkeley: University of California Press.

Hemming, John. 1978. *Red Gold: The Conquest of the Brazilian Indians*. London: MacMillan.

Henry, P. J. 2009. "Low-status Compensation: A Theory for Understanding the Role of Status in Cultures of Honor." *Journal of Personality and Social Psychology* 97: 451–66.

Hilberg, Raul. 1992. *Perpetrators, Victims, Bystanders: The Jewish Catastrophe 1933–1945*. New York: Harper.

Hinde, Robert. 2007. *Bending the Rules: Morality in the Modern World from Relationships to Politics and War*. Oxford: Oxford University Press.

Hinton, Alexander Laban. 2002. *Annihilating Difference: The Anthropology of Genocide*. Berkeley: University of California.

———. 2005. *Why Did They Kill? Cambodia in the Shadow of Genocide*. Berkeley: University of California Press.

——— (ed). 2002. *Genocide: An Anthropological Reader*. Oxford: Blackwell.

Hironaka, Ann. 2005. *Neverending Wars: The International Community, Weak States, and the Perpetuation of Civil War*. Cambridge: Harvard University Press.

Hirsch, Herbert. 2002. *Anti-Genocide: Building an American Movement to Prevent Genocide*. Westport, CT: Praeger.

Hitchcock, Robert K., and Wayne A. Babchuk. 2011. "Genocide of Khoekhoe and San Peoples of Southern Africa." In *Genocide of Indigenous Peoples, Genocide: A Critical Bibliographic Review*, vol. 8, eds. Samuel Totten and Robert K. Hitchcock. New Brunswick: Transaction Publishers. Pp. 143–71.

Hitchcock, Robert K., Charles Flowerday, and Thomas E. Koperski. 2011. "The Ache of Paraguay and other 'Isolated' Latin American Indigenous Peoples: Genocide or Ethnocide?" In *Genocide of Indigenous Peoples, Genocide: A Critical Bibliographic Review*, vol. 8, eds. Samuel Totten and Robert K. Hitchcock. New Brunswick: Transaction Publishers. Pp. 173–94.

Hitler, Adolf. 1940. *Mein Kampf*. München: F. Eher.

Ho, Arnold K., Jim Sidanius, Daniel T. Levin, Mahzarin R. Banaji. 2011. "Evidence for Hypdescent and Racial Hierarchy in the Categorization and Perception of Biracial Individuals." *Journal of Personality and Social Psychology* 100: 492–505.

Hobbes, Thomas. 1950. *Leviathan*. New York: E. P. Dutton.(Orig. 1651.)

Hoffer, Eric. 1963. *The True Believer: Thoughts on the Nature of Mass Movements*. New York: Time Inc.

Hoffman, Danny. 2011. *The War Machine: Young Men and Violence in Sierra Leone and Liberia*. Durham, NC: Duke University Press.

Hoggan, James, with Richard Littlemore. 2009. *Climate Cover-Up: The Crusade to Deny Global Warming*. Vancouver: Greystone Books.
Homer-Dixon, Thomas F. 1999. *Environment, Scarcity, and Violence*. Princeton: Princeton University Press.
Hume, David. 1969. *A Treatise of Human Nature*. Original edition 1739–1740. New York: Penguin.
Humphreys, Macartan, Jeffrey Sachs, and Joseph Stiglitz (eds.). 2007. *Escaping the Resource Curse*. New York: Columbia University Press.
Huntington, Samuel. 1996. *The Clash of Civilizations and the Remaking of World Order*. NewYork: Simon & Schuster.
Jackson, Lynne M. 2011. *The Psychology of Prejudice: From Attitudes to Social Action*. Washington, DC: American Psychological Association.
Jonassohn, Kurt, and Karin Solveig Björnson. 1998. *Genocide and Gross Human Rights Violations in Comparative Perspective*. New Brunswick, NJ: Transaction Publishers.
Jones, Adam (ed.). 2004. *Genocide, War Crimes and the West*. London: Zed.
Jones, Dan. 2008. "Killer Instinct." *Nature* 451: 512–15.
Jost, John T. 2006. "The End of the End of Ideology." *American Psychologist* 61: 651–70.
Jost, John T., Jack Glaser, Arie W. Kuglanski, and Frank Sulloway. 2003. "Political Conservatism as Motivated Social Cognition." *Psychological Bulletin* 129: 339–75.
Juergensmeyer, Mark. 2003. *Terror in the Mind of God: The Global Rise of Religious Violence*. 3rd edition. Berkeley: University of California Press.
Juhasz, Antonia. 2008. *The Tyranny of Oil: The World's Most Powerful Industry—and What We Must Do to Stop It*. New York: William Morrow (HarperCollins).
Kahin, George McT. 1970. *Nationalism and Revolution in Indonesia*. Ithaca, NY: Cornell University Press.
Kaiser, Cheryl, and Jennifer Pratt-Hyatt. 2009. "Distributing Prejudice Unequally: Do Whites Direct Their Prejudice toward Strongly Identified Minorities?" *Journal of Personality and Social Psychology* 96: 432–45.
Keeley, Lawrence. 1996. *War before Civilization*. New York: Oxford University Press.
Kelly, Raymond. 2000. *Warless Societies and the Origin of War*. Ann Arbor: University of Michigan.
Kemper, Theodore D. 2006. "Power and Status and the Power-Status Theory of Emotions." In *Handbook of the Sociology of Emotions*, eds. Jan E. Stets and Jonathan H. Turner. New York: Springer. Pp. 87–113.
Khan, Shahryar. 2000. *The Shallow Graves of Rwanda*. New York: St. Martin's Press.
Kidder, Tracy. 2009. *Strength in What Remains*. New York: Random House.
Kiernan, Ben. 2004. *How Pol Pot Came to Power: Colonialism, Nationalism and Communism in Cambodia*. 2nd edition. New Haven: Yale University Press.
———. 2007. *Blood and Soil: A World History of Genocide and Extermination from Sparta to Darfur*. New Haven: Yale University Press.
———. 2008. *Genocide and Resistance in Southeast Asia: Documentation, Denial and Justice in Cambodia and East Timor*. New Brunswick, NJ: Transaction Publishers.
Kirsch, Stuart. 2006. *Reverse Anthropology: Indigenous Analysis of Social and Environmental Relations in New Guinea*. Stanford: Stanford University Press.
Kissi, E. 2006. *Revolution and Genocide in Ethiopia and Cambodia*. Lanham, MD: Rowman & Littlefield.
Koenig, Walter D., and Ronald L. Mumme. 1987. *Population Ecology of the Cooperatively Breeding Acorn Woodpecker*. Princeton: Princeton University Press, Monographs in Population Biology 24.
Köhler, Joachim. 1998. *Nietzsche and Wagner: A Lesson in Subjugation*. Translated from German by Ronald Taylor. New Haven: Yale University Press.
Kolin, Andrew. 2008. *State Structure and Genocide*. New York: University Press of America.
Kuper, Leo. 1983. *Genocide: Its Political Use in the Twentieth Century*. New Haven: Yale University Press.
———. 1985. *The Prevention of Genocide*. New Haven: Yale University Press.

References

Kyokai, B. 1966. *The Teaching of Buddha*. Tokyo, Japan: Kosaido Printing Co., Ltd.
Langenbacher, Eric. 2009. "Ethical Cleansing? The Expulsion of Germans from Central and Eastern Europe." In *Genocides by the Oppressed: Subaltern Genocide in Theory and Practice*, eds. Nicholas Robins and Adam Jones. Bloomington: Indiana University Press. Pp. 58–83.
Langer, Ellen. 1983. *The Psychology of Control*. Beverly Hills: Sage.
Las Casas, Bartolomé de. 1992. *A Short Account of the Destruction of the Indies*. Edited and translated from Spanish by Nigel Griffin. London: Penguin.
LeBlanc, Stephen, and Katherine E. Register. 2002. *Constant Battles: The Myth of the Peaceful, Noble Savage*. New York: St. Martin's Griffin.
LeDoux, Joseph. 1996. *The Emotional Brain: The Mysterious Underpinnings of Emotional Life*. New York: Simon & Schuster.
———. 2002. *Synaptic Self: How Our Brains Become Who We Are*. New York: Viking Penguin.
Leland, Kevin N., Kim Sterelny, John Odling-Smee, William Hoppitt, and Tobias Uller. 2011. "Cause and Effect in Biology Revisited: Is Mayr's Proximate-Ultimate Dichotomy Still Useful?" *Science* 334: 1512–16.
Lenkersdorf, Carlos. 1996. *Los hombres verdaderos: Voces y testimonios tojolabales*. Mexico: Siglo veintiuno editores.
Levene, Mark. 2005. *Genocide in the Age of the Nation State*. Vol. 2: *The Meaning of Genocide*. London: I. B. Tauris.
Levenstein, Aaron. 1983. *Escape to Freedom: The Story of the International Rescue Committee*. Westport, CT: Greenwood.
Lewis, Bernard. 1961. *The Emergence of Modern Turkey*. Oxford: Oxford University Press.
Lewis, Mark Edward. 2009. *China's Cosmopolitan Empire: The Tang Dynasty*. Cambridge: Harvard University Press.
Lewis, Sinclair. 1935. *It Can't Happen Here*. Garden City, NY: Doubleday Doran.
Lewy, Gunter. 2005. *The Armenian Massacres in Ottoman Turkey: A Disputed Genocide*. Salt Lake City: University of Utah Press.
Leys, Simon (Pierre Ryckmans). 1985. *The Burning Forest*. New York: New Republic Books.
Lim, May, Richard Metzler, and Yaneer Bar-Yam. 2007. "Global Pattern Formation and Ethnic/Cultural Violence." *Science* 317: 1540–44.
Lindner, Evelin. 2009. "Genocide, Humiliation, and Inferiority: An Interdisciplinary Perspective." In *Genocides by the Oppressed: Subaltern Genocide in Theory and Practice*, eds. Nicholas Robins and Adam Jones. Bloomington: Indiana University Press. Pp. 138–58.
Lowenstein, George, Elke U. Weber, Christopher K. Hsee, and Ned Welch. 2000. "Risk as Feelings." *Psychological Bulletin* 127: 267–86.
Mamdani, Mamood. 2001. *When Victims Become Killers: Colonialism, Nationalism, and the Genocide in Rwanda*. Princeton: Princeton University Press.
Manne, Robert (ed.). 2003. *Whitewash: On Keith Wildschuttle's Fabrication of Australian History*. Melbourne: Schwartz.
Marcus, George E. 2002. *The Sentimental Citizen: Emotion in Democratic Politics*. University Park, PA: Pennsylvania State University Press.
Marquand, Robert. 2007. "When Can It Be Called Genocide?" *Seattle Times* (from *Christian Science Monitor*), April 30, p. A3.
Marzluff, John M., and Russell P. Balda. 1992. *The Pinyon Jay: Behavioral Ecology of a Colonial and Cooperative Corvid*. London: T. and A. D. Poyser.
McCarthy, Justin, Esat Arslan, Cemalettin Taşkıran, and Ömer Turan. 2006. *The Armenian Rebellion at Van*. Salt Lake City: University of Utah Press.
McNeill, David. 2007. "Japan's History War." *Chronicle of Higher Education*, April 27, pp. 53–56.
Meacham, A. W. 1875. *Wigwam and Warpath*. Boston: John Dale.
Mejia, Robin. 2006. "Grim Statistics." *Science* 313: 288–90.

Melvern, Linda. 2006. *Conspiracy to Murder: The Rwanda Genocide*. London: Verso.
Mencius. 1970. *Mencius*. Translated from Chinese by D. C. Lau. London: Penguin.
Mendes Pinto, Fernao. 1990. *The Travels of Mendes Pinto*. Translated from Portuguese by Rebecca Catz. Chicago: University of Chicago Press.
Midlarsky, Manus. 2005. *The Killing Trap: Genocide in the Twentieth Century*. Cambridge: Cambridge University Press.
Miller, Virginia P. 1979. *Ukomno'm: The Yuki Indians of Northern California*. Socorro, NM: Ballena Press.
Mills, Nicolaus, and Kira Brunner (eds.). 2002. *The New Killing Fields: Massacre and the Politics of Intervention*. New York: Basic Books.
Mintz, Sidney. 1985. *Sweetness and Power*. New York: Penguin.
Mobbs, Dean, Pedrag Petrovic, Jennifer Marchant, Demis Hassabis, Nikolaus Weiskopf, Ben Seymour, Raymond Dolan, and Christopher Frith. 2007. "When Fear Is Near: Threat Imminence Elicits Prefrontal-Periaqueductal Gray Shifts in Humans." *Science* 317: 1079–83.
Monroe, K. 2004. *The Hand of Compassion: Portraits of Moral Choice during the Holocaust*. Princeton: Princeton University Press.
Mooney, James. 1991. *The Ghost-Dance Religion and the Sioux Outbreak of 1890*. Lincoln:University of Nebraska Press. (Orig. in Bureau of American Ethnology, Annual Report 14 for 1892–1893, published in 1896.)
Moses, A. Dirk (ed.). 2004. *Genocide and Settler Society: Frontier Violence and Stolen Indigenous Children in Australian History*. New York: Berghahn.
Mote, Frederick. 1999. *Imperial China 900–1800*. Cambridge: Harvard University Press.
Mutua, Makau. 2002. *Human Rights: A Political and Cultural Critique*. Philadelphia: University of Pennsylvania Press.
Nagengast, Carole. 1994. "Violence, Terror, and the Crisis of the State." *Annual Review of Anthropology* 23: 109–36.
Naimark, Norman. 2001. *Fires of Hatred: Ethnic Cleansing in Twentieth-Century Europe*. Cambridge: Harvard University Press.
Neumann, Franz. 1943. *Behemoth: The Structure and Practice of National Socialism*. London: Victor Gollancz.
———. 1957. *The Democratic and the Authoritarian State*. Glencoe, IL: Free Press of Glencoe.
Nordstrom, Carolyn. 1997. *A Different Kind of War Story*. Philadelphia: University of Pennsylvania Press.
———. 1998. "Deadly Myths of Aggression." *Aggressive Behavior* 24: 147–59.
———. 2004. *Shadows of War: Violence, Power, and International Profiteering in the Twenty-First Century*. Berkeley: University of California Press.
Nowak, Martin A. 2006. "Five Rules for the Evolution of Cooperation." *Science* 314: 1560–63.
Oliner, Samuel P., and Pearl M. Oliner. 1988. *The Altruistic Personality: Rescuers of Jews in Nazi Europe*. New York: Free Press.
Olson, Mancur. 1965. *A Theory of Collective Action*. Cambridge: Harvard University Press.
Oreskes, Naomi, and Eik M. Conway. 2010. *Merchants of Doubt: How a Handful of Scientists Obscured the Truth on Issues from Tobacco Smoke to Global Warming*. New York: Bloomsbury Press.
Orwell, George. 1945. *Animal Farm*. London: Secker and Warburg.
———. 1949. *1984: A Novel*. New York: New American Library.
O'Shea, Stephen. 2002. *The Perfect Heresy: The Revolutionary Life and Death of the Medieval Cathars*. New York: Walker and Co.
Osman, Ysa. 2006. *The Cham Rebellion: Survivors' Stories from the Villages*. Phnom Penh: Documentation Center of Cambodia. Documentation Series no. 9.
Otterbein, Keith. 2003. "Does Territorial Expansion Lead to the State? I Say No!" Paper, American Anthropological Association, annual meeting, Chicago, IL.
———. 2004. *How War Began*. College Station, TX: Texas A&M Press.

———. 2011. "Warfare and Its Relationship to the Origins of Agriculture." *Current Anthropology* 52: 267–68.
Paddock, Richard C. 2003. "An Awful Truth Sinks In." *Los Angeles Times*, December 5, A1–A12–13.
Parks, Craig D., and Asako B. Stone. 2010. "The Desire to Expel Unselfish Members from the Group." *Journal of Personality and Social Psychology* 99: 303–10.
Peterson, Christopher, Steven Maier, and Martin E. P. Seligman. 1993. *Learned Helplessness*. New York: Oxford University Press.
Pilkington, Doris, and Nugi Garimara. 1996. *Follow the Rabbit Proof Fence*. Revised edition. Brisbane: University of Queensland Press.
Pinker, Stephen. 2011. *The Better Angels of Our Nature: Why Violence Has Declined*. New York: Viking.
Pinto, Isabel R., José M. Marques, John M. Levine, and Dominic Abrams. 2010. "Membership Status and Subjective Group Dynamics: Who Triggers the Black Sheep Effect?" *Journal of Personality and Social Psychology* 99: 107–19.
Polgreen, Lydia. 2007. "How Much Is Ecology to Blame for Darfur Crisis?" *Seattle Times* (from *The New York Times*), July 22, p. A17.
Pottier, Johan. 2002. *Re-Imaging Rwanda: Conflict, Survival and Disinformation in the Late Twentieth Century*. Cambridge: Cambridge University Press.
Potts, Rick. 1996. *Humanity's Descent*. New York: William Morrow and Co.
Power, Samantha. 2003. *"A Problem from Hell": America and the Age of Genocide*. New York: Perennial.
Prunier, Gérard. 1995. *The Rwanda Crisis: History of a Genocide*. London: Hurst.
———. 2007. *Darfur: The Ambiguous Genocide*. 2nd edition. Ithaca: Cornell University Press.
———. 2008. *Darfur: A 21st Century Genocide*. Ithaca: Cornell University Press.
Putnam, Robert. 2001. *Bowling Alone: The Collapse and Revival of American Community*. New York: Simon and Schuster.
Pynchon, Thomas. 1973. *Gravity's Rainbow*. New York: Viking.
Qiu, Jane. 2011a. "China Faces up to 'Terrible' State of Its Ecosystems." *Nature* 471: 19.
———. 2011b. "China to Spend Billions Cleaning Up Groundwater." *Science* 334: 745.
Raffles, Hugh. 2010. "Jews." In *Insectopedia*, by Hugh Raffles. New York: Vintage. Pp. 141–61.
Rawls, John. 1971. *A Theory of Justice*. Cambridge: Harvard University Press.
Rejali, Darius. 2008. "A Painful History." *Chronicle of Higher Education Review*, January 25, pp. B6–B9.
Rensink, Brendan. 2011. "Genocide of Native Americans: Historical Facts and Historiographic Debates." In *Genocide of Indigenous Peoples, Genocide: A Critical Bibliographic Review*, vol. 8, eds. Samuel Totten and Robert K. Hitchcock. New Brunswick: Transaction Publishers. Pp. 15–36.
Richerson, Peter, and Robert Boyd. 2005. *Not By Genes Alone: How Culture Transformed Human Evolution*. Chicago: University of Chicago Press.
Riddle, Jeff. 1974. *The Indian History of the Modoc War*. Eugene, OR: Urion.
Rilke, Rainer Maria. 1957. "The Panther." In *Rilke: Selected Poems*, edited and translated by C. F. MacIntyre. Berkeley: University of California Press.
Rittner, Carol, John K. Roth, and James M. Smith (eds.). 2002. *Will Genocide Ever End?* St. Paul, MN: Aegis in Association w Paragon House.
Robarchek, Clayton. 1977. "Frustration, Aggression, and the Nonviolent Semai." *American Ethnologist* 6: 555–67.
Robarchek, Clayton A. 1989a. "Hobbesian and Rousseauan Images of Man: Autonomy and Individualism in a Peaceful Society." In *Societies at Peace*, eds. Signe Howell and Roy Willis. New York: Routledge. Pp. 31–44.
———. 1989b. "Primitive War and the Ratomorphic Image of Mankind." *American Anthropologist* 91: 903–20.
Robarchek, Clayton, and Carole Robarchek. 1998. *Waorani: The Contexts of Violence and War*. Fort Worth, TX: Harcourt Brace.

Robins, Nicholas A., and Adam Jones (eds). 2009. *Genocides by the Oppressed: Subaltern Genocide in Theory and Practice.* Bloomington: Indiana University Press.

Roscoe, Paul. 2007. "Intelligence, Coalitional Killing, and the Antecedents of War." *American Anthropologist* 109: 485–95.

Rosen, David M. 2007. "Child Soldiers, International Humanitarian Law, and the Globalization of Childhood." *American Anthropologist* 109: 296–306.

Rosenbaum, Alan. 2000. *Is the Holocaust Unique? Perspectives on Comparative Genocide.* Boulder: Westview.

Roth, Anthony, and Peter Fonagy. 2005. *What Works for Whom? A Critical Review of Psychotherapy Research.* 2nd ed. New York: Guilford.

Roth, John K. (ed). 2005. *Genocide and Human Rights: A Philosophical Guide.* New York: Palgrave MacMillan.

Roux-Perino, Judith, and Anne Brenon. 2006. *The Cathars.* 2nd ed. Vic-en-Bigorre, France: MSM.

Rummel, Rudolph. 1994. *Death by Government.* New Brunswick, NJ: Transaction Books.

———. 1998. *Statistics of Democide.* Munchen, Germany: LIT.

Russell, Frank. 1908. *The Pima Indians.* Washington, DC: United States Government, Bureau of American Ethnology, Annual Report XXVI: 3–390.

Sahlins, Marshall. 1962. *Stone Age Economics.* Chicago: Aldine.

Santayana, George. 1905. *Reason in Common Sense.* New York: Charles Scribner's Sons.

Satir, Virginia. 1983. *Conjoint Family Therapy.* 3rd ed. Palo Alto, CA: Science and Behavior Books.

Schaller, Dominik J. 2011. "Genocide in Colonial South-West Africa: The German War against the Herero and Nama, 1904–1907." In *Genocide of Indigenous Peoples, Genocide: A Critical Bibliographic Review,* vol. 8, eds. Samuel Totten and Robert K. Hitchcock. New Brunswick: Transaction Publishers. Pp. 37–60.

Schulz, Richard. 1976. "Some Life and Death Consequences of Perceived Control." In *Cognition and Social Behavior,* eds. John S. Carroll and John W. Payne. New York: Academic Press. Pp. 135–53.

Schwartz, E. A. 1997. *The Rogue River Indian War and Its Aftermath, 1850–1980.* Norman: University of Oklahoma Press.

Scott, James. 1976. *The Moral Economy of the Peasant: Rebellion and Subsistence in Southeast Asia.* New Haven: Yale University Press.

———. 1985. *Weapons of the Weak.* New Haven: Yale University Press.

Scudder, Thayer. 2005. *The Future of Large Dams.* London: Earthscan.

Semelis, Jacques. 2007. *Purify and Destroy.* New York: Columbia University Press.

Sen, Amartya. 1992. *Inequality Reexamined.* Cambridge: Harvard University Press.

———. 1999. *Development as Freedom.* New York: Knopf (Random House).

———. 2006. *Identity and Violence.* New York: W. W. Norton.

———. 2009. *The Pursuit of Justice.* Cambridge: Harvard University Press.

Shaw, Martin. 2003. *War and Genocide: Organized Killing in Modern Society.* Oxford: Polity Press.

Shell-Duncan, Bettina. 2008. "From Health to Human Rights: Female Genital Cutting and the Politics of Intervention." *American Anthropologist* 110: 225–36.

Sidel, John. 2006. *Riots, Pogroms and Jihad: Religious Violence in Indonesia.* Ithaca: Cornell University Press.

Sidgwick, Henry. 1907. *The Methods of Ethics.* London: MacMillan.

Singer, Peter. 2000. *Animal Liberation.* 2nd edition (1st ed. 1975). New York: HarperColins.

Slovic, Paul. 2007. "'If I Look at the Mass I Will Never Act': Psychic Numbing and Genocide." *Judgment and Decision Making* 2: 79–95.

Smith, David Livingstone. 2011. *Less Than Human: Why We Demean, Enslave, and Exterminate Others.* New York: St. Martin's Press.

Smith, E. O. 2009. "Evolution, Primates, and Subaltern Genocide." In *Genocides by the Oppressed: Subaltern Genocide in Theory and Practice*, eds. Nicholas Robins and Adam Jones. Bloomington: Indiana University Press. Pp. 159–84.
Smith, Roger W. 1998. "Scarcity and Genocide." In *The Coming Age of Scarcity: Preventing Mass Death in the Twenty-First Century*, eds. Michael N. Dibkowski and Isidor Wellimann. Syracuse: Syracuse University Press. Pp. 197–214.
———. 2004. "American Self-Interest and the Response to Genocide." *Chronicle of Higher Education*, July 30, p. B6–B9.
Smokowski, Paul, Rachel Buchanan, and Martica Bacallao. 2009. "Acculturation and Adjustment in Latino Adolescents: How Cultural Risk Factors and Assets Influence Multiple Domains of Adolescent Mental Health." *Journal of Primary Prevention* 30, 3–4: 371–93.
Staub, Erwin. 1989. *The Roots of Evil: The Origins of Genocide and Other Group Violence*. New York: Cambridge University Press.
———. 2003. *The Psychology of Good and Evil*. Cambridge: Cambridge University Press.
Steele, Claude M. 2010. *Whistling Vivaldi and Other Clues to How Stereotypes Affect Us*. New York: W. W. Norton.
Steinberg, Ted. 2006. *Acts of God: The Unnatural History of Natural Disaster in America*. New York: Oxford University Press.
Steller, Georg. 2003. *Steller's History of Kamchatka*. Translated from German by Margritt Engel and Karen Willmore. (German original 1774.) Fairbanks: University of Alaska Press.
Stepakoff, Shanee, Jon Hubbard, Maki Katoh, Erika Falk, Jean-Baptiste Mikulu, Potiphar Nkhoma, and Yuvenalis Omagwa. 2006. "Trauma Healing in Refugee Camps in Guinea: A Psychosocial Program for Liberian and Sierra Leonean Survivors of Torture and War." *American Psychologist* 61: 921–32.
Sternberg, Robert J., and Karin Sternberg. 2008. *The Nature of Hate*. New York: Cambridge University Press.
Stets, Jan E. 1988. *Domestic Violence and Control*. New York: Springer-Verlag.
Stets, Jan E., and Jonathan H. Turner, eds. 2006. *Handbook of the Sociology of Emotions*. New York: Springer.
Stiglitz, Joseph. 2003. *Globalization and Its Discontents*. New York: W. W. Norton.
Stocking, George (ed). 1988. *Bodies, Bones, Behavior*. Madison: University of Wisconsin Press.
Stoll, David. 1993. *Between Two Armies in the Ixil Towns of Guatemala*. New York: Columbia University Press.
———. 1999. *Rigoberta Menchú and the Story of All Poor Guatemalans*. Boulder, CO: Westview.
Stone, Norman. 2007. "Two Sides to the Story." *Cornucopia* 6, 37: 20–24.
Straus, Scott. 2006. *The Order of Genocide: Race, Power, and War in Rwanda*. Ithaca: Cornell University Press.
Szathmáry, Eörs. 2011. "To Group or Not to Group?" *Science* 334: 1648–49.
Tashiro, Ty, and Laura Mortensen. 2006. "Translational Research: How Social Psychology Can Improve Psychotherapy." *American Psychologist* 61: 959–66.
Tatz, Colin. 2011. "The Destruction of Aboriginal Society in Australia." In *Genocide of Indigenous Peoples, Genocide: A Critical Bibliographic Review*, vol. 8, ed. Samuel Totten and Robert K. Hitchcock. New Brunswick: Transaction Publishers. Pp. 87–116.
Taylor, Christopher C. 2010. "Rwandan Genocide: Toward an Explanation in Which History and Culture Matter." In *Questioning Collapse: Human Resilience, Ecological Vulnerability, and the Aftermath of Empire*, eds. Patricia A. McAnany and Norman Yoffee. Cambridge: Cambridge University Press. Pp. 239–68.
Taylor, Michael. 2006. *Rationality and the Ideology of Disconnection*. New York: Cambridge University Press.
Thompson, E. P. 1963. *The Making of the English Working Class*. New York: Random House.

Tilly, Charles. 2003. *The Politics of Collective Violence*. Cambridge: Cambridge University Press.
Totten, Samuel (ed). 2008a. *The Plight of Women During and Following Genocide*. New Brunswick, NJ: Transaction Publishers.
———. 2008b. *The Prevention and Intervention of Genocide*. New Brunswick, NJ: Transaction Publishers.
———. 2011a. "The Darfur Genocide." In *Genocide of Indigenous Peoples, Genocide: A Critical Bibliographic Review*, vol. 8, eds. Samuel Totten and Robert K. Hitchcock. New Brunswick: Transaction Publishers. Pp. 229–70.
———. 2011b. "Genocide in Guatemala." In *Genocide of Indigenous Peoples, Genocide: A Critical Bibliographic Review*, vol. 8, eds. Samuel Totten and Robert K. Hitchcock. New Brunswick: Transaction Publishers. Pp. 271–98.
Totten, Samuel, and Robert K. Hitchcock, eds. 2011. *Genocide of Indigenous Peoples*. New Brunswick, NJ: Transaction Publishers.
Totten, Samuel, and Steven Leonard Jacobs, eds. 2002. *Pioneers of Genocide Studies*. New Brunswick, NJ: Transaction Publishers.
Totten, Samuel, William Parsons, Israel W. Charny, eds. 1997. *Century of Genocide: Eyewitness Accounts and Critical Views*. New York: Garland.
Tuchman, Barbara. 1984. *The March of Folly: From Troy to Vietnam*. New York: Knopf.
Tullis, Paul. 2011. "The Death of Preschool." *Scientific American Mind*, November–December, pp. 36–41.
Turchin, Peter. 2003. *Historical Dynamics: Why States Rise and Fall*. Princeton: Princeton University Press.
———. 2006. *War and Peace and War: The Life Cycles of Imperial Nations*. New York: Pi Press.
United Nations Environment Programme. 2007. Sudan: Post-Conflict Environmental Assessment. United Nations Environment Programme, web posting.
United Nations, UNICEF. 2004. "James P. Grant Biography." Posted online December 2004 at www.unicef.org .
Van Vugt, Mark, Robert Hogan, and Robert B. Kaiser. 2008. "Leadership, Followership, and Evolution." *American Psychologist* 63: 182–96.
Vansina, Jan. 2004. *Antecedents to Modern Rwanda: The Ninginya Kingdom*. Madison: University of Wisconsin Press.
Victor, David, et al. 2008. "The World Is Not Enough." *The National Interest* 93: 25–36.
Waller, James. 2002. *Becoming Evil: How Ordinary People Commit Genocide and Mass Killing*. New York: Oxford University Press.
Weatherford, Jack. 2004. *Genghis Khan and the Making of the Modern World*. New York: Three Rivers Press.
Weber, Max. 1958. *The Protestant Ethic and the Spirit of Capitalism*. Translated from German by Talcott Parsons. New York: Free Press.
Wedel, Janine. 2010. *Shadow Elite: How the World's New Power Brokers Undermine Democracy, Government, and the Free Market*. New York: Basic Books.
Weinstein, Henry. 2005. "Nazi Hunter Loyal to the Dead." *Los Angeles Times*, September 21, A1, A13–16.
Weitz, Eric. 2003. *A Century of Genocide: Utopias of Race and Nation*. Princeton: Princeton University Press.
Werner, Emmy. 1989. "Children of the Garden Island." *Scientific American* 260, 4: 106–11.
Werner, Emmy, and Ruth S. Smith. 1982. *Vulnerable but Invincible: A Longitudinal Study of Resilient Children and Youth*. New York: McGraw-Hill.
Westen, Drew. 2007. *The Political Brain: The Role of Emotion in Deciding the Fate of the Nation*. New York: Public Affairs.
Wiesenthal, Simon. 1998. *The Sunflower: On the Possibilities and Limits of Forgiveness*. Expanded edn. (orig. 1976). New York: Schocken.

Wildschut, Tim, Brad Pinter, Jack Leven, Chester Insko, and John Schopler. 2003. "Beyond the Group Mind: A Quantitative Review of the Interindividual-Intergroup Discontinuity Effect." *Psychological Bulletin* 129: 698–722.

Wildschuttle, Keith. 2002. *The Fabrication of Aboriginal History.* Vol 1: *Van Diemen's Land, 1803–1847.* Sydney: Macleay.

Woolford, Andrew, and Jasmine Thomas. 2011. "Genocide of Canadian First Nations." In *Genocide of Indigenous Peoples, Genocide: A Critical Bibliographic Review*, vol. 8, eds. Samuel Totten and Robert K. Hitchcock. New Brunswick: Transaction Publishers. Pp. 61–86.

World Almanac and Book of Facts. 2012. Senior Editor, Sarah Janssen; editor, M. L. Liu. New York: Infobase Learning.

World Briefings. "Bishop Guilty of Holocaust Denial," *Los Angeles Times,* April 17, 2010, p. A–11.

Xenophon. 1998. *Anabasis.* Translated from Greek by Carleton Brownson; revised by John Dillery. Revised edition (original edition 1922). Cambridge: Harvard University Press (Loeb Classical Library).

Xunzi. 1999. *Xunzi.* Translated from Chinese by John Knoblock. Changsha and Beijing, China: Hunan People's Publishing House and Foreign Language Press.

Youst, Lionel, and William Seaburg. 2002. *Coquelle Thompson, Athabaskan Witness.* Norman, OK: University of Oklahoma Press.

Yunus, Mohammed. 1999. *Banker for the Poor: Micro-lending and the Battle against World Poverty.* New York: Public Affairs: Perseus Books Group.

Zitek, Emily M., Alexander H. Jordan, Benoît Monin, and Federick R. Leach. 2010. "Victim Entitlement to Behave Selfishly." *Journal of Personality and Social Psychology* 98: 245–55.

Zucchino, David. 2011. "One War, Two Perspectives." *Los Angeles Times,* December 18, pp. A1, A14–15.

Index

abandonment, fear of, 30
Aborigines. *See* Australia
accountability, 146; and governance, 147–152
Aceh, 167
Adams, B., 145
Afghanistan, 107, 151, 158; predictions for, 123
aggression, 2, 16, 17, 29; versus genocide, 67; intergroup, 45–51
agrarian countries, and genocide, 188–189
agrarianism, as noncause, 70–73
Akçam, T., 102
Albania, 158
Albigensian crusade, 7, 91–92
Alexander, M., 27
Algeria, 158–159, 175
Alinsky, S., 48
Allport, G., 37
altruism, 24–25, 27; parochial, 28
Amazon, 160
amygdale, 17
Anderson, B., 29
Angola, 146, 159, 175
animal rights, 131
anocracy, term, 84
anthropomorphization, 61
Arab Spring, 122
Arendt, H., 47, 70
Argentina, 159
Arizona, 36, 124
Armenians, 102
Arnaud Amaury, 5, 91
atheism, 52
Atran, S., 54–55
Australia, 6, 11, 84, 100, 159–160
authoritarianism, 144
autocracies, 81, 84, 115; and civil wars, vigilance and, 143;
recommendations for, 144–147

Bagosora, Theonest, 147
Bangladesh, 122, 160
Barnaby, W., 77
Baumeister, R., 59
Beah, I., 89
Beck, Aaron, 43
Belarus, 122
Bhutan, 184
Biafra, 170
bin Laden, Osama, 56
Bolivia, 183
Borger, J., 77
Bosnia-Herzegovina, 6, 27, 180–181
Botswana, 183
boundary phenomena, 14
Bowles, S., 25, 28
Brazil, 95, 160
Brown, D., 95
Bulgaria, 161
bullying, 4, 9, 63; and leadership, 87; responding to, 136
Burger, J., 41
Burkino Faso, 183
Burma. *See* Myanmar
Burnett, Peter, 96
Burundi, 121, 161, 175
Butler, D., 77

Cambodia, 2, 5, 37, 89, 112, 108, 117, 161–162
Canada, 95
cannibalism, 111
Čapek, Karel, 104
Carthage, 9, 72
Cathars, 7, 91–92
Catholic Church, 53, 91–92
Cato, 72

207

causation models: causes of, 115–119; inadequate, 67–73; Stanton on, 2
Central African Republic, 162
Chad, 120, 162, 176
cheating, detection of, 26–27
Chechenya, 180
children: and definitions of genocide, 6; and fear, 29–31; as soldiers, 110
Chile, 145, 162–163
China, 48, 52, 86, 89, 93, 106, 117, 163–164, 189; and accountability, 149; civility versus violence in, 128; Japan and, 106, 168; and oil, 146; predictions for, 121, 133; and structural violence, 66; and Sudan, 77
Chirot, D., 82
Christia, F., 27
Christianity, 52–53, 139; and Albigensian crusade, 7, 91–92
civility, 75, 128–129
civil rights, 147–150
civil wars, 3–4, 117; decrease in, 151; definition of, 13; Hobbes on, 19; poverty and, 79, 81; prevalence of, 12–13; vigilance during, 143
clash of civilizations thesis, 69
climate change. *See* environmental issues
Clinton, Hillary, 41
Collier, P., 1, 79
Colombia, 117, 164; predictions for, 121
colonialism, 12, 100, 107–111; versus human rights, 133
Communism, 106, 115
compassion fatigue, 61
competition, 39–41, 46; and gender discrimination, 41
complicity, 87–89
conflict, justification of, 67–70
conflict resolution, 137
Confucius, 128
Congo-Brazzaville, 146; predictions for, 120
Congo (D. R.), 110, 176; predictions for, 120, 123
conquest, territorial, 70–73, 93–101
Conrad, Joseph, 59
control, 4, 32, 39, 42

cooperation, 22
coping mechanisms, alternative, 137–138, 154
corruption, 22, 49
Cote d'Ivoire, 150, 177–178
Crisp, R., 139
critical thinking skills, 138
Crook, George, 99
Cuba, 164
culture, 28; and human rights, 134
culturocide, 6
Czechoslovakia, 164

Darfur, 13, 77, 111, 181–182
dehumanization, 59–67; term, 59
demagoguery, 48–49, 65; and dehumanization, 62. *See also* leadership; propaganda
de Man, P., 103
democide: term, 7. *See also* genocide
democracy, 147–152; corruption of, 149; degree of, 148; and famine, 65; and genocide, 187; and noncitizens, 84; as protective, 131, 147, 150; recovering, 148
denial, of genocide, 112, 136
de Waal, F., 1, 77
diamonds, 79–80, 111, 146
dictatorships. *See* autocracies
Dies, M., 105
divide-and-rule strategy, 100, 109
Dobson, James, 53
doctors, genocide and, 2
domestic violence, 9, 39, 42, 118; control and, 4
dominance, 39
downward mobility, 3
drugs: and complicity, 89; Guatemala and, 95
Dulles, John Foster, 95
Dunbar, R., 22

Easterly, W., 12
East Timor, 107, 167
economic decline, 68, 85, 115; and genocide, 76–83; prevention of, 140–143
economic policies: and genocide, 77; open, as protective, 131, 150; as

structural violence, 63–64, 66
economic reparations, 146
Ecuador, 183
education, 81; recommendations for, 135–136, 138–140, 154
egalitarianism, 24
Egypt, 183; predictions for, 120, 123
Eichmann, A., 47, 70
Einstein, Albert, 75
Elias, N., 128
El Salvador, 9, 176
Enlightenment, 130
environmental issues, 77–79; and structural violence, 64
Equatorial Guinea, 146, 165
Eritrea, 183; predictions for, 121
Ethiopia, 63–64, 165
ethnic cleansing, 5, 109
ethnic diversity, as noncause, 69
Evans, G., 144, 151–152
exclusion, biological background of, 19–29
extractive industries: and genocide, 80; recommendations for, 142–143

fairness, 24, 27; economic, 141
famine, 64–65, 147
fascism, 68, 71, 103, 106; influence of, 104–105
fear, 2, 15–17; biology of, 17–31; as cause, 115; coping with, 32–33; infants and, 29–31; management of, 154; as noncause, 67–70; prioritizing, 31–32
Ferguson, N., 12
fictive kinship, 28–29
fight-or-flight arousal, 18
Fiji, 185
Fiske, A., 40
Foucault, M., 149
France, 91–92, 104, 165
Freud, Sigmund, 20
Friedman, B., 80, 83, 151
fundamentalism, 124; term, 52

gender discrimination, 41–42. *See also* women
Genghis Khan, 23, 129

genocide: causes of, 1–15, 115–119; comparative statistics on, 187–189; correlates of, 3–5; definitions of, 1, 5–14; dehumanization and justification and, 59–73; history of, 7–8, 91–112; immediate risk factors, 84–89; permanent nature of, 112; predictions of, 119–123; previous, effects of, 5, 84, 116; statistics on, 157–185; steps of, 75–89; versus structural violence, 67
Germany, 4, 86, 103–104, 112, 165–166; and banality, 47; and definition, 5; and dehumanization, 60; economic decline and, 83; and fascism, 68; and Guatemala, 95; and Herero massacre, 101; and imagined hurt, 35; propaganda in, 65; tradition and, 89; and Turkey, 102
Ghana, 183
Gibbon, E., 51, 85
Gintis, H., 25, 28
Goebbels, J., 65, 103
Gourevitch, P., 47
governance, accountable, 147–152
government insecurity, 3
Grant, James, 128
Grant, Ulysses, 98
greed, 49, 82
groups: expansion of identification with, 131; fluidity of, 23; hatred of, 43–44; social, 19–29. *See also* target groups
Guatemala, 2, 4, 13, 95, 166, 176–177; predictions for, 121
Gusterson, H., 5

Haiti, 177
Han Feizi, 20
Han Yu, 149
Harff, B., 84
hate crimes, 136
hate speech. *See* propaganda
hatred, 3, 35–57; versus aggression, 17; as cause, 115; components of, 43; culture of, creating, 75–76; dehumanization and, 59–67; and greed, 82; group sociability and, 29; and imagined hurt, 35–36;

individual versus group, 43–44; as noncause, 67–70; psychological traits and, 44; recommendations for, 135–140; subculture of, 86
Heidegger, M., 103
Heine, H., 140
Henry, P. J., 37
Herero massacre, 101
Hinton, A., 108
Hiroshima, 9
history, revisionist, 86, 100, 136
Hitler, Adolf, 4, 35, 71, 86, 145
Hobbes, Thomas, 19, 130
Holocaust: term, 8. *See also* Germany
Honduras, 9, 183
honey pot, 81
honor, 4, 15, 27, 108
hope, 80, 83, 85, 138, 150, 155
human nature, biology and, 19–29
human rights, 130–135
Hume, David, 21
humiliation, 60–61
Hungary, 122, 166
Huntington, S., 69
hurt, imagined, and hatred, 35–36
Hutus. *See* Rwanda
hypocrisy, 72

identity, and hatred, 45
ideology, 40; and group hatred, 44; Nazi, 104–105; as noncause, 68; religion and, 52–54
imagined communities, 28–29
imagined hurt, and hatred, 35–36
impunity, culture of, 145–146
indoctrination, 54–57
Indonesia, 4, 107, 145, 166–167; predictions for, 120, 123
industrial cooperation, 68, 71, 80, 104, 124, 145; recommendations for, 142–143
industrialized/industrializing nations, and genocide, 188
Inquisition, 92
integration, 27
international engagement, as protective, 131, 150
intervention, 150–151
Iran, 167–168; predictions for, 121

Iraq, 151, 168, 177; predictions for, 121
Ireland, 52
Irian Jaya, 107, 167
Islam, 46, 52–54, 92; bin Laden and, 56; perpetrator characteristics in, 55; predictions for, 122
Italy, 104
Ivory Coast, 150, 177–178

Jackson, Andrew, 10, 96
Japan, 106, 112, 168
Jenkins' Ear, War of, 9
Jews: and settler wars, 94. *See also* Germany
Juergensmeyer, M., 52
Jung, C., 105
justification, of violence, 67–70

Kagame, Paul, 147
Kant, Immanuel, 131
Karadzic, Radovan, 146
Karemera, Edouard, 147
Kenya, 183
Kiernan, B., xii, 8–9, 94, 100, 108; critique of, 70–73
killers, formation of, 54–57
King, Martin Luther, Jr., 46–48
kin selection, 23
Köhler, J., 87
Korean War, 107
Kuper, L., 144
Kyrgyzstan, 178

Laos, 169
Lawrence, D. H., 105
leadership, 55; and aftermath, 145–147; and dehumanization, 62; religious, 53; ruthless, rise of, 85–88; threatened, 3, 85, 115. *See also* demagoguery
Lebanon, 178
Lemkin, R., 5–6, 144
Lewis, S., 104
Liberia, 111, 178
Libya, 121–122
Lindbergh, Charles, 105
Lindner, E., 61
Locke, John, 130

Madagascar, 66, 183
Mahathir bin Muhamad, 184
Malawi, 183
Malaysia, 122, 184
Mali, 183; predictions for, 121
Mallery, Garrick, 99
Mao Zidong, 68, 71, 86, 106, 117
Marxism-Leninism, 68
massacres, 4
Matthews, Washington, 99
McCauley, C., 82
McFadden, Bernarr, 105
Meacham, William, 97
media. *See* propaganda
Mencius, 19–20
Mendes Pinto, F., 100
messaging. *See* demagoguery; propaganda
Mexico, 98–99, 112, 169, 183
Middle Ages, stereotypes of, 76, 128
Milgram, S., 41
militarism, 150
Milosevich, Slobodan, 5, 109
Mladic, Ratko, 146
Modoc War, 97
Mongols, 93, 129
Mooney, J., 97
morality, 40–41
Morocco, 183
Mosely, Osbert, 104
Mozambique, 169–170
Mugabe, Robert, 116
multiculturalism, 138–139
Muslims. *See* Islam
Mussolini, Benito, 68, 71, 103
Myanmar, 161; predictions for, 120, 123
My Lai, 9

Nagasaki, 9
Native Americans, 10, 94–99, 112; population decline among, 98
Nazi Germany. *See* Germany
near-genocide, 111
Nepal, 179
network reciprocity, 23
Ngirumpatse, Matthieu, 147
Nicaragua, 179
Nietzsche, Friedrich, 87
Niger, predictions for, 120

Nigeria, 146, 170; predictions for, 120
nonconformity, 35, 38
North Atlantic Treaty Organization, 6
North Korea, 64, 169; predictions for, 121

oil, 79–80, 142, 145–146
open economies, as protective, 131, 150
ordinary people, and genocide, 47; mechanisms of complicity, 54–57, 88–89, 119, 137
Orwell, G., 65
Ottoman Empire, 92
oxytocin, 46

Pakistan, 170; predictions for, 121–122
Papua-New Guinea, 185
Paraguay, 179, 189
parochial altruism, 28
passivity, 137
peace, 16, 127–133; recommendations for, 152–155; religion and, 54
peacekeepers, 152
Peru, 180
Philippines, 116, 144, 171
Pinker, S., xii, 2, 39–40, 54–55, 70, 84, 127–132, 141, 174
Pinochet, Augusto, 145
plantation agriculture, 80
Poland, 171
Polgreen, L., 77
political exploitation of hatred, 85–88; recommendations for, 135–140, 153
politicide, 6–7, 106. *See also* genocide
pollution, as justification, 69
Pol Pot, 145
poor: condemnation of, 50; structural violence and, 63–67
population growth, 81
Pound, Ezra, 105
poverty, 76, 78–79, 83
prejudice, 36–37
propaganda, 65, 87, 93, 125; effectiveness of, 88; jamming, 152; responding to, 135–136, 140, 153. *See also* demagoguery
protection, responsibility of, 151
protective factors, 44, 127–155; accountable governance as, 147–152;

economic growth as, 80; hope as, 83; Kant and, 131
protectors, 105, 110; education on, 140
proxies, 107
Prunier, G., 13, 77, 111
public health, 81, 128
Puntland, 181
Putin, Vladimir, 122

Qin Shi Huang Di, 7, 68, 93

racism, and slavery, 11
Raffles, H., 60
rational self-interest, 20, 22
Rawls, J., 154
rebuilding, 148, 152
reciprocity, 23, 27
refugees, 150
religion, 46, 51–54; and tolerance, 139; and war, 91–101, 130
reparations, 146
Republican Party, 123–125
resource curse, 120, 142, 146
resource limits: future of, 132; and genocide, 76–83
Ricoeur, P., 103
Riefenstahl, Leni, 103
Rilke, Rainer Maria, 18
Rios Montt, Efrain, 95
Roma, 51, 122. *See also* Germany
Romania, 171
Roosevelt, Franklin Delano, 154
Roscoe, P., 54
Rummel, R., 6, 7, 115, 147, 157, 187
Rusesabagina, Paul, 110
Russia, 100, 122, 180. *See also* Union of Soviet Socialist Republics
Rwanda, 4–6, 109–110, 147, 180; and banality, 47; economic conditions and, 78; perpetrator characteristics in, 55; predictions for, 122; youth in, 86

Sahlins, M., 27
Santayana, George, 5
scapegoats, 36
Schindler, Oskar, 105
segmented opposition, 23
segregation, 27

Sen, A., 45, 65–66, 147
Senegal/Senegambia, 184
September 11, 2001, 46
Serbia, 5–6, 109, 146, 180–181
settler wars, 3, 9–11, 93–101
Shakespeare, William, 29, 145
Shoah. See Germany
Sierra Leone, 89, 111, 146, 181
Singapore, 184
slave trade, 11, 130
Slovakia, 122
Slovic, P., 61
Smith, D. L., 60
Soccer War, 9
sociability, 20–29
solidarity, 89
Somalia, 63, 181
South Africa, 76, 78, 171, 183
South Korea, 169, 184
Soviet Union. *See* Union of Soviet Socialist Republics
Spain, 172
Sri Lanka, 84, 148, 172; predictions for, 121
Stalin, J., 86, 106, 117, 173
Stanton, G., 2
Staub, E., 44
Steele, C., 138
Stellar, G., 100
stereotypes, 76, 125; common elements of, 51
Sternberg, K. and R., 43
Straus, S., 4, 47, 55, 62, 68, 88
Stroessner, Alfredo, 179, 189
structural opponents, 38, 46
structural violence, 63–67, 147; dehumanization and, 61, 63; versus genocide, 67; and Native Americans, 98–99; term, 63
Sudan, 13, 111, 144–146, 172, 181–182; economic conditions and, 77–78; predictions for, 120, 123
Suharto, 145
Sykes, Mark, 12
Syria, 120, 122, 184

Tadzhikstan, 182
talk radio, 47–49, 65, 125
Tamerlane, 7, 86

Tanzania, 183
target groups: all-or-none presentation of, 48; defining, 5, 118–119, 136; and definition of genocide, 11; dehumanization of, 59–67; development of hatred for, 43–44; killing, 45–51; provocation of, 11
Taylor, R., 139
territorial conquest, 70–73, 93–101
Thailand, 184
Tibetans, 77, 106
Tilly, C., 1, 6, 147
tipping point, 40
Togo, 184
tolerance, 137–138
totalitarianism, 68, 85–88, 115
trade-based societies, 80
tradition, and genocide, 89
trust, 17
Tunisia, 121, 184
Turchin, P., 67
Turkey, 102, 112, 122, 147, 172–173, 182
Tutsis. *See* Rwanda

Uganda, 173
Ukraine, 173
Union of Soviet Socialist Republics, 86, 106, 117, 173–174
United Nations, 6, 144
United States, 9; economic decline and, 80, 83; and fascism, 104; and Guatemala, 95; and Native Americans, 10, 84, 95–99, 112; predictions for, 123–126, 135–140, 153

us-versus-them mentality, 26, 28, 36, 48

Victor, D., 77
Vietnam, 107, 174
vigilance, 143, 152–155
violence, justification of, 67–70
Von Trotha, Luther, 101

war, 11–12, 25; decrease in, 127–133; versus genocide, 67; Hobbes on, 19; religion and, 91–101, 130; and sociability, 26
Weber, Max, 18
Weitz, E., 89
Werner, E., 55
Wiesenthal, Simon, 105, 135
Williamson, Richard, 136
Winema, 97
women: discrimination against, 41–42; education of, 81; and genocide, 16

Xenophon, 93
Xunzi, 20

Yeats, W. B., 105, 119
Yemen, 122
youth: and complicity, 89; organization of, 86
Yugoslavia, 109, 122, 174
Yunus, Mohammed, 66

Zaire. *See* Congo (D.R.)
Zambia, 150, 184
Zhu Yuanzhang, 4, 7, 68, 86, 93
Zimbabwe, 184

About the Authors

E. N. Anderson, PhD, is professor of anthropology, emeritus, at the University of California, Riverside. He received his PhD in anthropology from the University of California, Berkeley, in 1967. He has done research on ethnobiology, cultural ecology, political ecology, and medical anthropology, in several areas, especially Hong Kong, British Columbia, California, and the Yucatan Peninsula of Mexico. His books include *The Food of China* (1988), *Ecologies of the Heart* (1996), *Political Ecology of a Yucatec Maya Community* (2005), and *The Pursuit of Ecotopia* (2010).

Barbara A. Anderson, DrPH, RN, CNM, FACNM, FAAN, is director of the Doctor of Nursing Practice (DNP) at Frontier Nursing University. Her doctoral and post-doctoral work was at Loma Linda University and Stony Brook University. She is a public health specialist and nurse-midwife with extensive teaching, service, and consultation experience in Africa, South Asia, Southeast Asia, and Central and South America. She conducted doctoral work and has been a consultant with refugee health in the refugee camps along the Cambodian border, in Cambodia and for resettled refugees in the United States. She has numerous publications focusing on health issues among vulnerable populations. She co-authored both the second and third edition of *Caring for the Vulnerable, Perspectives in Nursing Theory, Practice and Research*, with Dr. Mary de Chesnay. The third edition won an American Journal of Nursing award as best nursing book of the year in 2012.